Widows and Dependent Wives

Widows and Dependent Wives

From Social Problem to Federal Program

Helena Znaniecka Lopata
Henry P. Brehm

PRAEGER SPECIAL STUDIES • PRAEGER SCIENTIFIC

New York • Philadelphia • Eastbourne, UK
Toronto • Hong Kong • Tokyo • Sydney

Library of Congress Cataloging-in-Publication Data

Lopata, Helena Znaniecka, 1925-
  Widows and dependent wives.

  Includes index.
  1. Survivors' benefits—United States.
2. Mothers' pensions—United States.   3. Social
security—United States.   4. Widows—United States—
Economic conditions.   I. Brehm, Henry P.   II. Title.
III. Title: Dependent wives.
HV699.L67   1985   362.8'382   85-16753
ISBN 0-03-046301-7 (alk. paper)

Published in 1986 by Praeger Publishers
CBS Educational and Professional Publishing, a Division of CBS Inc.
521 Fifth Avenue, New York, NY 10175 USA

Printed in the United States of America on acid-free paper

INTERNATIONAL OFFICES

Orders from outside the United States should be sent to the appropriate
address listed below. Orders from areas not listed below should be placed
through CBS International Publishing, 383 Madison Ave., New York, NY
10175 USA

Australia, New Zealand
Holt Saunders, Pty, Ltd., 9 Waltham St., Artarmon, N.S.W. 2064, Sydney,
Australia

Canada
Holt, Rinehart & Winston of Canada, 55 Horner Ave., Toronto, Ontario,
Canada M8Z 4X6

Europe, the Middle East, & Africa
Holt Saunders, Ltd., 1 St. Anne's Road, Eastbourne, East Sussex, England
BN21 3UN

Japan
Holt Saunders, Ltd., Ichibancho Central Building, 22-1 Ichibancho, 3rd Floor,
Chiyodaku, Tokyo, Japan

Hong Kong, Southeast Asia
Holt Saunders Asia, Ltd., 10 Fl, Intercontinental Plaza, 94 Granville Road,
Tsim Sha Tsui East, Kowloon, Hong Kong

**Manuscript submissions should be sent to the Editorial Director, Praeger
Publishers, 521 Fifth Avenue, New York, NY 10175 USA**

Dedicated to

Cornelia Bachandouris Toppses
Eileen Markley Znaniecki

Contents

Preface

This volume is the last in a three-volume sequence analyzing the relation between the societal definition of a situation as a social problem, and the policy formulation and subsequent development of a program designed as the solution to that problem. The series presents three areas of American life subject to this process: the economic needs of the disabled, the economic needs of dependent wives deprived by death of a male breadwinner, and the medical needs of the aged. The Social Security program is focused on as an attempt to deal with the first two, and the Medicare program is treated as a solution to the cost of medical care to the elderly.

The research was funded by the Social Security Administration. It examined the consistency with which the programs were designed to meet the needs of three different populations defined as ameliorable (at least in part) by government action. In each case, a general policy for solving the problem has been translated into a legislated program. However, there is an inadequate fit between general policy and the program designed to fulfill that policy. Nor does the policy necessarily reflect an accurate understanding and assessment of the conditions defined as the social problem.

In each of the three cases we examine two primary issues of policy. One is whether the policy is consonant with, or a mismatch to, the parameters of the underlying social problem. Is it based on an accurate conception of the nature and root causes of that problem and an adequate assessment of its scope and dimensions? The second issue is whether the formally instituted program legislated by government, with implementing procedures and administrative rules, actually accomplishes the generally stated objectives of the policy.

Inconsistency or mismatch between the policy and the problem or between the policy and the program may prevent socially defined "success" in ameliorating the problem, independent of the level of funding or the operating efficiency in program administration. No attempt is made here to assess program efficiency per se. The focus of these books is on the formulation and implementation of policy and the outcome of the program.

There are many reasons for a mismatch between problem and final legislated program designed to accomplish the goals of the policy. These include: a lack of appropriate knowledge of the nature and complexities of the problem or what actions might affect it and how; the influence of varying social philosophies and values surrounding the subject, especially the responsibility for the social problem; and political compromises negotiated between, or for, vested interest groups with varying degrees of power. In addition, the underlying situation leading to problem definition may change, making the program even less effective. A lack of success in the solution of a social problem is often treated by tinkering with details of the program when in actuality it is due to a mismatch reflecting a lack of clear understanding or definition of the problem itself. Strengthening elements of the program's administration or supplying additional funds for implementation, making minor changes in the legislative structure of the program or its implementing procedures and regulations will not meet policy goals. Only a reexamination of the basic problem and the corresponding policy and program can achieve an improvement in problem amelioration.

METHODS AND CASES

The four studies providing the major inputs for these three volumes use data collected by three separate and distinct methodological approaches. The analytical model is addressed to independent, although potentially overlapping, areas of social problems.

Medical Care for the Aged

The study of medical care for the aged involved surveys of households and medical facilities. Comparable cross-sectional data were collected at three points in time: immediately after the passage of Medicare, with a focus on the period prior to its implementation; two years after the implementation, and again two years later. The analysis reported in a companion volume, *Medical Care for the Aged: From Social Problems to Federal Policy*, co-authored by Henry P. Brehm and Rodney M. Coe (Praeger, 1980) uses data primarily from a major Midwestern metropolitan area. One conclusion of this analysis is that the policy of providing the aged with greater access to medical care by decreasing the financial cost does fit a limited perspective of the underlying social problem. The aged were given financial assistance in meeting the costs of health care.

However, a second conclusion is that the policy and program do not meet the unique health problems of the aged because the Medicare system has not altered the working relationships, organizational structure, planning, coordination, or decision-making apparatus of the providers of medical care. The particular needs of the aged are not being met because the existing system for the delivery of medical care has effectively co-opted the financial mechanism established under Medicare. While theoretically the aged are less responsible for financing their own medical care, they are still paying out-of-pocket costs which can be extensive, and there has not been any significant realignment among the providers of medical care to meet the needs of the aged.

Disability

The study of disability used data from the 1970 U.S. Census of Population, from the Social Security Disability Insurance (SSDI) program on applications for and awards of benefits, and on State Disability Determination Services (DDS) characteristics. The analysis compared differences among states in their rates of self-defined disability, and application for and award of benefits under the SSDI program, as these related to state economic and social conditions. The administrative characteristics of state DDS were also analyzed as these related to the rates of award.

The other companion volume, *Disability: From Social Problem to Federal Policy*, co-authored by Irving Howards, Henry P. Brehm, and Saad Z. Nagi (Praeger, 1980), reviews the background and developmental history of the legislation authorizing the SSDI program and describes the social problem toward which the underlying policy was aimed. The policy was based on a medical conception of disability. However, the study indicates that a person's self-definition as disabled and application for disability benefits are based in large measure on another factor: his or her inability to get and hold a job. Many people with specific health problems define themselves as disabled only when the social and economic circumstances of the state in which they live affect their ability to obtain an income from employment. This means that the state's social and economic circumstances, including labor market factors, affect the number of persons with health problems who apply for disability benefits.

The study also indicates that the rate of awards of benefits relative to the insured population is based on the rate of applications. In addition, the award of benefits is also related to the separate state-by-state administration of the process of disability determination. There are two possible interpretations of these data. One is the possibility that the award determination process gives more weight to the underlying social and economic characteristics of the state than was intended under the legislated program or its implementing regulation. Thus, the process by which a disability application is decided on is responsive to pressures within the state and not just to the characteristics of the applicant. The policy did not take this into consideration.

The second interpretation is that under a given negative economic situation in a state in which there are difficulties in getting and holding a job, more people with legitimate health or injury characteristics may apply for benefits. Since the population with one or more chronic diseases by far exceeds the number who report themselves as disabled, there is a vast reservoir of people who could define themselves as disabled if they found themselves in a restricted job market which, therefore, promoted and reinforced self-definitions of disability. The massive growth of the SSDI program may thus be a reflection of a misconception of the potential influence of social and economic factors more than a consequence of an increased frequency of disability impairment.

Widows and Dependent Wives

The third volume of the series, contained here, focuses on two themes. One is the process by which American women became economically dependent on a husband, if married, and the consequences of this historical shift on the lives and future projections of middle-aged urban women. The second is the societal definition of the situation of women and children deprived of the family breadwinner through his death as a social problem ameliorable through federal policy, specifically the programs arising from the Social Security Act's amendments of 1939.

Members of modern urban societies can maintain themselves economically through one or more of three methods: employment for pay, support by another person, or societal support systems. Few Americans are totally supported by inheritance or private investment. After the society decided that wives and children were economic dependents of husbands and/or fathers it became increasingly concerned over their condition in the absence of a male breadwinner, or in cases when he was unable to earn sufficient income for their maintenance. At the turn of the twentieth century, children were taken away from such households, charity programs abounded, and state governments attempted to provide funds for Mothers' Aid. Throughout, however, there has been no consistent program with which to meet the problem of all women deprived of a male breadwinner and who are unemployable themselves for any number of reasons. No program even addresses itself to all widows. By 1939 the Social Security Act was amended to cover older dependent women and mothers of the dependent children of deceased or retired workers. We shall examine closely the consequences of this policy in this volume. Families deprived of the economic support of a husband for reasons other than death or retirement and unable to earn sufficient income remain wards of the welfare state, with all of the negative implications of such status.

Data on the economic situation of widows comes from a project entitled "Support Systems Involving Widows in Non-Agricultural Areas"

(Lopata et al., 1975; see also Lopata, 1979, *Women as Widows: Support Systems*). Interviews were conducted with five random subsamples of Chicago-area widows: current beneficiaries of the old age Social Security program; mothers of dependent children who were receiving benefits; former beneficiaries who remarried; former beneficiaries who became ineligible because of the age of their children; and women who received only the lump sum benefit to help defray furneral costs. The interview focused on the economic, service, social, and emotional supports of the widows.

Data from a second study examine the economic situation of middle-aged women, cohort variations in their role involvement, the degree to which they are knowledgeable about the Social Security program, as well as their expected age of retirement and sources of income at that time. The study of the "Changing Commitments to Work and Family Roles Among American Women and their Future Consequences for Social Security" (Lopata and Norr, 1978, 1979, 1980; see also Lopata, Barnewolt, and Miller, 1985, *City Women: Work, Jobs, Occupations, Careers: Chicago*) indicates that many women are still dependent on the earnings of a husband. Even those who are employed earn only about one-third of the family income, and female household heads are very likely to be living on very restricted funds. In addition, women do not organize their lives around the possibility of future Social Security benefits on their own record. In fact, few know the policies and program of the Social Security Act and its amendments sufficiently to have this knowledge influence their current behavior. The mothers have inevitably interrupted their employment following the birth of children and in cases of family emergencies. The married women earn less than their unmarried occupational counterparts. Commitment to mothering prevents commitment to a career outside of the home for most women.

The sample for this study was obtained through a four-stage area probability design covering the Chicago Consolidated Area. It contains, when weighted due to an oversampling of nonmarried women, 1,877 respondents, aged 25 to 54. The interview focused on their background (school, employment, occupational, marital, and parental histories), their construction of reality concerning their self-concept and jobs, and their role clusters. Attitudes toward, and knowledge about, the Social Security Program and retirement expectations were also obtained.

REFERENCES

Brehm, Henry P., and Rodney M. Coe. 1980. *Medical Care for the Aged: From Social Problem to Federal Policy*. New York: Praeger.

Howards, Irving, Henry P. Brehm, and Saad Z. Nagi. 1980. *Disability: From Social Problem to Federal Policy*. New York: Praeger.

Lopata, Helena Z. 1979. *Women as Widows: Support Systems*. New York: Elsevier.

Lopata, Helena Z., Debra Barnewolt, and Cheryl Allyn Miller. 1985. *City Women: Work, Jobs, Occupations, Careers: Chicago*. New York: Praeger.

Lopata, Helena Z., Henry Brehm, Frank Steinhart, Gertrud Kim, and Gloria Heinemann. 1975. *Support Systems Involving Widows in Non-Agricultural Areas*. Final report to Social Security Administration.

Lopata, Helena Z., and Kathleen Fordham Norr. 1978, 1979. *Changing Commitments of American Women to Work and Family Roles and their Future Consequences for Social Security*. Preliminary and final reports to Social Security Administration.

———. 1980. *Changing commitments of American women to work and family roles*. *Social Security Bulletin* 43, no. 6 (June):3–14.

Acknowledgments

A large number of people were involved in the two major projects discussed in this book. The widowhood study was funded by the Social Security Administration, with Helena Lopata as principal investigator and Henry Brehm, formerly chief of Research Grants and Contracts, SSA, as project officer. The various contributors to the study are personally thanked in *Women as Widows: Support Systems*, but special recognition must go to members of the Center for the Comparative Study of Social Roles, especially Frank Steinhart, Marlene Simon, Suzanne Meyering, and Sister Gertrud Kim. Chapter 4 of this study is based on Sister Kim's chapter for the final report of the study to SSA. Special thanks also go to Gloria Heinemann and the staff of the Survey Research Laboratory of the University of Illinois, Circle Campus, for conducting the interviewing and helping with various stages of the project.

The study, *The Changing Commitments of American Women to Work and Family Roles*, was also funded by the Social Security Administration, with Helena Lopata as principal investigator and Kathleen Norr as deputy director. Dr. Brehm was again project officer. The members of the Office of Research and Statistics of the Social Security Administration, including Patience Lauriat, Lucy Mallan, Lola Irelan, Wayne Finegar, Virginia Reno, and Gayle Thompson were of considerable help in planning the interviews. The Survey Research Laboratory of the University of Illinois again conducted the interviews and data reduction. Special thanks go to Ron Czaja, Beth Eastman, Andy Montgomery, Richard Warnecke, and David Schoemaker for their assistance. The members of the Center for the Comparative Study of Social Roles at Loyola University of Chicago who were involved in this study (besides Kathleen Norr) included Deb Barnewolt, Marlene Simon, Sue Meyering, and Cheryl Miller. Monica Schoemaker and Jenny Ettling helped through numerous drafts of reports and books. Kathleen Norr co-authored both the preliminary and the final reports, and many sections of this book are based on her contributions to both of these.

Throughout, Helena's colleagues at the Department of Sociology and the administration of Loyola University have been patient and enthusiastic in their support. This volume has been helped by discussions with Kirsten Grønbjerg and Jill Quadagno, who are working in similar fields. Jill read over half of the manuscript and offered new sources of information and ideas. Peggy Cusick, Mary Ellen Folk, and Dorothy Blumental at Loyola; Nancy Gordy at the University of Maryland, Baltimore County; and Molly Brehm have assisted both of us, again through many drafts. Lynda Sharp has been a great and patient editor.

List of Tables

Widows and
Dependent Wives

1
Women and Children as Economic Dependents

This book was intended to meet several goals. In the first place, it seeks to establish the process by which American women and children became economic dependents of their husband/father, and the process by which the loss of income from that breadwinner through his death or retirement became defined as a social rather than a personal problem. It traces the creation of Social Security benefits to solve that social problem and examines the consequences of the program. It looks at the match between the program and the economic situation of female beneficiaries, mainly widows. Finally, it presents the economic situation of younger urban women of all marital status in America in the 1970s to determine which areas of economic dependence have not been solved adequately by personal or societal efforts.

INTRODUCTION

In 1939, the leaders of the United States government amended the 1935 Social Security Act to include benefits for economically dependent wives of insured workers aged 65 or over, for older widows of insured workers, and for father-orphaned children and their mothers. This action, officially defining the wives and children of male workers as economically dependent on the husband/father's earnings or social security benefits, and the public insurance system as responsible for at least partial replacement of this income, was an outgrowth of years of social debate and reflected the American value system. The view of wives and children as legally dependent on the husband/father goes back to English common law, adopted in the United States in its early years of existence. However, it was not until the 1930s that this society officially

1

realized that sources of income of married or widowed women and young children of the past were no longer available so that many, if not most, had become completely dependent on the male breadwinner. The debate over the possible solutions of the economic problem of women without a male provider focused on the attempt to establish the responsiblility for their support. The value system that entered both the debate and the solution derives from the English Elizabethan Poor Laws and the American feeling that the poor are responsible for their own plight (Quadagno, 1984). The solution reflects this idea in that women and children became defined as having a right to federally distributed benefits if they are or were related to "worthy" men, who became disabled or retired through no fault of their own or who died. Women and non-adult children of men who deserted, divorced, or were imprisoned did not fall into this category and were thus ineligible for social security benefits. Such indigents were relegated to the public welfare program with all of its stigma. As we shall see throughout this book, other aspects of the social security program fail to solve the problems of many economically dependent wives and children. The economic system of this society does not allow women, especially mothers of children or "displaced homemakers," to earn enough on their own through jobs to lift them out of poverty in the absence of a male earner. Husbandless women are thus disproportionately represented among the poor. Let us now examine the backgrounds to our analyses.

THEORETICAL BACKGROUND

The basic concepts to be used in this volume need definition. For the purpose of our analysis we are defining a *social problem* as any situation or condition that negatively affects a significant portion of a society's population and is defined as a problem to be resolved by collective action.

Blumer (1971:301) has been insistent that social problems are a matter of collective definition:

Social problems are not the result of an intrinsic malfunctioning of a society but are the result of a process of definition in which a given condition is picked out and identified as a social problem. A social problem does not exist for a society unless it is recognized by that society to exist.

Julian (1973:9) develops this thesis further:

In order for a social condition to become a social problem, a significant number of people—or a number of significant people—must agree both that this condition violates an accepted value or standard *and* that it should be eliminated, resolved or remedied.

The importance of the process by which a condition becomes redefined into a social problem and some segment of the society becomes willing to take some sort of public action cannot be emphasized enough. Horton and Leslie (1960:5) exemplify the conversion process:

> Child labor was no social problem as long as most people thought child labor was acceptable. Only when a considerable number of people decided that child labor was harmful and began saying "Isn't it awful"—only then did child labor become a social problem.

We would add to the above statement that the definition of a condition as awful is an insufficient prerequisite since it is also necessary that the society, or at least its governing bodies or other organized groups decide that public action should be directed toward eliminating, or at least alleviating it. Thus, the decision that a condition is a *social problem* is followed by some general statement of *policy*, of goals and objectives for its elimination, including a definition of the criteria of successful resolution. The general policy has to be embodied, implicitly or explicitly, in legislation or official pronouncements designed to address the problem (Brehm and Coe, 1980; Howards, Brehm, and Nagi, 1980). The next step necessary in the societal attempt to alleviate the problem is a specific *program* through which the policy is put into action. In a large and complex society such as in the United States, such a program usually involves setting up social structures with personnel and bureaucratic procedures, by which the federal, state, or local community policy is so implemented as to reach the population affected by the problem or to protect the rest of society from its consequences. Private agencies allegedly fill the gap not covered by the governmental system (Grønbjerg 1983).

This definition of a social problem follows Blumer's (1971) theory rather than that of Merton (1971) which has been further developed by Manis (1974a,b) and others. The latter theory focuses on "the objective condition" and classifies it as either manifest (that is, publicly recognized) or latent (not defined as a social problem by society, although it may actually be "dysfunctional" to its goals or functional integration):

> Apart from manifest social problems—those objective social conditions identified by problem-definers as at odds with social values—are latent social problems, conditions that are also at odds with values current in the society but are not generally recognized as being so. The sociologist does not impose his values upon others when he undertakes to supply knowledge about latent social problems (Merton 1971:806).

The conversion of a social condition into a social problem requires leadership in bringing to public attention the fact that the condition exists and that its existence goes against many, or at least some, of society's values. However, the presence in each society of diverse interest groups, some of which may benefit from a condition that adversely affects others, means that not all such situations become subjects of a consensus. Fuller and Myers (1941) explained in excellent detail why many social conditions brought to public attention as logical potentials for redefinition as social problems never reach the stage of being the subject of public policy and programs. In addition, many social problems are not solved or even alleviated because of the inadequacy of the definition, lack of understanding of all the variables that contribute to their existence, inadequacy of the policy or its mismatch with the problem, and/or failures in the development and implementation of the program. The whole process takes considerable time, especially in a democracy, so that externalities may modify the condition before the program is put into effect. As Kunza (1975) points out, there can be a policy lag over the years, so that a policy that matched the problems at one period in a society's history may no longer fit them. Long-range consequences of policies and programs may also have been unforeseen, especially in large and complex societies and when the planners cannot control all the variables affecting the social problem (Dyckman, 1968).

ECONOMIC DEPENDENCY AS A SOCIAL PROBLEM

The inability of many members of societies to maintain themselves economically emerged as many aspects of production moved out of the home and from the family work group. These were combined with economic and political management into jobs in large-scale organizations. This necessitated the movement of people out of the home for most of the day in order to perform these jobs and support themselves. However, not all persons have been able, for a variety of reasons, to enter the labor force. With industrialization and modernization in general came societal values that decreed certain societal members, those with proven mental and physical disabilities, as incapable of earning a living (Howards, Brehm, and Nagi, 1980). Small children were defined as needing to be supported by others, and child labor laws extended the number of years they were to be free from working. The aged, those of a specifically defined age, have been removed from, or encouraged to leave, employment. Finally, of relatively recent time in human history, women, especially those who have children, have been unable to support themselves in the home and have been discouraged from taking full-time jobs outside of the home in societies such as England and the United States. Wives of men deemed important by virtue of ascribed status or occupation have, until recently, taken on the back-up function in the "two-person" career (Finch, 1983; Papanek, 1973). Some jobs (such as that of religious minister) have required a wife who is not encumbered by occupational demands of her own.

The dependence on a job for income in the absence of many other sources of support has made difficult the life of people unable to earn money outside of the home or even inside its walls. In other words, the current organization of economic life has made a large number of people *economically dependent* on others, people personally responsible for them, or on societal action. American society has been reluctant to undertake responsibility for such non-employed members because of its individualistic nonintervention ideology. However, the reality of life, of the system that makes it impossible for so many people to support themselves, has entered this consciousness at various times. The adult male, that is, the man between school age and retirement, is defined as having to work for as much money as he can earn. Strong censure faces a "healthy" adult male who is not employed full time, forcing men to declare themselves disabled if they have a physical handicap that can be used as an excuse by employers for not hiring them (Howards, Brehm, and Nagi, 1980). The healthy adult male is not only supposed to work for pay but also to devote most of his energies to that effort, not allowing distraction from other needs. The "marketing mentality" (Fromm, 1947) developed in American society evaluated the total worth of an individual only in terms of how much he was worth to the employer or client in the allegedly open labor market.

American society gradually realized that people who, for various physical and social reasons, were unable to work for pay were not being supported by people who did earn an income. The problem, looming ever larger as the number of such dependents increased especially in times of economic depression, became defined in terms of responsibility. Who is responsible for supporting those children, mothers, disabled, or old people deprived of an earning adult male? Society has a convoluted history of attempting to define the situation as a social problem, to assign responsibility for its solution, to develop policy and programs. One of the complications has been the inconsistent way society has looked on its women. The Victorian ideal would have made them economically dependent first on the father, then the husband. However, women were expected to support themselves if they were not married. Does this apply only to unmarried women, or to those deprived of an earning husband through death, divorce, desertion or the inability to work? Also, women are often mothers, and the society has at least recently wanted them to stay home and care for the children, rather than taking a job. Women are also among the aged who are not wanted in the labor force.

As we shall see throughout this book, the problem of dealing with the economically dependent members of American society has been variously defined and acted on. Of special interest to us here are the complications and consequences of American policy formulations concerning women. Allegedly, the Social Security Act of 1935, but especially of 1939, alleviated some of the problem. However, the deeper we delved into the study of the economic situation of American women and social security as an attempt to solve it, the more we realized that there is no single policy or program that focuses on them. Married women are basically defined as being dependent on the earnings of their husbands, but there is no consistent program by which they are covered. Social Security aims at the male breadwinner and his dependents if he can no longer provide support. However, only certain categories of dependents are considered. Concern for widows of beneficiaries is defined only in terms of old age, as is concern for wives whose husbands are living but retired. The wife or widow can obtain benefits only if she herself reaches old age. Otherwise, a woman can receive benefits only if she is caring for non-adult children of the deceased or retired husband. Women not old enough to qualify for old-age benefits who have no eligible children in their care are not entitled to a widow's benefit, nor to a benefit based on being the husband's dependent if he were retired. Divorced women are not defined as a problem for policy or program concern unless the man had retired or died and they met either the condition of care of his eligible children or of old age. Nowhere in the policy or program statements is there any indication of an effort to deal with dependent women and their needs for economic security as a social problem that in its own right warranted or deserved a comprehensive approach. To do so would have required dealing with widows, divorced women, and the wives of retired husbands as women whose economic security was affected by the loss of income when earnings of the male breadwinner were no longer available. The difficulties created by the withdrawal of economic security from women could have been defined as a social problem for resolution when the Social Security program shifted focus in 1939. However, this was not the case. The focus was on men and the replacement of lost wages under specifically defined conditions, not on women. This is still the orientation to the problem definition and the policy of Social Security.

ANTHROPOLOGICAL BACKGROUND

In pre-industrial and non–wage-organized societies, women and children old enough to work in the family economic system were not economically dependent. Rather, they formed part of a mutually interdependent labor force, all of whose members made important contributions, which were divided by age and gender (Cowgill and Holmes, 1972).

In family production for subsistence, the general rule for the division
of labour is for each sex to specialize in a particular type of goods and
services, and to have as helpers children and young persons of the same
sex as the adult person who is responsible for the production (Boserup,
1970:140)

Recent work by comparative anthropologists points to the fact that the
content of the division of labor has varied considerably at different times
and places so that it is impossible to predict which tasks fall into the male
or female province in any one group. Although the elderly are usually
assigned physically easier tasks, such as grazing the animals, their current and prior contributions are recognized as important (Simmons, 1945).
In most of the food gathering, hunting, and subsistence agricultural societies that comprise 90 percent of human history, members of the same
group also pooled resources and loosened work boundaries in times of
emergency or peak season (Boserup, 1970; O'Kelly, 1980). Pastoral and
early agrarian societies often involved men in forays, wars, or trade away
from the home territory, necessitating women's takeover of their tasks
during their absence (O'Kelly, 1980).

The next stage of human modernization occurs when "non-
agricultural goods are produced for sale by handicraft or home industry at the village level" (Boserup, 1970:140).

At this stage, women often continue to be independent producers and
to train younger women in the craft. At a somewhat later stage, though
still at the village level, whole families may, as a full-time occupation,
specialize in the production for sale of some commodity or in the per-
formance of some service for the general public (Boserup, 1970:140–141).

The division of labor in such communities usually follows traditional lines
of activities, but less rigidly than in modern industry (Boserup, 1970).

Most societies have been patriarchal, in that authority rested with the
eldest male until he passed on his role to the next generation, and patrilineal, in that descent also followed the male family line. Families also
tended to be patrilocal, the sons settling with their wives and children
with, or near the father's land or housing. Each nuclear family was thus
embedded into the larger family unit which served as the basic economic
system, with cooperative sharing of work and product. This also means
that the wife who comes into the unit must generally leave her own family of orientation, to which she was born and in which she was brought
up (Goode, 1963; Ward, 1963). Only relatively recently have people been
able to support themselves economically through paid employment, thus
freeing themselves from the extended family's control, but simultaneously losing many of its supports in the form of economic goods and

services. Independence from the patrilineal unit was also made possible by migration into new territories, when new land was available and arable.

Paul Bohannan (1963) concluded from a comparative study of many societies that men universally acquire certain rights vis-à-vis their wives at marriage (see also Lopata, 1972:280; 1979). These include the right to share with the wife a domicile, be it a room, part of a house, or a whole separate home and a division of labor by which it is maintained. Second, the man acquires the right of sexual access to the wife. Third, patrilineal societies grant him the right of filiation of the ensuing children with his family line. This means that these are technically not the wife's children and that, should she decide to go away, she must leave them with the husband or his family. Finally, and this set of rights varies considerably throughout the world, the man can have rights to the economic goods the wife brings with her, those they jointly create during marriage, and even those she obtains through her own efforts. Barbara Ward (1963) and William Goode (1963) point out that the status of women in a particular group is strongly influenced by the degree of their economic dependence on the husband and his family. Women in some societies in West Africa or Asia have had considerable power as a result of their activities in the marketplace and the right to retain their own goods and earnings. The economic contribution to the extended and nuclear families by wives is influenced by cultural constraints introduced with religions and the class system in complex societies (Boserup, 1970; Goode, 1963; Ward, 1963). Generally speaking, the higher the contribution to family life and status a woman was judged as making, the higher was her personal status, although this did not necessarily widen her freedom of action (Boserup, 1970; Goode, 1963; Sicherman, 1975). It is, of course, difficult for outsiders to estimate the evaluated worth of the work of members of any social unit, so it is necessary to know the criteria used by the unit itself. An example of this is the low status of housewives in American earnings valuing society.

The complementary to the rights of the husband are those acquired by the wife. If she leaves her family's territory to move in with, or near, her husband and his family of orientation she must be guaranteed a domicile and the cooperation of others in maintaining it. If she is expected to bear children in filiation with the male line, she has the right to the shared rearing of these offspring. The division of labor by which the family is maintained must include her and her children, as well as the other family members in mutual exchange. She also has the right to have her contribution to the family welfare through reproduction positively valued. Children of such family systems were used very early as economic assets, not as dependents, and wives gained status as they contributed children, especially boys, to the family line and as they themselves aged and gained power.

The nature of marital and extended kin rights and obligations becomes very visible when a member dies or is otherwise permanently removed from the unit. This is especially true if the person who is removed is making a definite contribution to the family by carrying forth major social roles without which the unit cannot survive in its original form. The death of a husband/father or a wife/mother is particularly traumatic in any society in which these roles are considered central to family welfare and where the replacement of the deceased is not easily accomplished (Lopata, 1972; 1973; 1979). The rights and duties of these roles must be carried out by others, or the system must be modified so that they are no longer needed.

The solutions to the problems faced by widows or widowers and by father- or mother-orphans vary considerably in different societies and according to the identity of the deceased. In patriarchal, patrilineal, and patrilocal family systems, the death of the wife/mother is generally less traumatic than that of the husband/father, because of the importance of maintaining the family line. The widower is usually encouraged to remarry as soon as the mourning period is over, and the new wife simply moves in to replace the deceased. The problem with widows is different, in that their children must continue to be in filiation with the male line and future offspring must also be so identified. Other norms for ensuring that a widow will continue to contribute children to the late husband's family line include widow remarriage to a male agnate of the deceased or the levirate system. According to the latter, referred to in the Old Testament, a male relative of the late husband "enters the hut" of the widow in order to "raise up the seed" of the deceased, who remains the social and legal father of the children (Bohannan, 1963).

The situation of the widow in pre-modern societies, thus, depended on her age and the presence and ages of her children, especially sons. In the patriarchal family of all but modern times, at least one son is expected to stay in the ancestral home and take over the work and other nonsexual obligations of the dead father, since he inherits whatever property is left. It is often the widow without children who is allowed to return to her family of orientation. If she must remain with the husband's family without remarriage or a levirate to ensure her childbearing status, she may become more like a servant than a family member. The status of the child widow in traditional India was a very demeaning one (Lopata, 1972; 1973; 1979; Sarasvati, 1888).

HISTORICAL BACKGROUND

Moving now to Western Europe, from which much of American culture emerged, we find the economic situation of women varied considerably by time and place, influenced by and in turn influencing, her rights of inheritance and property management. According to McNamara and Wemple (1974:103), during the time of the Roman republic "women lived in complete subjection to the patria potestas (paternal power), being classed as alieni juris (minors). The power over them was transferred from the father to the husband." Although women of the Roman Empire "were excluded from civil and public offices," they had numerous private rights. The bureaucratic structure of the empire "weakened the power of the family and of the father... and the private rights of wives and children came to be protected by the laws of the state." Herlihy (1962/1976:13) agrees that "The history of Roman law is the history of progressive improvement in the legal rights of the woman."

In early Germanic and English life the position of women changed with modifications of property ownership. Tribe or clan ownership was replaced by male bloodline inheritance, and women varied in their rights to inherit or manage the land and goods of their father or husband. There is some disagreement among historians as to the rights and activities of women during the Middle Ages. Stuard (1976:10) concludes that

> The tendency, as the Middle Ages progressed, was toward a lessening of the public activity of women, a lower place in ecclesiastical opinion, fewer roles in guild organizations and less agricultural administration if not less agricultural labor.... The late eleventh and twelfth centuries stand in many ways as a watershed between the greater opportunity of women in early medieval times and the more confining circumstances of life in the later Middle Ages.

On the other hand, other authors found women quite active in the economic sphere of life during the fourteenth (Tuchman, 1978) and seventeenth centuries (Aries, 1962; Laslett, 1971; and Oakley, 1974).

> In everyday life women of noble as well as non-noble class found equality of function, if not of status, thrust on them by circumstances. Peasant women could hold tenancies and in that capacity rendered the same kinds of service for their holdings as men, although they earned less for the same work. Peasant households depended on their earnings. In the guilds, women had monopolies of certain trades, usually spinning and ale-making and some of the food and textile trades. Certain crafts excluded females except for a member's wife or daughter; in others they worked equally with men. Management of a merchant's household— of his town house, his country estate, his business when he was absent—in addition to maternal duties gave his wife anything but a leisured life (Tuchman, 1978:216).

Herlihy (1976:24) also points out "that the woman during the Middle Ages everywhere and always had some importance in the management of the household economy." There were great class variations in the type of work wives and daughters undertook, but they were active both in and out of the home, in guilds and crafts. Queens and manor ladies often held a great deal of power, but the majority of the people (80–90 percent) were peasants or serfs, the latter being distinguished by a set of rights and obligations tying them to a particular manor lord (Burke, 1978; Kamen, 1971).

The economic situation of many Europeans began to worsen as early as the beginning of the sixteenth century.

> During the closing years of the fifteenth century, the emergence of the wool industry in England began to transform the economic and social arrangements governing agriculture. As sheep raising became more profitable, much land was converted from tillage to pasturage, and large numbers of peasants were displaced by the emerging entrepreneurial gentry which either bought their land or cheated them out of it (Piven and Cloward, 1971:12).

The increasing poverty and displacement of the population led to vagrancy, migration, and social disorders, which were responded to by government with increasingly restrictive legislature, as exemplified by the Elizabethan Poor Laws (Piven and Cloward, 1971). Societies such as that in England began to define poverty as a social problem. However, its solution required overcoming two completely different attitudes. The traditional "Christian feeling was that the poor had a right to alms and the propertied had an absolute moral obligation to help them" (Kamen, 1971:403). Alms giving was the province first of individual families and later of parishes, with parish taxes or "poor rate" used to cover the expenses. However, as the number of poor increased, and they became depersonalized through migration and vagrancy, embarrassing through begging, and dangerous through increased crime and social unrest, the Protestant attitude of the Reformation won over. According to this viewpoint, work is a virtue akin to saintliness and idleness a sin; poverty became redefined as a result of laziness and immorality. The seventeenth century saw a "shift of emphasis from private charity as a spiritually beneficial act to the public control and institutionalization of charity in the interest of social order" (Kamen, 1971:406). Then, as later, charity functioned as "no more than an attempt to stave off social unrest" (Kamen, 1971:396; see also Piven and Cloward, 1971).

> Relief arrangements were reactivated and expanded again...during the massive agricultural dislocations of the late eighteenth century. Most of the English agricultural population had by then lost its landholdings (Piven and Cloward, 1971:17).

The main way by which the last of the land was lost for many people as a means of self- and family maintenance was the Enclosure Acts, by which common land became unavailable for use, animal husbandry and modern agriculture deprived people of even "gleaning rights" of picking "the fields clean after the harvest" (Piven and Cloward, 1971:18). The inability to farm for needed self-maintenance goods especially hit women and children who, as repeatedly stated by observers of Western Europe during the centuries prior to the full establishment of industrialization, were the majority of the poor.

> The drift from the land to the towns, which was aggravated by the enclosure of commons, conversion of arable to pasture, and reimposition of old seigneurial dues, created a drifting and workless proletariat. What we know of urban poverty suggests that it was women and children who made up the bulk of the poor (Kamen, 1971:387, 389).

The Elizabethan Poor Laws were added and expanded from the sixteenth to the end of the eighteenth centuries in their harsh and detailed punishment, much of it physical, to be meted out to the category of people defined as vagrants, especially if they were judged to be able-bodied and capable of earning a living (Burn, 1973). "The vagrant acts of late years have distinguished the offenders into three kinds: idle and disorderly persons, rogues and vagabonds, and incorrigible rogues" (Burns, 1973:125).

Other statutes specified the obligations of masters and "servants labourers and artificers" to each other (Burn, 1973:7), while a major portion of the laws were devoted to the "impotent poor" (Burns 1973:60–103). The latter category was allowed to beg, but only within their own home town, that is, where they were born or "the place where they made last their abode by the space of three years" (Burns 1973:61). The settlement law forcing people to return to their home community guaranteed that each parish was responsible for the care of only "its own" people. All means were used by the local community under the direction of an overseer appointed by the justice of the peace to put the poor to work. "The poor became victims, not of circumstances or God's greater design for man, as they were seen earlier, but of their own 'idle, irregular and wicked courses' " (Smith and Zietz, 1970:12). Workhouses were erected and the "overseers were to be responsible for setting to work all children whose parents were unable to keep and maintain them" (Smith and Zietz, 1970:13). English society was particularly interested at that time (early seventeenth century) in removing the children of the poor from their homes in order to teach them the virtues of hard work. The attitude is evidenced in a scheme of Sir Josiah Child to modify some of the Poor Law statutes, because

> ...the children of our poor, bred up in beggary and idleness, do by that means become unhealthy, and more than ordinarily subject to loathsome

diseases, of which very many die in their tender age; and if any of them do arrive to years and strength they are by their idle habits contracted in their youth, rendered for ever after indisposed to labour, and serve but to flock the kingdom with thieves and beggars (Burn, 1973:161).

The philosophy behind the Poor Laws, as evolved from 1601 on, is important for our analysis of American definition of deserted wives, widows, and father-orphans as a social, or at least an economic, problem and the whole debate over how this problem was to be solved. England's attempt over the years to deal with the situation of extreme poverty affecting so many of its people resulted in a moralistic definition of the poor, with some separation into the "worthy" and the "unworthy." The care of the former, or any help offered them was to be given only if they met the test of being worthy, in that their situation was not created through any fault of their own, and that they were at least attempting a somewhat middle-class life style, especially in relation to their children. Supervision of the poor became part of the program but this could be accomplished most easily through "indoor relief," that is, "assistance given in institutions such as the almshouse or the workhouse." (Smith and Zietz, 1970:13) "Outdoor relief" was assistance given to individuals and families in their own homes (See also *Encyclopaedia Britannica* 1926:74–80; Loch 1926:860–91). English public officials and the emerging charitable organizations did not favor "outdoor relief" because of the difficulty of supervising recipients. They had the power to remove father-orphans or children from homes lacking a male worker if they judged the mother as unable to support them adequately, or to supervise them if she worked for pay outside of the home. Few attempts were made to keep the family together in their own home if the father was absent, a result of the early definition of wives and children as dependent on a male provider.

The Economic Activities of European Women Since the Seventeenth Century

Obviously, not all women of the Western European countries in the centuries since the Middle Ages were poor, in spite of tremendous changes in the economic and political structures of these societies. The commercial revolution, the scientific revolution, wars of centralization and capitalism with early industrialization shifted many bases of economic maintenance of families. Although in much of Europe, especially in the eastern part of the continent, the support of many families was still tied to work and goods arrangements with manor lords, the English system removed most family wage opportunities. Cottage industries slowly began to move out of the home from the seventeenth to the nineteenth centuries. Although English common law made a woman legally dependent on her husband, men had been highly dependent economically on the work of their wives and children. Many interdependent activities were involved in running a home, especially above the bare subsistence level.

> ...brewing, dairy-work, care of poultry and pigs, production of vegetables and fruit, spinning flax and wool, nursing and doctoring, all formed part of domestic industry...men were also more occupied with domestic affairs than they are now, educating children, apprentices and servants (Clark, 1919/1968).*

Servants were numerous; almost a third of the homes in English communities were listed as having servants and/or apprentices living on the premises (Laslett, 1971:13). These servants were young girls from poorer families who could not be supported at home, or young people sent to equal-status families in order to be "properly trained"; the English especially feared that too much lenience in the treatment of their own children would prevent the acquisition of good habits and strength of character (Laslett, 1965; 1971; Oakley, 1974; Tilly and Scott, 1978; see also Queen, Habenstein and Quadagno, 1985, for medieval and later English families).

> In the seventeenth century, in an English parish studied by Macfarlane, two-thirds of the boys and three-quarters of the girls between puberty and marriage were living away from home, and some began leaving at age 10 (Gordon, 1978:58).

Many women worked with their husbands, assisting with the work itself, or handling the "financial side of business, and seen in the role of salesman, receiving payments for which her receipt was always accepted as valid and even acting as buyer" (Clark, 1919/1968:156). In fact, Oakley (1974:27) concludes that "In the seventeenth-century family women were not subject to the arbitrary authority of their husbands; they were equal partners." At the same time, some historians examining everyday life of seventeenth-century England state that women and children were expected to support themselves, first through the efforts of the mother, and later with the help of the offspring as young as age seven if there were no family business (Clark, 1919/1968; Laslett, 1973). If the hus-

---

*Throughout this volume, the date of the first publications of a work will be given first, followed by the date of the edition being used here in cases where there is an important time gap between these dates, so that the reader will know the setting in which the author was writing.

band/father were present in the family, he and the mother were seen as equal providers for the children, who were too young to work themselves. "In the seventeenth century the idea is seldom encountered that a man supports his wife; husband and wife were then mutually dependent and together supported their children (Clark, 1919/1968:12).

The manner by which people supported themselves and mothers provided for their children varied by social class and the resources available for family use or for family industry (Clark, 1919/1968:7). Wage earners who had insufficient property to support themselves and others obtained only individual, not a family wage, because employers assumed that their families were supporting themselves through other means during the early capitalist period (Clark, 1919/1968:12). Some of the activities for women listed by Hill (1896), Oakley (1974), or Clark (1919/1968) included commerce and trade, manufacture of objects for sale, ale making, midwifery, and so forth. Mayhew (1861) described many women among the "street people" in *London Labor and The London Poor*:

> It must be remembered that, except for those who were classed as servants, all grown-up women were either married or widows (Clark, 1919/1968:156).

The need for women to work for pay or barter increased in widowhood, and the probability of this situation was high. Men tended to marry much younger women and marriage tended to be relatively short because of the high death rate. Combined nutritional and hygienic deficiencies aged people early, so that a man in his forties was already considered old (Lutz, 1973). Lutz (1973:398) estimates that husbands and wives lived together about a dozen years, and that families thus contained many widows, widowers, and orphans and, because of the frequency of remarriage, step-parents and step-children. Few people saw the marriage of their youngest child and very few the birth of a grandchild.

It was often difficult for a widow to continue the business in which she worked with her husband because of the inheritance laws which, depending on the century, deprived her of direct ownership or guaranteed only a fraction. The latter situation usually meant that she had to sell the business, since she could not buy out the other beneficiaries. Some cases have been known in which she was able to retain the establishment with the help of an apprentice, who sometimes even married her (Laslett, 1971). Medieval Europe had assigned male guardians to father-orphans, who took control of their fate and removed property from the mother's hands, so that she often needed a male guardian in order to complete business transactions, a tradition passed on to later English history (Walker, 1976).

The opportunities for earning money expanded with the introduction of cottage industries. Early capitalists brought up raw goods, such as wool, and "put it out" to families working in their own homes. The distribution of work to provide a finished product depended on custom and the type of activity required. Very young children were usually employed by the parents in certain tasks, and the hours were long, although the pay was meager. Thus, such work, called family economy, involved all members of the family, with a division by age and sex and often with the assistance of young apprentices (Boserup, 1970; O'Kelly, 1980; Oakley, 1974; Tilly and Scott, 1978). Gradually, however, the introduction of centralized capital and power in factories and the need for standardized products expanded industrialization and removed much of the productive work from the home and family economy.

> The factory won its victory by outproducing the working family, taking away the market for the product of hand labour and cutting prices to the point where the craftsman had either to starve or take a job under factory discipline himself (Laslett, 1971:18).

Ann Oakley, writing in 1974 about England, documents the separation of most of productive work from family life as taking place for two centuries from the start of industrialization, involving three periods:

> 1. From 1750 until the early 1840s, when the family was increasingly displaced by the factory as the place of production, but women followed their traditional work out of the home.
> 2. From the 1840s until 1914, when a decline in the employment of married women outside the home was associated with the rising popularity of a belief in women's natural domesticity.
> 3. From 1914 until the 1950s, when there is a discernible, though uneven, tendency toward the growing employment of women, coupled with a retention of housewifery as the primary role expected of all women (Oakley, 1974:34).

In spite of the use by Laslett of the male pronoun, most of the early factory workers were women and children. Oakley (1974:37) found that 46 percent of the factory workers in 1835 were women, and 15 percent were children of both sexes under the age of thirteen. In earlier years, and especially in the textile industries, the proportion of women and children was even higher. However, men became more and more interested in factory work as the ability to maintain themselves through agriculture decreased, especially in England. "Protective" legislation developed in the 1800s, first to modify the work of small children, spurred by the outcry of social reformers such as the Webbs (Abbott, 1929) or writers such as Charles Dickens. As Horton and Leslie (1960:2) stated, child labor gradually became redefined from being desirable as a means of teaching them good habits or as an economic necessity to being a social problem. The redefinition was slow in crystallizing, as we shall see when discussing American history, since it was fought by employers who wanted cheap labor and by some charitable organizations feeling that children should be kept busy.

Women began to be pushed out of English industry—out of most occupations, in fact—in the 1850s. Guilds started refusing membership even to widows. Protective legislation made them less and less attractive to employers who now had an increasing labor supply in men. Employers preferred male workers for a variety of reasons, including supposedly steady employment and the gradually consolidating male control of the public domain (Lipman-Blumen, 1976; Rosaldo and Lamphere, 1974; Sanday, 1974). The removal of women from public life became accompanied by a new ideology and the "emergence of the role of housewife as the dominant mature female role" (Oakley, 1974:32).

> The shift from domestic to industrial production in the nineteenth century increased women's dependence on men, not only in economic terms, but in the psychological subtleties of their relationships (Meacham, 1977:64).
>
> Capitalism and industrial revolution and mass production wages and money to buy services liberated the man from kin control and the family as a work group. Before, man needed a wife and children; now he can get a divorce and buy services. [Woman's situation is opposite]— went into economic dependence upon the husband since domestic industry broke down and has little opportunity to earn money (Clark, 1919/1968:1).

Motherhood and Childhood

The expansion of industrialization to other areas of life was accompanied by masculinization of occupations and public life outside of the home, as well as by increasing identification of the province of women with private family life. Many factors contributed to the separation of the world into two spheres—the home, with the mother and small children, and the outside world of male control—as men moved into factory work.

The creation of politically centralized national states dependent on the loyalty of members rather than control by manor lords, increased interest in the education of children. Nationalism, as identification with a national culture and society, as well as the evolution of democratic political ideologies, made societies much more interested in an expanded literate population than in the past (Znaniecki, 1952).

Both Aries (1962) and Shorter (1975) point to beginning of the eighteenth century for the definition of childhood as a special stage in the life course. Prior to that time, children were treated as miniature adults (Aries, 1962). The high mortality rates of infants and young children discouraged strong emotional involvement by parents with their children. Middle-class women often sent newborns to wet nurses in villages, although they were aware of even higher death rates in such conditions (Shorter, 1975). Sussman (1977) reports the continuation of the "wet nursing business" in France as late as World War I, and Coleman (1976) and deMause (1974a,b) document the occurrence of infanticide and neglect until recent decades (see also Illick, 1974). According to Aries (1962) childhood became defined as an important stage of life requiring protective care and freedom from work around the turn of the eighteenth century, and became established with the organization of the school system. Shorter (1975) identified the redefinition of motherhood at about that time into an important child maintenance and socialization role. This dual movement of romantization of both childhood and motherhood had important consequences for women, especially those living above the poverty level in Western Europe and England, and later in America. Books on child care emerged in Europe, and official policies gave power to representatives of private charities and government to judge the quality of care being given to children, even by their parents. Such representatives were given the right to take children away from a "bad parent" and the protection of the children became more of a concern than just the assurance that s/he obtain virtuous socialization. Parents were judged to be bad if they

> a) abandoned or deserted his child or b) allowed his child to be brought up by another person at the person's expense, or by guardians of poor law union for such a length of time and such circumstances as to satisfy the court that the parent was unmindful of his parental duties, the court shall not make an order for the delivery of the child to the parent unless the parent has satisfied the court that, having regard to the welfare of the child, he is a fit person to have the custody of the child (*Encyclopadia Britannica*, 1926:76).

As motherhood increased in importance in the value system of Western Europe, and as mothers were encouraged to remain home with their children, the home itself became much more restricted than in the past. Productive work for other than family use had already been removed, and few economically gainful activities could be carried forth from this location. Also, as Aries (1962) points out, life prior to the eighteenth century was very public and family boundaries were not clearly demarcated. People lived in villages, manor homes, and towns or cities. Villagers interacted frequently, while on their way to the fields or working nearby, often pausing to chat; all negotiations and play took place in public places. Manor homes were complex, with as many as 200 persons living inside or nearby; large common rooms housed servants, scribes, the family, and others contributing to its maintenance, while visitors came in at all times of the day and night. Homes in towns or cities such as London usually contained nonrelatives, the English especially believing that children past the age of seven could best be socialized in homes other than those of their own family (Laslett, 1971). Thus, children were placed for years in the homes of other families as servants or apprentices (Oakley, 1974; Shorter, 1975). For a variety of reasons pointed out by different historians, the family began to withdraw from public life and to define member roles more strictly in the eighteenth century than before, privatizing itself and even its members from each other. The common room became divided into smaller rooms for fewer members and specialized activities. Aries (1962) and Shorter (1975) both consider the privatization of the family as accompanying the romanticization of motherhood and childhood, but within the narrow confines of the new home.

These changes restricted the lives of widows as much as they had those of married women. Although there was greater tolerance for the employment of widows than for married women, few occupations were open to them. Midwifery, ale making, and home services were still available, but there was little other choice. Few households in England contained more than two generations, even before the industrial revolution, let alone after its development, according to the Cambridge Group for the History of Population and Social Structure. These historians have reconstructed household composition in prior centuries from parish and town records (Laslett, 1971; Laslett and Wall, 1972; Shorter, 1975).* In spite of the reduced size of the household with the vanishing of the child-servant and decreasing family size, there is considerable evidence that relatives tended to live within what Townsend (1957) now calls "soup carrying distance." Even Laslett (1971:117), who provides the main documentation of the absence of the three-generation family in the last three or so centuries of English history, describes one woman as follows: "She was another of the solitary widows we have already referred to...she managed to get within an easy walk of a member of her family." In fact, she lived next door to her son, who helped with her home maintenance.

---

*Demos (1973), Hareven (1977a,b; 1978) and Hareven and Langenbach (1978) have done the same for U.S. communities.

SUMMARY

It is important for us to understand the historical background of European life since the early Middle Ages because of its influence on the American process of defining the situation of wives, widows, and father-orphans as a social problem requiring public action, although this society did so quite late in its own history. The changes in life in Europe (particularly in England) and the way these changes were interpreted, formed a foundation not only for American social and cultural systems but also for its laws and public policy. The common law that defined married women and children as dependents of the husband/father and as requiring a guardian at his death was incorporated into all the Elizabethan Poor Laws, even in their latter-day revisions (Walker, 1976). The independence of the nuclear family from the control of the male-extended network may have been the reason, or the justification, for this system of guardianship. It made the orphan a ward of the state or its subdivisons and allowed those groups to take the child away from the mother if they defined her as unfit, or even as incapable of providing what the guardian considered an adequate environment (Walker, 1976). The Poor Laws and related statutes not only defined the poor as a social problem, but also created workhouses which would insure that they did not live "in idleness," but "earned" their relief. As many observers noted, the English, and other societies as well, made it a crime to be poor and established the obligation of the society to decrease this poverty through the provision of work. Ideology regarding the poor as somehow morally inferior traveled across the ocean to America. "Outdoor" relief or any support system that bypassed charity groups or, later, the social worker by providing money directly to the recipient was strongly disapproved of. "Indoor relief" became the favorite method of caring for the deserving poor, such as father-orphans, deserted children, the aged (often widowed), although it meant removing them from their families.

In the meantime, family-economy, providing work and maintenance to all family members, gradually but inevitably vanished from most of Western European life with increased urbanization and industrialization, and with changes in agricultural production, which grew in scope from family subsistence to societal needs. Women, active in such cooperative economy or working as entrepreneurs providing services, serving as middle-level suppliers, or running businesses and craftshops, were no longer able to maintain themselves and their children. Even cottage industries, originally providing income with which to buy goods for home and family maintenance, were replaced by factory industries. Children and then women were gradually pushed out of both the entrepreneurial and the cottage occupations, becoming increasingly dependent on an adult male breadwinner. Childhood became redefined as a time for learning and play, motherhood as a vital role for women, the home as the domain of women, and public life as the domain of men.

REFERENCES

Abbott, Edith. 1929. The Webbs on the English Poor Law. *Social Service Review* 3:252–269.

Aries, Philippe. 1962. *Centuries of Childhood: A Social History of Family Life.* New York: Vintage Books.

Becker, Howard S. 1966. *Social Problems: A Modern Approach.* New York: Wiley.

Blumer, Herbert. 1971. Social Problems as Collective Behavior. *Social Problems* 18, no. 3 (Winter): 298–306.

Bohannan, Paul J. 1963. *Social Anthropology.* New York: Rinehart and Winston.

Boserup, Ester. 1970. *Women's Role in Economic Development.* New York: St. Martin's Press.

Brehm, Henry and Rodney Coe. 1980. *Medical Care for the Aged: From Social Problem to Federal Program.* New York: Praeger.

Burke, Peter. 1978. *Popular Culture in Early Modern Europe.* New York: New York University Press.

Burn, Richard. 1973. *The History of the Poor Laws with Observations.* Clifton, NJ: Augustus M. Kelley.

Clark, Alice. 1919/1968. *Working Life of Women in the Seventeenth Century.* New York: Augustus M. Kelley Reprints of Economic Classics.

Coleman, Emily. 1976. Infanticide in the early Middle Ages. In *Women in Medieval Society*, edited by Susan Mosher Stuard. Philadelphia, PA: University of Pennsylvania Press.

Cowgill, Donald O., and Lowel D. Holmes. 1972. *Aging and Modernization.* New York: Appleton-Century-Crofts.

deMause, Lloyd. 1974a. *The History of Childhood.* New York: Psychohistory Press.

———. 1974b. The evolution of childhood. In *The History of Childhood*, edited by Lloyd deMause, pp. 1–73. New York: Psychohistory Press.

Demos, John. 1973. *A Little Commonwealth: Family Life in Plymouth Colony.* New York: Oxford University Press.

Dyckman, John W. 1968. Social planning, social planners and planned societies. In *Vital Problems for American Society*, edited by J. Alan Winter, Jerome Rakow, and Mark Chester, pp. 462–478. New York: Random House.

Encyclopaedia Britannica. 1926. 13th ed., v. 22:74–80. "Poor Law."

Finch, Janet. 1983. *Married to the Job: Wives' Incorporation in Men's Work.* Boston: George Allen Unwin.

Fromm, Erich. 1947. *Man for Himself.* New York: Holt, Rinehart and Winston.

Fuller, Richard C., and Richard R. Myers. 1941. Some aspects of a theory of social problems. *American Sociological Review* no. 6 (February): 24–32.

Goode, William. 1963. *World Revolution and Family Patterns.* New York: The Free Press.

Gordon, Michael. 1978. *The American Family, Past, Present and Future.* New York: Random House.

Grønbjerg, Kirsten. 1977. *Mass Society and the Extensions of Welfare*. Chicago, IL: University of Chicago Press.

——. 1978. *Poverty and Social Change*. Chicago, IL: University of Chicago Press.

Hareven, Tamara K. 1977a. Family time and historical time. *Daedalus* 106 (Spring): 57–70.

——. 1977b. *Family and Kin in Urban Communities, 1700–1930*. New York: New Viewpoints.

——. 1978. *Family and Population in Nineteenth-Century America*. Princeton, NJ: Princeton University Press.

—— and Randolph Langenbach. 1978. *Amoskeag: Life and Work in an American Factory-City*. New York: Pantheon Books.

Herlihy, David. 1962/1976. Land, family and women in continental Europe. In *Women in Medieval Society*, edited by Susan Mosher Stuard, pp. 13–45. Philadelphia, PA: University of Pennsylvania Press.

Hill, Georgiana. 1896. *Women in English Life: From Medieval to Modern Times*. London: Richard Bentley & Sons.

Horton, Paul, and Gerald Leslie. 1960. *The Sociology of Social Problems*, 2d ed. New York: Appleton-Century-Crofts.

Howards, Irving, Henry P. Brehm, and Saad Z. Nagi. 1980. *Disability: From Social Problem to Federal Program*. New York: Praeger.

Illick, Joseph. 1974. Child-rearing in seventeenth-century England and America. In *The History of Childhood*, edited by Lloyd deMause, pp. 303–350. New York: Psychohistory Press.

Julian, Joseph. 1973. *Social Problems*. New York: Appleton-Century-Crofts.

Kamen, Henry. 1971. *The Iron Century: Social Change in Europe, 1550–1660*. New York: Praeger.

Kuhza, Elizabeth Ann. 1975. *Policy Lag: Its Impact on Income Security for Older Women*. University of Chicago School of Social Service Administration, occassional paper no. 6 (June).

Laslett, Barbara. 1973. The family as a public and private institution: An historical perspective. *Journal of Marriage and the Family* 35, no. 3 (August): 480–492.

Laslett, Peter, 1971. *The World We Have Lost*, 2d ed. New York: Charles Scribner & Sons.

Laslett, Peter, and Richard Wall, eds. 1972. *Household and Family in Past Time*. Cambridge, England: Cambridge University Press.

Lipman-Blumen, Jean. 1976. Toward a homosocial theory of sex roles: An explanation of the sex segregation of social institutions. In *Women and the Workplace*, edited by Martha Blaxall and Barbara Reagan, pp. 15–31. Chicago, IL: University of Chicago Press.

Loch, Charles Stewart. 1926. *Encyclopaedia Britannica*, 13th ed, s.v. "Charity and Charities."

Lopata, Helena Znaniecki. 1972. Role changes in widowhood: A world perspective. In *Aging and Modernization*, edited by Donald O. Cowgill and Lowell D. Holmes, pp. 275–303. New York: Appleton-Century-Crofts.

——. 1973. *Widowhood in an American City*. Cambridge, MA: Schenkman.

——. 1979. *Women as Widows: Support Systems*. New York: Elsevier North Holland, Inc.

Lutz, K. Berkner. 1973. Recent research on the history of the family in Western Europe. *Journal of Marriage and the Family* 35, no. 3 (August): 395–405.

Manis, Jerome G. 1974a. The concept of social problems: Voc populi and sociological analysis. *Social Problems* 21, no. 3: 305–315.

——. 1974b. Assessing the seriousness of social problems. *Social Problems* 22, no. 1 (October): 1–15.

Mayhew, Henry. 1861. *London Labor and the London Poor*. London: Charles Griffin and Company.

McNamara, Jo Ann, and Suzanne Wemple. 1974. The power of women through the family in medieval Europe: 500–1100. In *Clio's Consciousness Raised*, edited by Mary Hartman and Lois W. Banner, pp. 103–118. New York: Harper & Row Torchbooks.

Meacham, Standish. 1977. *A Life Apart: The English Working Class, 1890–1914*. Cambridge, MA: Harvard University Press.

Merton, Robert K. 1971. Social problems and sociological theory. In *Contemporary Social Problems*, edited by Robert K. Merton and Robert Nisbet, pp. 793–845. New York: Harcourt Brace Jovanovich.

Oakley, Ann. 1974. *Woman's Work: The Housewife, Past and Present*. New York: Vintage Books.

O'Kelly, Charlottee G. 1980. *Women and Men in Society*. New York: D. Van Nostrand.

Papanek, Hanna. 1973. Men, women and work: Reflections on the two-person career. *American Journal of Sociology* 78: 852–872.

Piven, Frances Fox, and Richard A. Cloward. 1971. *Regulating the Poor: The Functions of Public Welfare*. New York: Pantheon Books.

Quadagno, Jill S. 1984. From poor laws to pensions: The evolution of economic supports for the aged in England and America. *Milbank Fund Quarterly* 62, no. 3: 112–153.

Queen, Stuart, Robert Habenstein, and Jill S. Quadagno. 1985. *The Family in Various Cultures*. New York: Harper & Row.

Rosaldo, Michelle Zimbalist, and Louise Lamphere, eds. 1974. *Women, Culture & Society*. Stanford, CA: Stanford University Press.

Sanday, Peggy R. 1974. Female status in the public domain. In *Women, Culture and Society*, edited by M.Z. Rosaldo and L. Lamphere, pp. 189–205. Stanford, CA: Stanford University Press.

Sarasvati, Pundita Ramatai. 1888. *The High-Caste Hindu Woman*. Philadelphia, PA: James B. Rodgers Printing Co.

Shorter, Edward. 1975. *The Making of the Modern Family*. New York: Basic Books.

Sicherman, Barbara. 1975. Review Essay: American History. *Signs* 1, no. 2 (Winter): 461–485.

Simmons, Leo W. 1945. *The Role of the Aged in Primitive Society*. London: Oxford University Press.

Smith, Russell E., and Dorothy Zietz. 1970. *American Social Welfare Institutions*. New York: John Wiley & Sons.

Stuard, Susan Mosher, 1976. *Women in Medieval Society*. Philadelphia, PA: University of Pennsylvania Press.

Sussman, George D. 1977. The end of the wet-nursing business in France, 1874–

1914. *Journal of Family History* 2:237-258.

Tilly, Louise A., and Joan W. Scott. 1978. *Women, Work and Family*. New York: Holt, Rinehart and Winston.

Townsend, Peter. 1957. *The Family Life of Old People*. London: Routledge and Kegan Paul.

Tuchman, Barbara W. 1978. *A Distant Mirror: The Calamitous 14th Century*. New York: Alfred A. Knopf.

Walker, Sue Sheridan. 1976. Widow and Ward: The Feudal Law of Child Custody in Medieval England. In *Women in Medieval Society*, edited by Susan Mosher Stuard, pp. 159-172. Philadelphia, PA: University of Pennsylvania Press.

Ward, Barbara, ed. 1963. *Women of New Asia*. Paris: UNESCO.

Znaniecki, Florian. 1952. *Modern Nationalities*. Urbana, IL: University of Illinois Press.

2
Economic Dependency of Women and Children in America

In order to better understand the economic and social situation of women and children in America at the present time, we must trace the development of personal and family economic dependency. As in England, so in America vast areas of economic life have been converted into paid jobs, and anyone unable to earn money has become dependent on paid workers or the society. Few people can live on inheritance or investment. People discouraged or prevented from earning a living in urban America include: children, mothers of dependent children, the elderly, the disabled, and those otherwise unemployed. Thus the main wage earners until recently were the post-school, pre-retirement men and women without dependent children, especially if they were young and/or unmarried. Inflation and changing values have pushed many mothers into the labor force, but the sex segregation of that force and the traditional underpaying of women have resulted in a wage scale that offers women about 60 percent of what men receive. The result of all these changes has been the creation of a large segment of the U.S. population that is economically dependent on others. Some forms of this dependency are defined as "natural," as in the case of young children, others as a social problem to be solved by societal action, as in the case of deserted or widowed mothers of small children. The whole subject of economic dependency is heavily laden with emotionality.

AMERICAN HISTORICAL BACKGROUND

Colonial America adopted a large portion of its values and behavioral patterns from England, modifying them to fit its situation, developing others independently, and weaving its own cultural fabric, often with inconsistent elements (Boorstin, 1958, 1965, 1973). It could not duplicate the English social structure and culture for a variety of reasons. It was impossible to transplant sufficient segments of the mother country to clone it, and the life English immigrants could create in the new environment was necessarily very different. Many characteristics of the new land—especially its size and natural resources as well as the absence of a social structure acceptable to the early settlers—removed many of the constraints of the past, while simultaneously forcing the creation of new systems. The Indian way of life was not understood and was flatly rejected. This necessitated a slow build-up of the social structure from land-based families and small communities. Families worked together to clear the land, moving westward to conquer new territory. Although initially able to maintain only their own families on the new land, with mutual interdependence of neighboring settlers, farmers soon were also able to feed the increasing town population. Communities, organized politically and religiously, usually took care of families in trouble who were without kin support (Leiby, 1978). Once industrialization began, it expanded rapidly, without much of the social dislocation experienced in societies established on other economic traditions. The new nation could thus draw on European heritage, yet it was freed from the "hampering drag of centuries-old social and cultural habits and attitudes to impede its advances" (Davidson, 1951/1974:ix).

American society moved away from English culture through revolutionary and democratic ideology, emphasis on individualism, freedom from tradition when it interfered with the economic institution, laissez-faire policy, and states' rights (Brinker and Klos, 1976). These values combined with Puritanism to promote among its members high regard for hard work and its visible products. Its own history pushed the society into a variety of unique paths, merging at times into a united effort and world view, at other times diverging. As Leiby (1978:7) points out, American culture consolidated its focus on democracy during the 45 or so years of isolation from England following the Revolutionary War. This view of democracy did not, however, include a concern for the civil rights of children, women, Indians, or the increasing number of slaves (Leiby, 1978). The society itself changed considerably with mass migrations, bringing new cultures and new social problems, often crowded into the rapidly growing urban-industrial centers (see also Grønbjerg et al., 1978).

THE STATUS OF WOMEN IN PRE-INDUSTRIAL AMERICA

The Status of Married Women

One of the influences transplanted from England to America was British common law, which disenfranchised married women and left them without legal rights (Chapman and Gates, 1977; Demos, 1973; Riegel, 1975; Ryan, 1979).

> At common law, marriage made the wife legally incapable and laid on the husband the duty of supplying her with what the lawyers called "necessities," that is, with those things that seemed essential for her existence and such other things as accorded with the standard of life he was able to maintain.... The custody of the child belonged, with his earnings, to the father (G. Abbott, 1938:600).

The fact that the husband was the legal guardian of the family, including the wife, meant that

> In the nineteenth century, females were not allowed to testify in court, hold title to property, establish businesses, or sign papers as witnesses (Chafe, 1972:5).

The patriarchal nature of the family under this legal system is reflected in the fact that

> when a woman marries, she "loses her domicile and acquires that of her husband, no matter where she resides or what she believes or intends.... As of 1974, only four states allowed married women to have separate domiciles from their husbands for all purposes; another 15 allowed women to have separate domiciles for voting, six for election to public office, five for jury service, seven for taxation and five for probate (Babcock et al., 1975:575-576).

Another characteristic of the patriarchal family system in the United States was its insistence on patrilineal descent for inheritance and identity of women and children in the form of the male surname.

> However, it was apparently not until Victorian times that her [wife's] loss of identity generally included the loss of both her first and last names. And even then, it was a matter of widespread custom, not *law* in England (Babcock, 1975:579).

Ramay (1977:350) summarized the legal situation of women in America as follows:

> The majority of American women live their lives without ever being recognized by law as legal persons. In most jurisdictions until recently a woman was a minor until age 21. Most women marry at about age 21, and since man and wife are one in the eyes of the law, and that one is the man, the woman may never become a legal person.

Historians, however, do not agree on the social status of women in pre–twentieth-century United States. They initially viewed the former status of women to be much higher than common law would lead one to presume. The argument stated that women's social standing was enhanced by their scarcity (because immigration involved more men than women) and by the need for their work in the family and community. Norton (1979:335) and others have recently questioned the likelihood that need of women in colonial times translated to high social status:

> It has often been asserted that colonial women, especially those who lived in the seventeenth century, had a "high" status relative to their sisters in England and their descendants in the United States. Because females were relatively few in number (and therefore presumably in demand as marital partners) and because their labor was vital to the survival and maintenance of the household, it has been believed that colonial women probably wielded power within the home and that they were valued members of society. Current scholarship describes a more complex picture.

Demos (1973:84–93), who studied family life in Plymouth colony, believes that American circumstances led to a modification of the British common law, especially in "the transfer of land in inheritance, joint responsibility for the putting out of children into foster homes and business management." On the other hand, Norton (1979:336) claims that

> American women were denied some common-law protections enforced in England, and thus that the colonists' failure to follow prescribed law did not always work to women's benefit.

Ryan (1979) points out that many of the women who entered the United States as unmarried migrants were indentured servants and thus did not raise the status of their gender. Sicherman (1975) adds that the need for a person's labor does not necessarily translate itself into status and power, as evidenced by the situation of slaves or of unskilled workers.* In fact, Sicherman (1975) devotes her review essay on American history and the status of women to the complexities of past and current situations. Rosaldo (1974:36) develops a structural model which suggests

> that women's status will be lowest in those societies where there is a firm differentiation between domestic and public spheres of activity and where women are isolated from one another and placed under a single man's authority, in the home.

---

*The situation of slaves and of the whole world of work in America's South appears to have been very different from that in the North, but this volume concentrates on the urban North, since much of the data comes from metropolitan Chicago (see Quadagno, 1985).

This model ensures a low status for American women, especially after the eighteenth century. The assumption underlying the definition of wives and children as dependent on the husband/father is that the size of the earnings, not the work in maintaining a family, is the determining variable. Once the family no longer functioned as an interdependent productive unit, but began to live on earnings obtained from outside work, the work remaining in the home and confined to maintaining a personal family became defined as economically nonproductive (Glazer, 1980; Glazer-Malbin, 1977).

> The actual economic dependency of a homemaker is not inequitable in itself but is made so by the law. The refusal to value homemaking services in economic terms unfairly brands her as a socially nonproductive person. The supposed right to be supported by the husband without regard to her contributions to the family categorizes her as a parasite. . . . Having chosen dependency (through marriage), the traditional legal rules serve to keep the wife dependent (Krauskopf, 1977:105–106).

The economic dependency of wives became reinforced through the changes in the United States since colonial times. Industrialization, mass immigration, urbanization, and all the components of American modernization continued to move economically productive labor out of the home and created an employee rather than an entrepreneurial work structure (Hareven, 1975; Mills, 1956). Although "two-thirds of the nation's population still lived in rural areas in 1890, and nearly half of its families still made their living from the soil" (Smuts, 1959/1971:4), the northeastern part of the country experienced major occupational changes much earlier that that. This was accompanied by a change in the composition of the family (as women decreased their fertility) and in the ideology of the relative positions of women and men (Sicherman, 1975:468). The removal of productive work from the home into occupations performed in large organizations led to its masculinization, especially in jobs and at levels in which women were absent. Protective legislation and the action of male-dominated unions removed women even further from income or earnings-producing activities, and the public sphere became increasingly identified in masculine terms. Societal life became more and more focused on economic activity as the focal institution. Ware (1977:12) attributes the change in the labor force, as women became limited to a few sex-segregated occupations, partially to the union movement:

> The basic demand of the unions, led by the Western Federation of Miners, was for a living wage, which could enable a man to support his family in comfort and decency . . . They shared the perception of manhood and womanhood which had become popular during the nine-

teenth century when industrialization had destroyed the household as a productive unit based on shared activity and substituted the dichotomized world of work which was the domain of men and the home now defined as women's "natural" sphere.

The ideological definition of the life of women in the home had several consequences. These were evident to de Tocqueville (1835/1969) as early as the 1830s:

> In America, more than anywhere else in the world, care has been taken constantly to trace clearly distinct spheres of action for the two sexes, and both are required to keep in step, but along paths that are never the same. You will never find American women in charge of the external affairs of the family, managing a business, or interfering in politics; but they are also never obliged to undertake rough laborer's work or any task requiring hard physical exertion (601)...they seem to take pride in the free relinquishment of their will, and it is their boast to bear the yoke themselves rather than to escape from it.... In America a woman loses her independence forever in the bonds of matrimony. While there is less constraint on girls, there more than anywhere else , a wife submits to stricter obligations (599).

Dulles (1965) also reports European observers who were surprised at the absence of women from American public life, including recreation, as well as the absence of street life in general. The seriousness of life and the obligation to save human energy for work pushed this society away from leisure orientation, the function of recreation being only to re-create energy for the next day's work.

A growing ideological base gave support to the religious encouragement of women's home roles by the middle of the nineteenth century. This movement has been labeled "the cult of true womenhood," or the theory of the "spheres" (Douglas, 1977). According to this social ideology, the world is divided into two spheres, the domestic (dominated by women) and the public (dominated by men) (Sicherman, 1975; Welter, 1966).

> Any review of the now familiar evolution of the "woman's sphere" must start with the decline of economic production in the home and the transformation of domestic work into an activity with no commercial value. This trend was first visible in affluent middle-class families where women supported by their husbands could afford to stay home and devote themselves to the primary care of their families.... By the middle of the nineteenth century the vast majority of working-class mothers apparently were no longer gainfully employed (Block, 1978:246).

The division of the world into domestic and public spheres was accompanied by the redefinition of the personalities of women and men within their own cultural provinces. The men's world was defined as physically dangerous, competitive, and harsh, the men who lived in it as "uncultured," crude, and amoral. The world of the home and the hearth, supervised by the true woman, was redefined as economically dependent, submissive, physically in need of protection, and non-societally involved but warm, pure, and delicate (Cott, 1977; Dulles, 1965; Hartman and Banner, 1974; Sicherman, 1975; Welter, 1966). Although originally based on the Victorian romanticization of the upper-class woman as economically unproductive, delicate to the point of fainting but devoted to the arts and literature as "high culture," womanhood became so represented in America for all women who could afford such a life. It was particularly popular among east coast cities and nonfrontier and nonagricultural homes. In spite of the fact that early suffragettes fought the stereotype of women as fragile, passive, and lacking in mental ability and stamina, the weight of the image, reinforced later by Darwinism and Freudianism, retained its hold on American culture well into the 1950s in the form of the "feminine mystique" (Friedan, 1963; Harris, 1979; LaPierre, 1959). the rigors of pioneer life and the existence of immigrant women working hard to help the family survive in a strange land were neglected in this image of women (Cott, 1977).

There were several developments within the "woman's sphere" that had long-range repercussions. As the society grew in economic wealth, distributed unevenly but a visible proof of the "virtue of hard work," and men's interest remained focused on economic institutions, idealization of the home increased the importance of motherhood, even more than it did in Europe (Sicherman, 1975). Childrearing guides, originally written for fathers, now directed their attention to mothers. The harshness of discipline of the Puritan years, when parents were taught the importance of "breaking the wills" of children, became replaced with a more sentimental mothering (Demos, 1973; de Mause, 1974a, b; Lantz et al., 1968, 1973, 1975; Sicherman, 1975). The second long-range consequence of the segregation of women to the domestic sphere was what Douglas (1977) calls "the feminization of American culture." The increasingly educated and affluent middle-class women with time to do so, combined with the Protestant clergy which had been gradually deprived of status and power over the society, began a campaign of sentimentalizing the role of women and the aspects of culture that were their province. Women who no longer needed to "feed, clothe and equip the nation" (Douglas, 1977:57) turned their attention by the 1830s to a monopolization of "high culture" and the dissemination of its values and attitudes. They were helped by the clergy.

Between 1820 and 1875, the Protestant Church in this country was gradually transformed from a traditional instituation which claimed with certain real justification to be a guide and leader to the American nation to an influential ad hoc organization which obtained its power largely by taking cues from the nonecclesiastical culture on which it was dependent (Douglas, 1977:25).

Middle-class women devoted to full-time homemaking and economic dependency on the husband, who were both the creators and the consumers of popular culture, together with Protestant ministers began a joint campaign to reform American society, trying to remove many of the characteristics that were identifed with the male world, such as alcohol and the accompanying tavern life, "the vices," and exploitation of workers, particularly women and children. Feminine "influence" on culture was seen as a moral one, designed to soften the harshness of public life with an ideology emerging from the private sphere. Not surprisingly, this definition of the situation was often resented by men, increasing the schism between the genders.

Regardless of the woman's influence over the home and over the private organizations determined to cleanse society and relieve the lot of the poor, the American woman's position in the nineteenth century and in all but recent years remained upon marriage that of a "personal dependent" (Eichler, 1970). Her means of economic support, legal status, and social position were "tied to another person who has authority over her as a personal dependent" (Eichler, 1973:47; see also Nilson, 1978). This was true even if she was able to earn some income through such activities as running a boarding or rooming house, a rather frequent source of money until the 1930s (Modell and Hareven, 1973; Vogel, 1977). The large and increasing number of immigrants as well as unattached people needing housing and food because of personal crisis or community action created a market for such services, one of the few remaining income-producing sources when industry moved out of the home (Smuts, 1959/1971:14). Morgan and Golden (1979:64–65), for example, describe the household composition of Mount Holyoke families of 1880:

Just over one-third of all households included non-related persons— boarders, domestic servants, or other resident employees of the household head—but few households included more than one of these. The presence of domestic servants was the most frequent in households with native-born heads, probably reflecting their higher occupational status, while households with Canadian-born heads were most likely to include a boarder. The prevalence of boarding, and particularly the widespread tendency for private households to contain boarders appears to be characteristic of towns during the early industrial period of both Western Europe and North America, and probably represents a short-term response to the housing shortage created by rapid population growth and migration into town.

The Status of Husbandless Women

Thus employment of married women outside of the home acquired a social stigma in post-colonial America. However, girls between the end of schooling (when that institution was developed) and marriage, whose families did not need them for work around the home or farm, often went to the "factory cities" or towns where housing and protection of virtue were provided by employers. Hareven and Langenbach (1978) describe Amoskeag, founded in 1837, and similar communities up and down the Connecticut Valley (see also Easton, 1976; Hareven, 1977; Hareven and Vinovskis, 1978). Life for the "mill girls" was very different from that of the emerging middle-class wife, as Lerner (1969) explains. The numbers of such young women and their proportion in the female population of nineteenth-century America was quite large. For example, between 36 and 38 percent of the women aged 15 or over living in New York State in the years 1855, 1865, and 1875 were single, according to Vinovskis (1978:53). Whether living in specially constructed dormitories with chaperones or as boarders with town families, these young women generally contributed their wages after expenses to their families' total income and were thus regarded as an economic asset, enabling their mothers to stay home and take care of the family, even at times when the father was not earning a steady income (E. Abbott, 1913). The economic situation of many families in early industrialized America was precarious due to the instability of the business life, seasonal fluctuations, and the policies of employers. As a result, the earnings of each member were needed and parents were willing to have even very young children work in factories or otherwise earn money. The other main source of income for unmarried women was domestic service, which was usually rewarded with small wages but which ensured housing and food, as well as training in homemaking skills. It was often the only occupation available to young immigrant or second-generation women (Lopata, 1976).

An entirely different life faced women who had been married but whose husbands had died.* However, historians do not agree on the social status of widows in pre-industrial America. Until fairly recently it was assumed that their status was high.

> Widows were quite popular, even those with children. One reason was their economic status. The European custom of leaving the major portion of an estate to the eldest son did not survive in the colonies. In the

---

*Orloff and Skocpol (1984) believe that "many old and young widows" of the Civil War were receiving survivors' pensions from the 1870s on.

typical family, the widow, guaranteed at least one-third of her husband's estate, was the main beneficiary. Her second husband automatically acquired the product of these lands during her lifetime. Further, since children were a definite economic asset in the largely agrarian society, her proven fertility was no detriment to remarriage. Benjamin Franklin aptly noted that "a rich widow is the only kind of second-hand goods that will always sell at a prime cost" (Murstein, 1974:300).

The last statement of the above quotation certainly does not reflect a high personal status for widows. Sicherman (1975:466) reports on a study by Keyssar (1974) that questions the assumption that many colonial widows were rich. His study of widows in a town in Massachusetts finds their estate to be smaller than the town's average. They were often unable to maintain a farm or business because they did not inherit it whole or due to lack of sufficient funds to hire workers, the going rate being influenced by a shortage of labor (see also Sussman et al., 1970). His conclusion was that widows were "relatively poor, dependent and lacking other options" (Sicherman 1975:466), since so few occupations and ways of earning a living were open to women. Other descriptions of life in the nineteenth century and earlier make references to various activities for money or barter carried out by widows. Edith Abbott (1913:13) found them in work such as: keeping taverns and "ordinaries"; shopkeeping; running businesses; in trade; running dame schools; in service where they spent most of their time in manufacturing (i.e., as spinners or tailoresses); printing; bakers and wine makers; and knitting, spinning, and weaving in household industry.*

Kleinberg (1973) studied the life situation of working-class women in Pittsburgh, in the period between 1800 and 1890, and found widows to be frequently beset by problems. They often lived in the older part of town.

> The old section of the city had one of the highest percentages in the city of household heads who were widows (19 to citywide 14).... Their widowhood was not a result of the natural aging processes but of the hazards of the mills and mill neighborhoods.... As difficult as it was for women generally to find work, the widows in the mill area were isolated in parts of the city which had no jobs for them at all. The proportion of residents in these areas who might require their services as seamstresses, washerwomen or servants was low since these were precisely the areas which had few middle or upper class residents.... Instead they depended upon meager savings, the labor of their children or hand-

---

*For detailed discussion of the occupations of American women, see the two companion volumes to this study.

outs from charitable agencies (49-50)....Forty percent of all widows' sons were working at ages ten to fourteen (205), 27 percent of the widows' daughters worked (206).... If women worked at all, they did so as an interlude between childhood and marriage or after the death or desertion of their husbands (227).

THE FAMILY AND POVERTY

As U.S. society increased its insistence that married women should not seek employment outside the home and marriage became more attractive as a wish and possibility, girls were trained for a trade or profession less frequently than they had been in the past. When these trends were combined with the high economic dependence of wives and children on the breadwinning function of the husband/father, we find a high incidence of poverty in families in which the man was unable to earn this support or in families with female heads due to desertion, divorce, or the death of this breadwinner. Unemployment because of disability, the economic situation in the nation at large or in the area of residence, desertion, or widowhood was common (see Howards, Brehm, and Nagi, 1980). In spite of the consistent fear of Americans that charity or public welfare programs were supporting mainly able-bodied men who could be economically independent if they had the right "moral fiber," the majority of the poor in this society as in Europe have been wives and children of disabled workers, widows, and deserted wives or single mothers and their children (Leiby, 1978). Just as Americans adopted the principles of the Elizabethan Poor Laws, they accepted the whole attitude toward poverty as a crime, an evidence of "bad habits" and an immoral life style. The whole history of social welfare prior to the Social Security Act of 1935, particularly in its amended form of 1939, reflects this constant concern over, and suspicion toward the country's poor. This attitude was accompanied by the fear of "pauperism," the assumption that economic help to the poor would make the person "dependent and demoralized, unwilling to take care of himself" (Leiby, 1978:112). Although this attitude was incorporated in the Poor Laws of 1815-1845, it reached its height in the United States at the end of the nineteenth century.

Prior to attempts to recognize poverty as mainly a consequence of events beyond the control of the victims and therefore as a responsibility of the society, various attempts were made to identify the poor and assign their care to others. The insistence that the poor are to be cared for by the parish was transferred from England to America in the colonial period. The funds came from an assessment on property, called a "rate," and they were administered by a specific committee (Anderson, 1977).

People unable to take care of themselves were "put out" into the homes of others or contracted for care, the community covering their costs (G. Abbott, 1938). According to Coll (1969) there were

> ....four major means being used to care for the needy: the contract system, auction of the poor, the almshouse and relief in the home. Under the contract system all dependent persons were placed under the care of a townsman or farmer and his wife who offered to care for them for a lump sum, fixed as low as possible. The second system, which became increasingly subject to adverse comment, was to auction off the poor to the couple who agreed to take care of them for the smallest amount.... Placement in an almshouse was the third important means for caring for the indigent (Coll, 1969:21).

"Outdoor relief" was given in the form of money or "in kind," meaning as goods necessary for living. Finally, the poor were increasingly being housed in the United States, as they were in England, in workhouses. Each state, and sometimes each community, developed its favorite method of handling problems with its poor. Of course, the initial response of the community to finding poverty among some of its residents was to demand that relatives take care of them.

> The poor laws commonly required that the economic resources of certain relatives be tapped to support their dependent kinfolk. Colonial poor laws specified these relatives as the parents, grandparents, or children. By 1836 all states on the Atlantic seaboard except New York and the Southern states had added grandchildren to the list. Stipulations were later expanded in many states beyond the consanguine line to the collateral line to make brothers and sisters liable. However, litigation to enforce relatives' responsibility has never reached the higher courts to the same extent as suits about settlement laws. Poor persons usually have poor relatives (Coll, 1969).

The policy of "relative's responsibility" became narrowed down in turn over the years:

> The old poor law adopted a firm attitude toward relatives' responsibility: public aid was not given if there were relatives who were capable of supporting the needy family members and the span of the family for this purpose was very wide. Modern public assistance has greatly narrowed this concept of the family. In many states today (1954) brothers and sisters, uncles, aunts, cousins and grandchildren are not typically expected to contribute to the support of needy family members. But the laws still generally reflect the view that children should be responsible for the support of their parents (Burns, 1954/1970:138).

Even this narrowing of the persons who should contribute to the care of the needy to children of elderly parents was unsuccessful in preventing poverty in America. Edith Abbott (1938) discussed at length the problems old parents have had over the years in obtaining support from their adult children, problems that some brought to court as litigants, a difficult situation for all involved. Community agencies also tried to sue adult children who were not contributing to the support of their parents, but not as often as parishes brought cases against other communities for support of people who legally belonged as their residents. Burns (1954/1970:138) further pointed out that the 1950s brought pressure to limit even the children's responsibility because of the recognition that the expanded "economic responsibility of parents for their minor children" makes it "unreasonable also to expect the adult to support his needy parents." The policy of familial responsibility has been the subject of debate and legislation through the years, as evidenced by the fact that the state of Minnesota did not declare the removal of such responsibility from "grandparents, sisters and brothers of children receiving aid to families with dependent children for contribution to the necessary care and support of the recipient" (Minnesota House, 1980:11).

The removal of kin responsibility for the care of needy family members was an unsurprising consequence of the failure of the system. Anderson (1977:45) lists the following reasons for this failure:

1. It is difficult or impossible to enforce kin contribution in a society where some adults claim poverty or other obligations while others of equal income offer help.
2. The heterogeneity of the population makes a single policy impossible to formulate or impose.
3. The attempts to enforce kin help resulted in tensions within the families.
4. Dependence upon family members is not a good base for family relations, especially in a society with such a strong emphasis on independence.

Kreps (1977:22) develops this last point. She states that the official removal of family responsibility for the care of the aged contributes positively to intergenerational relations. It removes a source of conflict, changes the base of the interaction to mutual interest, affection and psychological support, and provides the middle generation the freedom of control over its own financial planning.

Thus, American society has moved a considerable distance from the old poor laws in its view of the best source of economic aid to the poor. However, the ideological shift of responsibility of such care of needy citizens to the federal system took a great deal of time and much heated debate. The shift from family and parish to larger unit responsibility, the community turning into a city, the state, and then the federal system, focused on several different types of indigent: children, mothers deprived of a male breadwinner, and the elderly. Each of these groups was the concern of different segments of the U.S. public and public policy, with a resultant absence of a uniform system.

Children and their Mothers*

The ideological position concerning childhood has also shifted dramatically in U.S. society, as in Western Europe, over the last three centuries. Children were seen as miniature adults in early history. The American Puritanical system also defined them as "heathen" by natural inclination, needing harsh methods of socialization in order to turn them into hard-working adults (Illick, 1974; de Mause, 1974a, b; Walzer, 1974). Their education was in the hands of the fathers, who, as we saw before, had legal rights to their earnings. Continuing the practice of using children for work in the home and farm as early in their lives as possible, families also utilized their labor in the cottage industries, as well as "putting them out" into the homes of others as apprentices or servants. In fact, as seen in the discussion of Plymouth colony (Demos, 1973), parents could send their children out for foster care if they felt they could not maintain them. The almshouses and workhouses were filled with children and other dependents. Their presence in such public institutions did not necessarily mean that they had no parents, only that the parents, or the mother or father left alone, felt they could not care for them or that the community defined the home of their parent(s) to be a "bad influence" or "unfit" to socialize them into proper virtue.

> In all colonies dependent children were indentured by local township, city or county poor authorities for care until a certain age (Fredericksen, 1950).

If not "put out" for the lowest bidder or placed in foster care, each child was expected to contribute labor to the family business (if there was one), do farm work, or earn income through outside employment (Wittner, 1977). For example, New York state, finding itself with many children defined as dependent on public care "sent out little companies of emigrants...after thoroughly cleaning and clothing them...to a village with an agent" (G. Abbott, 1938:140). According to Grace Abbott, New York City itself sent in 1872 "between twenty and twenty-four thousand children who have been placed in homes or provided with work" (140). Most of these children were sent to "Western states," meaning the Mid-

---

*Part of this section has been used for an article, "Social Construction of Social Problems over Time," by Helena Z. Lopata. *Social Problems* 31 (1984): 249–272.

west, and the state of Michigan "passed the first law regulating inter-state placement in 1895."

> It required that any person, society, or asylum placing children from an-other state in Michigan must file with the county probate judge a bond protecting the county from future support of the child (G. Abbott, 1938:133).

At the time when American society was rapidly industrializing but before unionization and federal actions forced employers to pay living wages, the employment of children was an economic necessity if the fa-ther could not earn enough to maintain the family. Child labor was also favored by the employers themselves. Children formed a cheap labor force and the societal redefinition of childhood as a time for learning and growth rather than for work had not developed sufficiently to pressure those who benefited from such labor. Widows and other mothers and children deprived of breadwinning husband/fathers frequently left the home together to go to their jobs. Tattler (1970:27) reports that in 1820

> according to the Digest of Manufactures, children comprised 43 percent of the labor force in the textile mills of Massachusetts, 47 percent in Con-necticut, and 55 percent in Rhode Island.... Massachusetts in 1842 limited the workday for children under twelve to 10 hours (30).

Child labor laws were slow to develop and were initially declared un-constitutional by the Supreme Court because they interfered with "nat-ural rights" of parents, "state rights" as against federal laws and "repub-lican" government in opposition to "federal" government (Rutledge, 1933). The case for a federal law was strongly made by Rutledge as late as 1933 in opposition to an address made by Clarence Martin, president of the American Bar Association. Rutledge (1933: 507) argued that state laws are totally inadequate, nonuniform and inconsistently applied.

> It may be admitted that there are some forms of child labor, particularly in the home or about the parent's business, which do not call for government control. But there are also vicious forms of child labor which may not constitute technical employment. The so-called family agree-ment (by which the parent contracts the labor of the entire family for a lump sum) is an example. Because the contractual relation of the em-ployer is with the parent rather than the child, it is possible that the child would not be technically an employee, though he would be a laborer subject to all the evils of employment.... Over two million children be-tween ten and seventeen were gainfully employed in 1930. State legis-lation in many instances is wholly inadequate and state enforcement is notoriously lax (507).

The pressure to abolish child labor, rather than just to control its hours and working conditions, mounted in the United States in the 1920s, with the help of what has now been called the "child-saving movement" (Platt, 1970) or "the crusade for children" (Chambers, 1963). The National Child Labor Committees debated the policy in 1918 and 1919, after the recent war

> .... revealed how debilitating of the national strength were lack of education, denial of opportunity, poor standards of health.... (it suggested that) Federal aid to education particularly in poorer states, would offer a positive alternative to employment in factory, field and mine by making schooling more attractive (Chambers, 1963:13).

Many groups joined to force a child labor law that survived the Supreme Court. This included the Consumer's League, the Women's Trade Union League, and the American Association for Labor Legislation, as well as the American Federation of Labor's Child Labor Committee, the Women's Joint Labor Committee, the League of Women Voters, the National Federation of Business and Professional Women's Clubs, the Young Women's Christian Association, the General Federation of Women's Clubs, the National Congress of Mothers, and the Parent–Teachers Association. The list indicates some of the extent of the women's organizational thrust in the United States as well as its focus of interest. Opposed to the child labor law were the Sentinels of the Republic, Women Patriots, the Citizens' Committee to Protect Our Homes and Children, the Moderation League of Pennsylvania, the National Association of Manufacturers, the American Farm Bureau Federation, and some Roman Catholic groups (Chambers, 1963:35–46). According to Chambers, one of the major historians of Social Security in the United States, the White House provided no leadership in this fight for legislation, and Congress moved slowly during the 1920s.

In the meantime, another effort to change public policy was being organized without waiting for the outcome of the legislative battle. This focused on the problems of dependent mothers and their children and the best way of resolving them. Public policy after the 1840s increasingly favored "inside relief" as the concern with "pauperism" increased in the United States. Criticism of "outdoor relief" was spurred by a social Darwinist ideology promoted by the work of Herbert Spencer in England and sociologist William Sumner in this country (Coll, 1969:42). Spencer, who coined the phrase "survival of the fittest," favored the abolition of the poor laws because they supported the socially unfit instead of encouraging only the fittest to survive. Spencer retreated from this position as a result of public outcries against his stance, justifying voluntary charity because it "encouraged the development of altruism" (Coll,

1969:42). However, the influence of this ideology which reinforced prior values of Americans, was evident in the repeal in many states of all forms of public outdoor relief. The policy was to leave only "indoor" relief in almshouses or workhouses, closely supervised and devoted to training for work. Help to people in their homes was to become the province of voluntary charity organized by each city's Charity Organization Society. These societies were imported from London in the 1870s, the first formed in 1877 (Coll, 1969:44).

> To the COS all relief was at best a necessary evil.... Assistance could be given to a family whose breadwinner had died or was disabled, when it appeared best to keep the family together. The aged could be helped if they were without blame for their destination and had no children able to assume responsibility. Widows with young children could be aided, if aid were accompanied by diligent supervision from the agent or the friendly visitor (Coll, 1969:54).

New York City was particularly prone to pressures to stop outdoor aid, but other cities along the east coast experienced similar redefinitions of the best methods of solving the problems of economic dependency. The Charity Organization Society specified, as we saw above, the criteria for eligibility of the "deserving poor," all other people being assigned to public welfare in the supervised almshouses and workhouses. Grønbjerg and associates (1978) refer to the former as the "politically deserving."

"Almshouses often served as temporary residences for children without parents or for those who had been taken away from one or both parents after agency people had declared the home unfit to care for them" (Lopata, 1984:254). An example of such a place was studied in 1898, with the following facts reported. Of 523 children sent to the Hudson County Almshouse,

> Fifty-four of these children were less than three years old when sent from the almshouse. The average age was about 10 years for boys and nine years for girls. No investigation was made of the type of home maintained by a person applying for a child. Few written reports as to the child's condition had been received by local officials, nor was there a record of any attempt within twenty years to enforce the standard of child care specified in the indenture papers (Epstein, 1933/1968:623).

Many of the almshouses were designed to function as workhouses, able to support themselves through the labor of their residents. However, most were occupied by people too ill, too old, or too young to perform paid labor. They were often repositories for all types of deviants and handicapped people for whom there were no specialized facilities such as mental hospitals or detention homes. Some of those along the east coast served as temporary residences and hospitals for new immigrants who arrived sick from the conditions of travel across the Atlantic. Coll (1969:23–24) points out that many doctors received their training in these workhouses. However, social reformers became concerned over the exposure of children to such people and over their being deprived of a "normal childhood." The solution they suggested was the creation of facilities for children alone. This led to a move to build "enormous orphanages by religious and charitable groups and by individual philanthropists for the housing of large numbers of dependent children" (Epstein, 1933/1968:623).

Grace Abbott (1938:80) described the procedure by which one state legalized the formation of workhouses in the case of "industrial schools for girls." Illinois passed a law in 1897 allowing the organization of such schools.

> The object of Industrial Schools for Girls shall be to provide a home and proper training school for such girls as may be committed to their charge; and they shall be maintained by voluntary contributions, excepting as hereinafter provided.... Any responsible person who has been a resident of any county in this state, one year next preceding the time at which the petition is presented, may petition the county court of said county to inquire into the alleged dependency of any female infant then within the county, and every female infant who comes within the following descriptions shall be considered a dependent girl, vis.: Every female infant who begs or receives alms while actually selling, or pretending to sell any article in public, or who frequents any street, alley or other place, for the purpose of begging or receiving alms; or, who having no permanent place of abode, proper parental care, or guardianship, or sufficient means of subsistence, or who for other cause is a wanderer through streets and alleys, and in other public places; or, who lives with, or frequents the company of, or consorts with reputed thieves, or other vicious persons; or who is found in a house of ill-fame, or in a poor house.

The petition to declare the female infant a dependent had to list the name of the father, mother, or guardian, if any were living or in the county. If living, the petition "shall also show that the parent or guardian is not a fit person to have the custody of such infant." In other words, any "respectable" resident of a county had the right to petition not only that an orphan or abandoned child, but also a child with parents who he or she decided was unfit, be taken and placed in the school (Lopata, 1984:255).

The practice of taking children from a widow or deserted woman appears to have been frequent, the argument being that she neglects them if she works for pay or provides a "poor home" if she does not (G. Abbott, 1934:4). In addition, American Puritan attitudes toward "pauperism," as chronic dependency on charity and the moral condemnation of the poor as creating their situation because they lack habits of work, justified removal of children to surroundings where they could be socialized into better "character." Even the indenturing of child workers, or foster care were deemed preferential to having the child grow up in his or her own home if the latter were deemed "unfit" because of poverty or the absence of a parent. The few cases in which the Charity Organization Societies allowed financial or "in kind" help to mother-headed families, existed only with the constant supervision of an agent or the "friendly visitor."

A reform movement began, however, at the turn of the twentieth century that attempted to reverse this tendency to take children away from their mothers. Frequent statements to that effect began appearing in charitable and mass communication periodicals documenting that

> ....children thrive better in bad homes than in good institutions and why children with parents are, apparently unreasonably, so attached to them.... Those responsible for institutions have sometimes been resistant to acknowledging that children are often better off in even quite bad homes.... It is still common in Western communities to see in the removal of the child from the home the solution to many family problems without there being any appreciation of the gravity of the step and, often, without there being any clear plan for the future (Bowlby, 1951/1966:68–70).
>
> Foster and institutional care rested on identical assumptions; that the families of the poor were out of control and that a change in environment would make productive citizens out of a population of children who were potential criminals (Wittner, 1977:39).

The private charitable organizations, which had gained control over all "outdoor relief" (while the states were limited to "indoor relief" with some combination of private and county funds, depending on the location), were highly opposed to any change in the system, particularly to the granting of funds to people directly, without the intervention of their investigatory procedures. Reformers pushing for the standardization of benefits for people in difficult situations, such as "mothers' pensions" to enable husbandless women to care for their own children at home, social insurance to keep the elderly from poverty or dependence on charity, or family allowance to help cover the cost of each additional child, were constantly fought by the private charity organizations. The latter were not necessarily just protective of their control over charity and other vested interests. They sincerely believed their philosophy and the need to couple financial aid with supervision and attempts at reform of the poor. The provision of automatic benefits to specified categories of people, distributed through the mail and defined as their right although they had not worked for this money was defined by these groups as detrimental to moral character.

"The clash between the voluntary [social work] agencies and the advocates of mothers' pensions was among the bitterest ever to arise in American philanthropy" (Lubove, 1968:95). The social work profession fought hard against "mothers' pensions" and any program that would provide funds automatically rather than through the activities of social workers who also took the opportunity of advising mothers on how to maintain the home and rear the children. Some social workers, Jane Addams being the best know, were "early proponents of pensions to mothers of children who were orphaned or deserted by the father, without the interference of the 'friendly visitor,' but they were a minority" (see especially Leff, 1973; Lopata, 1984:256). Leff (1973) uses as an example of the attitudes of social workers in a quotation from the 1888 Proceedings of the National Conference of Charities and Correction. The speech, by a Buffalo charity organization leader, concerns the termination of outdoor relief in Brooklyn in 1879: "It was wonderful...how the refusal to give outside the institution develops grit, restores health, and brings relatives and friends from under cover."

In spite of the opposition of many charitable organization, a White House Conference on the Care of Dependent Children was held in 1909. Attenders heard many reports as to the sad situation of children without a father, most of whom were still being housed in almshouses or church-related orphanages, although fewer were placed as indentured servants than in the colonial period (Fredericksen, 1950:15; Lubove, 1968:97). Several observers of the U.S. scene pointed out that institutions such as orphan asylums, county poor farms, and workhouses had vested interests in keeping the children and opposing "outside relief." They were paid a specified sum for each ward in their care and disliked the idea of losing this money. Women in charge of foster homes, where some children were housed, were also paid for their care, and in addition, used them as workers with the justification that they were training them for proper work behavior (Wittner, 1977).

Not without controversy, the White House Conference of 1909 attempted to reverse the policy of institutionalizing children and diminish the use of foster homes if the parents of the child were available to care for them. The recommendations of the conference were based on a strong family-oriented statement.

> Home life is the highest and finest product of civilization. It is the great molding force of mind and of character. Children should not be deprived of it except for urgent and compelling reasons. Children of parents of

worthy character, suffering from temporary misfortune and children of reasonably efficient and deserving mothers who are without the support of the normal breadwinner should, as a rule, be kept with their parents, such aid being given as may be necessary to maintain suitable homes for the rearing of the children. This aid should be given by such methods and from such sources as may be determined by the general relief policy of each community, preferably in the form of private charity rather than of public relief. Except in unusual circumstances the home should not be broken up for reasons of poverty, but only for consideration of inefficiency or immorality (U.S. Congress, quoted by Leff, 1973:400).

The specific recommendations, paraphrased by Friedericksen (1950: 20-21) included the following:

children should not be taken away from their homes by reason of poverty alone;
causes of dependency should be studied and as far as possible removed or minimized;
foster homes provide the most desirable care for those removed from their homes;
when care at an institution is necessary, the cottage plan is recommended;
all child-caring agencies should be under state approval and inspection (see also Lubove, 1968:98).

The Conference had visible results in that state legislatures began passing "mothers' pension" or "funds to parents" acts. The state of Illinois was the forerunner, enabling families to keep their children and obtain funds for their care if they lacked other sources of income. The funds were available to both widows and other mothers without a supporting father, a major move since the public was much less sympathetic to "dependent mothers whose husbands had deserted or were divorced, imprisoned, confined to a mental institution or permanently disabled" (Lubove, 1968:99).

Observers labeled the rapid state-by-state expansion of mothers' pensions as a "wildfire spread" (Leff, 1973:400). There were several cogent reasons why statutes were passed by so many states within such a short period. In the first place, the emphasis on keeping the family together supported many values of American culture. It was not appropriate to pay a foster mother for care of a child while the real mother, who was assumed to have much greater emotional investment in such care, worked elsewhere. The argument that it was cheaper to keep the child in its home than to care for it in institutions could not have hurt the cause. Finally, there was growing evidence that children brought up in institutions without individualized affective care were unable to function adequately in society as adults. Concern over juvenile delinquency and mental health of the youth pushed for new forms of caring for them and many "experts," such as judges argued for the de-institutionalization of as many children as possible. Even then, the Puritanical nature of American culture was evident in the qualification that "to be eligible to receive this pension, a mother had to be a 'proper person, physically, mentally and morally fit' to bring up her children" (Leff, 1973:401). Thus, the poor were redefined from immoral and incapable parents to worthwhile citizens in an unfortunate state. However, recommendations and laws still retained the power of determining if the home were "suitable" and the parent "fit" to rear the child with the charitable organizations and the emerging social welfare profession. (See Cook, 1979; Grønbjerg, 1977; Grønbjerg, Street, and Suttles, 1978; and Costin, 1972 for more current attitudes toward "deserving" and "undeserving" clients of public assistance.)

A Children's Bureau was another second major result of the 1909 conference. Pressure for expanding the number of states with mothers' pension laws was applied by a coalition of the Child Welfare Committee of America, the National Congress of Mothers, the Parent–Teacher Association, the National Consumers' League, the American Federation of Labor, and similar groups with the help of major newspapers and magazines (Leff, 1973). The public nature of the debate preceding, during, and following the White House Conference established the "right" of widowed mothers to a steady pension, freeing them from the possibility of losing their children and the humiliation of dependency on unsystematic aid under the auspices of private philanthropy. "A mother caring for her children," according to the proponents of the pensions, "made greater contribution to society than if she engaged in some other employment" (Leff, 1973:411). The pension was defined as payment for service rather than as charity. This statement had important consequences in coming years for the definition of the economic situation of widows and father-orphans as a social problem to be dealt with through governmental policy. State laws, administered by counties, were, however, a compromise between the historically embedded attitude of charitable "help" to the "impotent poor" and a full recognition of the right of widows and their children to a steady income without proof of need.

The years following the 1909 White House Conference on the Care of Dependent Children saw American society pass through World War I, the suffragette movement, and the beginnings of the Great Depression. Women got the vote in 1920, but few organized efforts were made to raise the economic welfare of women workers or those with dependent children but without a male breadwinner (Rossi, 1965). The mothers' pension program was never really successful, but it took until the 1930s before it became publicly defined as completely inadequate to meet the problem of the economic situation of widows with dependent children, or mothers deprived of a husband-earner for other reasons. Statistics began appearing as documentation of its failure (Bucklin, 1939). As late as "....1923, 64.2 percent of all dependent children receiving care were receiving it in institutions," and although "by 1933 the figure had dropped to 48 percent," relatively few children were being cared for at home with the help of the mothers' pensions (Wittner, 1977:45). "At no point before the enactment of the Social Security Act did more than half of the counties in the United States provide mothers' pensions" (Leff, 1973:412). Black mothers were almost never recipients of pension funds (Epstein, 1933/1968:635).

The criteria by which a mother could be considered unfit by the investigator included "use of tobacco and lack of church attendance" (Leff, 1973:412). The investigators had a great deal of power over the families.

> Families were forced to move from "neighborhoods whose morality was questionable." Investigators "visited" to enforce home cleanliness and rules against male boarders. The eviction of incapacitated husbands could be ordered if they were deemed "a menace to the physical and moral welfare of the mother or children." Mothers were obliged to prepare monthly budgets showing how they spent their pensions and met such requirements as "nourishment, no extras," or "warm clothes, not fancy." The Massachusetts Board of Charity was quite forthright in its statement of objectives: "The public authorities can make adequate relief a powerful lever to lift and keep mothers to a high standard of home care" (Leff, 1973:413).

Thus, by the 1930s observers had defined the Mothers' Aid program as completely inadequate in preventing poverty and humiliation among fatherless households for several reasons. In the first place, only 20 "states have included in their legislation...what might be called approved mothers' aid families" policies (G. Abbott, 1934:195). States (and especially counties) varied considerably in the amount of aid they provided and in criteria for refusal to give aid (G. Abbott, 1934). A third reason for dissatisfaction with the program was the onus it put on women in spite of the fact that it was not their behavior but their inability to have or keep an economically providing husband that placed them in need. Finally, the depression created real problems because local administrating agents tended to cut back on this program as need of other families, especially ones with unemployed husbands, increased their demands (G. Abbott, 1934:204).

In spite of all of its drawbacks and the unfairness as well as arbitrariness of the program in actual application, its passage had a great impact on American society. It established the right of mothers to keep their children even if there were no father in the family; and the obligation of society to offer them money for the service they performed through the care of these children.

> Yet the impact of the mothers' pension legislation had a large positive component. The past practice of juvenile court-martials, with poverty as the charge and family separation as the sentence, was abandoned. On the eve of the Social Security Act, the number of children aided by mothers' pensions rivaled the total in foster homes and orphanages combined (Leff, 1973:416). . . .It laid a foundation for later contentions that government had the responsibility to establish welfare as a right, independent of the compassion, altruism or paternalism of the "better" members of society. It shattered the view of income support as a mere adjunct to more direct programs of social control. It undermined the prestige of private charities to such an extent that they never again so confidently asserted their prerogative to define the government-welfare role. The United States had reached a preliminary recognition of poverty as a public program requiring governmental remedies (417).

Aged Women

While a great deal of public attention in the United States was directed in the early years of the twentieth century to the problems of children, people with other dependencies or difficulties were receiving new types of care through the efforts of many people during the Progressive Era (1900–1917) (Boardman, 1970; Leiby, 1978). Mentally ill people were beginning to be housed in special facilities, and attempts were made to make them again able to live in society. Aid to the blind, mutual aid societies, fraternal orders, and life and casualty insurance programs began in a variety of locations. The first old-age pension law was passed in Arizona in 1914 (Leiby, 1978:214).* Unions organized more and more workers and the government started antitrust lawsuits. "Management accepts an obligation for the well-being of labor" (Brody, 1968:163). Although "at the start of the century only seven states required school attendance to the age of 16, by 1915 the number had increased to 31" (Boardman, 1970:36). Cities began garbage collection and sanitation improved considerably. However, the elderly still depended on "the traditional agents of relief—kith and kin, the poor house, old age homes, and, in some cases, veteran benefits" (Achenbaum, 1978). However, Achenbaum (1978:113) concludes from his history of old age in America since 1790, that it gradually became defined as a national problem toward

---

*The Arizona old age pension was later declared unconstitutional (Quadagno).

which studies and "articles in popular and scholarly journals" became directed. Of particular concern was the increasing inability of the older male worker to find or keep employment and thus to support himself and his wife. Labor and management initially opposed any attempt at helping the elderly through some form of social insurance. The depression removed some of the ideological objections to financial security programs, however, since it became apparent that the elderly had no control over their inability to find jobs or to retain their savings (Achenbaum, 1978).

A careful examination of the literature of U.S. history prior to, and even during, the passage of the Social Security Act of 1935 and its amendments of 1939 unearthed a very interesting fact. Older women are simply not discussed in this literature, or are referred to only in passing. Widows are a subject of interest in connection with their roles as mothers of dependent children. Older women are assumed to be taken care of by their husbands (in spite of statistics documenting how many have no husband) or by their children (in spite of all discussions as to the inability of adult children to contribute financially to the care of the aged). As attention turned away from dependent children with the increasing economic depression of the 1930s, it moved into concern for the unemployed man and his family, less so to the elderly segment of the population:

> Paradoxically, the major motivating force behind the passage of the Social Security Act in 1935 was not the provision of adequate income in retirement but the creation of jobs. Passed in a period that at one point witnessed more than a quarter of the labor force without jobs, the social security legislation was one of many New Deal laws aimed at job creation and relief for those out of work.... Old-age pensions were provided to help the elderly financially but also *to encourage them to leave or remain out of the work force* (Schulz, 1976:89).

If this really was the basic motivation for this act, then it is not surprising that there were no provisions for the dependents of a retired worker in the 1935 act. The welfare of older wives and older widows was not the purpose of the act, even tangentially. Such women were relatively invisible in the society at large and in the minds of policy makers or even social scientists.

SUMMARY

This chapter traces the development of economic and legal dependency of wives, children, the elderly, and the poor on the family member who can earn an income through employment in organizations outside of the home. As American society grew in complexity and size, distributing itself mainly in urban centers and industrial activity, kin responsibility for the economic needs of people who could not work for pay, because of society policy or personal inability, became narrowed to the roles of husband and father. The responsibility for the elderly rested on the shoulders of the son until recently, when community measures and finally federal policy took over. Widows were expected to work and take care of themselves, young unmarried women often worked for pay which they turned over to their families. Children were seen as economic assets, working at an early age in houses, farms, or factories. Young children were taken away from homes lacking an employed and out-of-poverty father, whether his absence was due to death or desertion, and his inability to support the family due to disability or behavioral problems. Such children were at first placed by the community as indentured servants, then assigned to almshouses or workhouses. Only in the twentieth century has American society decided that such dependent children should remain in the care of their mothers, with the help of funds provided through various government administrative agencies.

Aid to dependent and poor people thus moved over the last three centuries from private charity to public indoor relief, while "outdoor relief" was taken over temporarily in the nineteenth century by private but "scientific" charitable organizations with investigators and "friendly visitors" checking on the morality of the home and trying to reform the poor. Poverty gradually became redefined from a sin or proof of moral weakness to a socially induced condition over which many people did not have any control. Puritanical attitudes toward the poor remain, however, in the form of the distinction between the "deserving" poor, such as widows and orphans and the elderly retired workers and their wives, and those whose behavior led them to poverty, such as unwed or deserted mothers. As we shall see in the next chapter, this distinction was written into law with the Social Security Act's amendment of 1939.

REFERENCES

Abbott, Edith. 1913. *Women in Industry: A Study in American Economic History*. New York: D. Appleton and Co.

——. 1938. Poor law provision for family responsibility. *The Social Service Review* 12: 598–618.

Abbott, Grace. 1934. Recent trends in mothers' aid. *The Social Service Review* 8, no. 2 (June): 191–209.

——. 1938. *The Child and the State*. Vol. 2, *The Dependent and the Delinquent Child*. Chicago, IL: University of Chicago Press.

Achenbaum, Andrew W. 1978. *Old Age in the New Land: The American Experience Since 1790.* Baltimore, MD: Johns Hopkins University Press.

Anderson, Michael. 1977. The impact on the family relationships of the elderly of changes since Victorian times in government income-maintenance provision. In *Family, Bureaucracy and the Elderly: An Organizational/Linkage Perspective,* edited by Ethel Shanas and Marvin B. Sussman, pp. 36–59. Durham, NC: Duke University Press.

Babcock, Barbara Allen, Ann Freedman, Eleanor Holmes Norton, and Susan C. Ross. 1975. *Sex Discrimination and the Law: Causes and Remedies.* Boston, MA: Little, Brown.

Bloch, Ruth H. 1978. Untangling the roots of modern sex roles: A survey of four centuries of change. *SIGNS: Journal of Women in Culture and Society* 4, no. 2 (Winter): 237–252.

Boardman, F.W. 1970. *America and the Progressive Era, 1900–1917.* New York: Henry Z. Walck.

Boorstin, Daniel J. 1958. *The Americans: The Colonial Experience.* New York: Random House.

——. 1965. *The Americans: The National Experience.* New York: Random House.

——. 1973. *The Americans: The Democratic Experience.* New York: Random House.

Bowlby, John. 1951/1964. *Maternal Care and Mental Health.* Geneva: World Health Organization.

Brinker, Paul, and Joseph J. Klos. 1976. *Poverty, Manpower and Social Security.* Austin, TX: Austin Press.

Brody, David. 1968. The rise and decline of welfare capitalism. In *Change and Continuity in Twentieth Century America, the 1920s,* edited by John Braeman, Robert H. Bremner and David Brody. pp. 221-262, Columbus, OH: Ohio State University.

Bucklin, Dorothy R. 1939. Public aid for the care of dependent children in their own homes, 1932–1938. *Social Security Bulletin* 2, no. 4 (April): 24–35.

Burns, Eveline M. 1954/1970. Significant contemporary issues in the expansion and consolidation of government social security programs. In *Economic Security for Americans: An Appraisal of the Last 50 Years, 1900–1953,* pp. 65–77. New York: Books for Libraries Press.

Chafe, William H. 1972. *The American Woman: Her Changing Social, Economic and Political Roles, 1920–1970.* New York: Oxford University Press.

Chambers, Clarke. 1963. *Seedtime of Reform: American Social Services and Social Action, 1919–1933.* Minneapolis, MN: University of Minnesota Press.

Chapman, Rane Roberts, and Margaret Gates, eds. *Women Into Wives: The Legal and Economic Impact of Marriage.* Beverly Hills, CA: Sage Publications.

Coll, Blance D. 1969. *Perspectives in Public Welfare: A History.* Washington, D.C.: U.S. Department of Health, Education and Welfare.

Cook, Fay Lomax. 1979. *Who Should be Helped: Public Support for Social Services.* Beverly Hills, CA: Sage Publications.

Costin, Lela B. 1972. *Child Welfare: Politicies and Practice.* New York: McGraw-Hill.

Cott, Nancy F. 1977. *The Bonds of Womanhood: Women's Sphere in New England, 1780–1885.* New Haven, CT: Yale University Press.

Davidson, Marshall. 1951/1974. *Life in America: Bicentennial Edition.* Boston, MA: Houghton Mifflin.

de Mause, Lloyd. 1974a. *The History of Childhood.* New York: Psychohistory Press.
———. 1974b. The Evolution of Childhood. In *The History of Childhood,* edited by Lloyd de Mause, pp. 1–73. New York: Psychohistory Press.
Demos, John. 1973. *A Little Commonwealth: Family Life in Plymouth Colony.* New York: Oxford University Press.
Douglas, Ann. 1977. *The Feminization of American Culture.* New York: Avon Books.
Dulles, Foster Rhea. 1965. *A History of Recreation: America Learns to Play.* New York: Appleton-Century-Crofts.
Easton, Barbara L. 1976. Industrialization and femininity: A case study of nineteenth century New England. *Social Problems* 23, no. 4 (April): 389–401.
Eichler, Margrit. 1973. Women as personal dependents. In *Women in Canada,* edited by Marylee Stephenson, pp. 36–55. Toronto: New Press.
Epstein, Abraham. 1933/1968. *Insecurity: A Challenge to America.* New York: Agathon Press.
Fischer, David Hackett. 1980. Growing old in America. In *Aging, The Individual and Society,* edited by Jill S. Quadagno, pp. 34–49. New York: St. Martin's Press.
Fredericksen, Hazel. 1950. *The Child and His Welfare.* San Francisco, CA: W.H. Freeman and Company.
Friedan, Betty. 1963. *The Feminine Mystique.* New York: Norton.
Fromm, Erich, 1947. *Escape from Freedom.* New York: Rinehart and Co.
Glazer, Nona, 1980. Everyone needs three hands; Doing unpaid and paid work. In *Women and Household Labor,* edited by Sarah Fenstermaker Berk, pp. 249–273. Beverly Hills, CA: Sage Publications.
Glazer-Malbin, Nona. 1977. Housework. *SIGNS: Journal of Women in Culture and Society* 1, no. 4 (Summer) : 905–921.
Grønbjerg, Kirsten. 1977. *Mass Society and the Extension of Welfare, 1960–1970.* Chicago, IL: University of Chicago Press.
Grønbjerg, Kirsten, David Street, and Gerald D. Suttles. 1978. *Poverty and Social Change.* Chicago, IL: University of Chicago Press.
Hareven, Tamara K. 1975. Family time and industrial time. *Journal of Urban History* 1 (May): 365–388.
Hareven, Tamara K., ed. 1977. *Family and Kin in Urban Communities, 1700–1930.* New York: New Viewpoints.
Hareven, Tamara K., and Randolph Langenbach. 1978. *Amoskeag: Life and Work in an American Factory City.* New York: Pantheon Books.
Hareven, Tamara K., and Maris A. Vinovskis, eds. 1978. *Family and Population in Nineteenth Century America.* Princeton, NJ: Princeton University Press.
Harris, Barbara. 1979. Careers, conflict, and children: The legacy of the cult of domesticity. In *Career and Motherhood: Struggles for a New Identity,* edited by Alan Roland and Barbara Harris, pp. 55–84. New York: Human Sciences Press.
Hartman, Mary S., and Lois Banner, eds. 1974. *Clio's Consciousness Raised: New Perspectives on the History of Women.* New York: Harper & Row.
Howards, Irving, Henry Brehm, and Saad Nagi, 1980. *Disability: From Social Problem to Federal Program.* New York: Praeger.
Illick, Joseph. 1974. Child-rearing in seventeenth century England and America.

In *The History of Childhood*, edited by Lloyd de Mause, pp. 303–350. New York: Psychohistory Press.

Kleinberg, Susan. 1973. Technology's stepdaughters, the impact of industrialization upon working class women, Pittsburgh, 1865–1890. Unpublished dissertation, University of Pittsburgh, Department of History.

Krauskopf, Joan M. 1977. Partnership Marriage: Legal Reform Needed. In *Women Into Wives: The Legal and Economic Impact of Marriage*, edited by Jane Roberts Chapman and Margaret Gates, pp. 93–121. Beverly Hills, CA: Sage Publications.

Kreps, Juanita M. 1977. Intergenerational transfers and the bureaucracy. In *Family, Bureaucracy and Elderly: An Organizational/Linkage Perspective*, edited by Ethel Shanas and Marvin B. Sussman, pp. 21–34. Durham, NC: Duke University Press.

Lantz, Herman R., Margaret Britton, Raymond L. Schmitt, and Eloise C. Snyder. 1968. Preindustrial pattern in the colonial family in America: A content analysis of colonial magazines. *American Sociological Review* 33 (June): 413–426.

Lantz, Herman R., Jane Keyes, and Martin Schultz. The American family in the preindustrial period: From baselines in history to change. *American Sociological Review* 40 (February): 21–38.

Lantz, Herman R., Raymond Schmitt, Richard Herman. 1973. The preindustrial family in America: A further examination of early magazines. *American Journal of Sociology* 79 (November): 566–589.

LaPierre, Richard. 1959. *The Freudian Ethic*. New York: Duell, Sloan and Pearce.

Leff, Mark H. 1973. Consensus for reform: The mothers' pension movement in the progressive era. *Social Service Review* 47 (September): 397–417.

Leiby, James. 1978. *A History of Social Welfare and Social Work in the United States*. New York: Columbia University Press.

Lerner, Gerda. 1969. The lady and the mill girl: Changes in the status of women in the age of Jackson. *American Studies Journal* 10, no. 1 (Spring): 5–15.

Lopata, Helena Znaniecka. 1976. *Polish Americans: Status Competition in an Ethnic Community*. Englewood Cliffs, NJ: Prentice-Hall, Inc.

———. 1984. Social construction of social problems over time. *Social Problems* 31, no. 3 (February): 249–272.

Lopata, Helena Znaniecka, with Cheryl Allyn Miller and Debra Barnewolt. 1984. *City Women: Work, Jobs, Occupations, Careers. Volume 1: America*. New York: Praeger.

Lopata, Helena Znaniecka, Debra Barnewolt, and Cheryl Allyn Miller. 1985. *City Women: Work, Jobs, Occupations, Careers. Volume 2: Chicago*. New York: Praeger.

Lubove, Roy. 1968. *The Struggle for Social Security, 1900–1935*. Cambridge, MA: Harvard University Press.

Mayhew, Henry. c. 1850. *London Labor and the London Poor*. New York: Harper & Brothers.

Mills, C. Wright. 1956. *White Collar*. New York: Oxford University Press.

Minnesota House. 1980. File 408 2135, *Session Review* (May) 1980:11.

Modell, John, and Tamara K. Hareven. 1973. Urbanization and the malleable household: An examination of boarding and lodging in American families. *Journal of Marriage and the Family* 35 (August): 467–479.

Morgan, Myfanwy, and Hilda H. Golden. 1979. Immigrant families in an industrial city: A study of households of Holyoke, 1880. *Journal of Family History* 1 (Spring): 59–68.

Murstein, Bernard I. 1974. *Love, Sex and Marriage Through the Ages.* New York: Springer Publishing Co.

Nilson, Linda Burzotta. 1978. The social standing of a housewife. *Journal of Marriage and the Family* 40, no. 3: 541–548.

Norton, Mary Beth. 1979. American History Review Essay. *SIGNS: Journal of Women in Culture and Society* 5 (Winter): 324–333.

Orloff, Ann Shola and Theda Skocpol. 1984. Explaining the politics of public social spending. *American Sociological Review.* 49 no. 6 (December): 726–750.

Papanek, Hanna. 1979. Family status production: The "work" and "non-work" of women. *SIGNS: Journal of Women in Culture and Society* 4, no. 4 (Summer): 775–781.

Platt, Anthony M. 1970. The rise of the child-saving movement: A study in social policy and correctional reform. In *Crisis in American Institutions,* edited by Jerome H. Skolnick and Elliot Currie, Boston, MA: Little, Brown.

Quadagno, Jill. 1985. Personal correspondence.

Ramey, James W. 1977. Legal regulation of personal and family life styles. *The Family Coordinator* 26, no. 4 (October): 349–360.

Riegel, Robert F. 1975. *American Women: A Story of Social Change.* Madison, NJ: Fairleigh-Dickinson University Press.

Rosaldo, Michelle Zimbalist. 1974. Women, culture and society: A theoretical overview. In *Women, Culture and Society,* edited by Michelle Zimbalist Rosaldo and Louise Lamphere, pp. 17–42. Stanford, CA: Stanford University Press.

Rossi, Alice S. 1965. Equality between the sexes: An immodest proposal. In *The Woman in America,* edited by Robert Jay Lifton, pp. 98–143. Boston, MA: Houghton Mifflin Co.

Rutledge, Wiley. 1933. The federal government and child labor. *The Social Service Review* 7, no. 4 (December): 555–571.

Ryan, Mary. 1979. *Womanhood in America: From Colonial Times to the Present.* New York: New Viewpoints.

Schultz, James S. 1976. *The Economics of Aging.* Belmont, CA: Wadsworth.

Sicherman, Barbara. 1975. Review essay: American history. *SIGNS: Journal of Women in Culture and Society* 1, no. 2 (Winter): 461–485.

Smuts, Robert W. 1959/1971. *Women and Work in America.* New York: Columbia University Press.

Sussman, Marvin B., Judith N. Cates, and David T. Smith. 1970. *The Family and Inheritance.* New York: Russell Sage Foundation.

Tattler, Walter I. 1970. "Crusade for the children: A history of the National Child Labor Committee and the child." *Labor Reform in America.* Chicago: Quadrangle Books.

Tocqueville, Alexis de. 1835/1969. *Democracy in America.* Edited by J.P. Meyer. Garden City, NY: Doubleday and Co.

Vinovskis, Maris A. 1978. Marriage patterns in mid-nineteenth century New York State: A multivariate analysis. *Journal of Family History* 3, no. 1 (Spring): 51–61.

Vogel, Lise. 1977. Hearts to feel and tongues to speak: New England mill women in early nineteenth century. In *Class, Sex and the Woman Worker,* edited by

Milton Cantor and Bruce Laurie, pp. 64–82. Westport, CT: Greenwood Press.

Walzer, John. 1974. A period of ambivalence: Eighteenth century American childhood. In *The History of Childhood*, edited by Lloyd de Mause, pp. 351–382. New York: Psychohistory Press.

Ware, Caroline. 1977. Introduction. In *Class, Sex and the Woman Worker*, edited by Milton Cantor and Bruce Laure, pp. 3–19. Westport, CT: Greenwood Press.

Welter, Barbara, 1966. The cult of true womanhood: 1820–1860. *American Quarterly* 18, no. 2 (Summer): 151–160.

Wittner, Judith. 1977. Households of strangers: Career patterns of foster children and other wards of the state. Unpublished dissertation, Northwestern University, Department of Sociology.

3
The 1930s:
The United States
and the Social Security Act

Historian Carl Degler (1970:379) considers the events of the 1930s to be "the third American revolution," the first being the revolt against the British, and the second, the Civil War. The 1930s saw the ending of "laissez faire" policy on the federal level, the strengthening of the federal government and the Democratic party, a revolution in the organization of labor, and the creation of many policies under the rubric of the New Deal aimed at improving the welfare of U.S. citizens. The impetus for many of these changes was a serious depression and unemployment which hit the country in 1929 and progressively worsened.

> And, as the Civil War was precipitated from the political and moral tensions of the preceding era, so the Great Depression was the culmination of the social and economic forces of industrialization and urbanization which had been transforming America since 1865 (Degler, 1970:379).

A major segment of this "third revolution" was the movement of the federal government into problem definition, policy formulation, and program development on a national scale. Equally important was the shift in definitions of human dependency and citizen rights. As mentioned before, earlier U.S. history was characterized by a philosophy of "rugged individualism" and the refusal of government agencies to protect citizens from poverty or family problems. Calvinist Puritanism laid the foundation for the definition of the poor as unworthy of devine blessing, lazy, sinful, and immoral (Snowman, 1977:37–60). The expanding economy and the availability of land were seen as providing everyone opportunity and few people examined carefully the composition of the poor population. Social Darwinism discouraged aid for the "unfit" beyond the most demeaning level. The ideology of volunteerism, self-sufficiency, and superiority of voluntary institutions over government predominated (Brown, 1972; Leiby, 1978; Sanders, 1973; Snowman, 1977).

This whole ideology changed with the New Deal, although not without conflict and opposition, mainly from the conservatives, but also from a variety of positions left of center (Ekirch, 1969).

> The era of the New Deal thus marked a general attack upon the doctrines of laissez-faire individualism or Darwinian struggle for survival. No longer were poverty and unemployment to be condoned as the fruits of improvidence; no longer was competition considered superior to cooperation and association as a regulator of the national economy (107–108)....For the older isolated individualism there was not substituted, in the Beards' phrase "an interlaced system of exchange and mutuality correctly described as collectivism" (Ekirch, 1969:108).

A detailed view of the nation at the beginning of this decade will help us understand the significance of the changes in values and policies that took place during the 1930s.

AMERICA OF THE 1930s: A HISTORICAL–DEMOGRAPHIC VIEW

In 1930 the United States was still a young nation, created out of mass immigration, mainly from Europe. The native Indian population was quickly outnumbered and ignored in the culture and life of the society. The peak of foreign immigration occurred in the years between 1880 and the 1920s, when very small immigration quotas were imposed on most countries from which the people had emigrated. Although most of the immigrants from any country were young men, families followed and ethnic communities emerged in the United States (see Lopata, 1976). In the 1930s these communities housed both the foreign-born immigrants and their native-born children. Most Americans were of the second or third generation. The population, as well as the nation, was young. The median age was 26.5 years, but this was already nine years more than it had been a century ago. Overall, women were still younger than men, as they had been in prior decades. Their median age increased in the following years, with a decrease of mothers' deaths in childbirth and a slower improvement of health among men. There was in 1930 a gap of 3.3 years between white and black women, the latter group being disadvantaged by an imposed history and life style. The median age of women of "other races," was much younger. Native American women experienced a much shorter life span, and Asian women were new immigrants. The other foreign-born white population had a much higher median age, since the current generation was already aging and not being replaced by many younger immigrants.

The rapidity of urbanization is evident in the fact that only 22 percent of American families lived on farms in 1930, down from 31 percent in 1910. The peak was reached in 1935, while urban populations were also increasing, so that the proportion of farm to nonfarm families was 23 that year. The number of farm families did not vary much prior to 1960; but it dropped considerably that year, so that by 1970 only 4 percent of American families lived on farms. The numbers of households and the relative proportion of farm to nonfarm households reflects the history of this country, in which farming was an important activity for a large number of families, until modern technology developed into an agribusiness while the cities became filled with immigrants and the children of farmers.

The median years of school completed by Americans was difficult to establish before 1940 because, although public schools had been in existence for decades, attendance varied considerably by community. "In 1930 one of every seven persons of college age was in college and one of every two persons of secondary school age was in high school" (Sanders, 1973:44). By 1940 American men aged 25 and over had completed 8.3 years and American women 8.5 years of schooling. Fifty-seven percent of the women had not gone beyond grade school. The quality of education in all but middle- and upper-class schools was generally low, and parents were in the habit of taking children out of school to work for pay when the earnings of the father were insufficient or to care for younger siblings at home. As we shall see later, child labor was still in existence and many immigrant families did not value education to the degree that the ideology of democracy encouraged. For example, Polish immigrants in America, most of whom entered as young people between 1880 and 1924, used their children's earnings or work on the farm to increase their property and status (Lopata, 1976). Many people who were adults in 1940, it must be remembered, were likely to have obtained their schooling around the time of World War I. Trattner (1979:154) points out some of the consequences of this combination of child labor and lack of schooling from figures of military conscription during World War I:

> Approximately 31 percent of all Americans between the ages of twenty-one and thirty-one drafted for service were rejected because they were physically unfit. The draft also revealed an appalling amount of illiteracy in the United States. Of approximately 1,500,000 men who were tested, over 300,000, or 20 percent, were unable to read or write—one of the highest illiteracy rates of all the advanced countries in the world. The average level of education among the draftees was sixth grade (154).

Of course, many of the young men called up for the armed forces were immigrants who had entered in the great wave prior to the war. They and the sons of prior immigrants often attended foreign language schools. The education of others was affected by racial prejudice and the poverty of the South. American society was in an exaggerated pyramidal form, the lower classes far outweighing in numbers the middle and upper classes.

The economic dependence of unemployed women in a money economy is heavily influenced by not only their limited knowledge of the society and the attitudes of the community to the employment of different categories of women, but also by their marital and parental status. This is especially true of American urban women. Age at marriage and at the birth of the first child, as well as the number of children and household members for which a woman is responsible are, in turn, influenced by major events and trends of the society. Several such events experienced by American women have included World War I, the Great Depression (Elder, 1974), World War II, the baby boom, and the "feminine mystique" (Friedan, 1963). Women themselves undertook changing patterns of involvement in a changing occupational structure.

In 1930, the median age at first marriage for women was 21.3, a drop from 22 years in 1890; the median for men was 24.3 years in 1930, a drop of almost two years since 1890. Men in Western Europe and America have traditionally married younger women, but the gap between the ages of men and women had decreased until 1970. Modern family culture has resulted in the young couple having to support itself. A delay in marriage usually means the birth of fewer children to the woman and increases the probability of employment in youth as well as the length of attachment to the labor force.

A major difference between American women of 1930 and 1970 had been a large reduction in the proportion who remain single (i.e., never marry) (see Table 3.1). The decrease in the proportion of women who remain single is mainly due to the increase in married, rather than widowed or divorced women. However, the increase in the number of women in those two situations should not be ignored, since they are likely to be the "displaced" homemakers who had been dependent upon a man for economic support, which they then lost. Single women provided a pool of employees usually removed through marriage, of private servants in the pre- and early industrial eras, of factory workers, clericals, and professionals in the 1930s. In 1970 single women were more likely to become wives than were single women in the past, except in early colonial times, when there was a shortage of women. On the other hand, the pool of employees was increased in decades since the 1930s due to the growing number of married women and mothers who are willing to work outside of the home.

The cohort of women born between 1900 and 1910 was between 20

Table 3.1 Marital Status of Women in the U.S. Population at Large and the Labor Force 1890–1980

| Year | Number of women (1,000) | Percentage by marital status | | | | Percentage in civilian labor force[a] | | | |
| | | | | | | Percentage of female labor force | | Percentage of female population | |
		Single	Married	Widowed	Divorced[b]	Married	Widowed	Married	Widowed
1890[c]	20,239	34.1	54.9	10.6	0.4	14	18	5	30
1900[c]	24,951	33.3	55.2	10.8	0.5	15	18	6	32
1910[c]	30,905	31.8	57.2	10.2	0.6	25	15	11	34
1920[d,e]	36,190	29.4	58.9	10.8	0.8	23	—[e]	9	—
1930[d]	44,013	28.4	59.5	10.8	1.3	29	17	12	34
1940[d]	50,549	27.6	59.5	11.3	1.6	36	15	16	30
1950[d]	56,970	19.6	66.1	12.2	2.2	52	16	23	33
1960[d]	64,875	19.0	65.6	12.8	2.6	61	16	32	36
1970[d]	69,474	13.7	68.5	13.9	3.9	61	15	40	37
1980[d]	83,800	17.1	63.0	12.8	7.1	60	15	51	41

Figures for the period 1890–1960 refer to females aged 14 years and older; figures for 1970 and 1980 refer to females aged 18 and older. See original sources for explanations of changes in population base resulting from changes in the composition of the United States or in census definitions.

[a]Source: U.S. Bureau of the Census. 1975. *Historical Statistics of the United States: Colonial Times to 1970*. Bicentennial ed., Washington, D.C.

[b]Women identified as "marital status not reported" are omitted from this table.

[c]Source: U.S. Bureau of the Census. 1975. *Historical Statistics of the United States: Colonial Times to 1970*. Bicentennial ed. Washington, D.C. Part 1, Series A 160–171: 20–21.

[d]Source: U.S. Bureau of the Census. 1984. *Statistical Abstracts of the United States*, 104th ed.

[e]In that year, the category of "single" included the widowed or divorced.

and 30 years of age in 1930, when the Depression had already begun. The number of children they produced is lower than the cohort immediately before and the trend continues in the following age cohort. Large families of ten or more children practically vanished by the 1930s and families with seven to nine children dropped from 22 percent to 4 percent within about a decade. A very high proportion of women between the ages of 20 and 34 in 1940 were still childless, a reflection of the depression years. The drop in the number of children per woman reflects the social situation in that, as the Brownlees (1976) state, the colonists reproduced in high rates. Referring to the years between 1675 and 1929 they conclude that

Certainly the pivotal characteristic of the American population was its phenomenal rate of growth; during the eighteenth century the population more than doubled every twenty-five years—a rate at least twice that prevailing in Europe at the same time. The transatlantic movement of people was important in creating that higher rate of increase, but it was the reproduction of the existing population that accounted for most of the differential between the American and the European rates. Behind the remarkable rate of natural increase are two central factors that directly affected the role of women in America: (1) colonists, in response to greater agricultural opportunities, married somewhat earlier and thereby tended to have more children during the course of their marriages than did Europeans; (2) as a result of the more favorable conditions of land and climate in America, mortality rates, particularly for infants and children, were lower, perhaps by as much as half (Brownlee and Brownlee, 1976:8–9).

The decrease in the number of children per family by the 1930s was not uniform across the population. A simultaneous trend had been, and continues to be at an extremely high rate: the increase of illegitimate births. These are usually accompanied by the absence of the father from the home and neglect of economic support of the family. The sudden increase in illegitimacy occurred after World War II and has affected the lives of many Americans of the 1970s. It is particularly the uneducated, lower-class black and "other" social races that have experienced this trend of illegitimate births. The trend often followed the waves of migration to the northern urban centers, with its inevitable break-up of family and community social control, poverty, and community disorganization (Drake and Clayton, 1945; Thomas and Znaniecki, 1918). This trend put fatherless families very much in the minds of reformers and policy makers of the 1930s (this situation is discussed further in Chapter 6).

Looking now at the results of marital and parental status, we can briefly examine the composition of households managed by women in American cities. By the 1950s, the proportion of families with no children under 18 years of age hovered around 40–50. The ages of the children and the presence of other adults in the household are important features. The best way to understand what is meant by household composition is to obtain the definitions of households and classification of members used by the U.S. government. The Bureau of the Census (1975, Part 1:6) defines its basic concepts as follows:

> A household includes the related family members and all the unrelated persons, if any, such as lodgers, foster children, wards, or employees who share the housing unit.... Households classified as having a male head include those where the head of the household is a married man whose wife lives with him and all other households with a male designated as head. Female household heads include women who are not married or not living with their husband and who are designated as household heads. Data for families are shown only for 1940 and later years. Prior to 1940 the concept of "family" was basically synonymous with the present concept of "household" wherein a family comprised the head of the household and all other members of the household related to the head. The term "family," as shown here, refers to a group of two or more persons related by blood, marriage, or adoption and residing together in a household. Unrelated individuals refer to persons (other than inmates of institutions) who are not living with any relatives. A primary individual is a household head living alone or with nonrelatives only. A secondary individual in a household is a person such as a guest, lodger, or resident employee who is not related to any other person in the household.

There are a few aspects of these definitions that are worth noting for current and future reference. Feminists have objected strongly to the fact that a husband was automatically designated as the head of the household and have recently instituted a change, in that respondents are asked who is the head. The pre-1940 census classification of all persons living in a household as "family" has historical precedence. As Aries (1962), Laslett (1973, 1978), Shorter (1975), and other historians have pointed out, the idea of family as defined after 1940 is a relatively new concept. Boundaries between people related by blood, marriage, and adoption and the rest of the world started being drawn in the eighteenth century. The recent removal from the household of persons who do not form the nuclear family of one or both parents and minor children has further narrowed the idea of the family. Most Americans think of only the nuclear unit, of the family of orientation into which they were born and the family of procreation that they create, when the world "family" is introduced. The extended family is increasingly seen as a matter of choice in contact and interaction and is referred to as "kin." Recent redefinitions of the family have removed the interior of single residence and are otherwise attempting to broaden the concept of family.

The shrinking household size from the 1920s reached 3.67 in 1940 and, in spite of the baby boom of the 1950s and 1960s, continued to decrease until 1970. At the time of that census, the proportion of "primary individuals" living away from families had increased considerably, while that of unrelated individuals living with others had gone down. This dual trend is especially true of women. The expanding numbers of divorcees and widows has been accompanied by their increased independence of attitude and economic situation, thanks to an expanded labor market in specialties drawing their gender, and to social security. This enables more women than ever to live alone. In the 1930s the majority lived in the homes of their married children (see Lopata, 1979).

The differentials in death rates between men and women, and the cultural norm encouraging men to marry down in age, make it much more likely that elderly males live in families, or at least with a wife, while women are more apt to be widowed and living alone. Moreover, the number of younger women who were heads of families in 1970 was much higher than that of 1940 families (Table 3.2).

The figures in Table 3.2 are dramatic, because they mean that as early as 1940, 26 percent of the families lacked a male head. Women heads of families or subfamilies and those living alone had to gain some means of economic support other than the wages of a husband, in spite of the dominant ideology which defined a woman's basic roles as those of companion to her husband, mother to developing children, and homemaker (Brownlee and Brownlee, 1976; Rothman, 1978). The figures for 1970,

Table 3.2 American Female-Headed Households, 1940 and 1970 (in thousands)

Year	1940	1970
Total number of families	32,166	51,586
Female heads of families[a]	3,616	5,591
Female heads of subfamilies[a]	464	484
Primary individuals[b]	1,859	7,882
Secondary individuals[c]	2,476	1,412
Total	8,415	15,369
Percentage of families	26	30

Source: U.S. Department of Commerce, Bureau of the Census, *Historical Statistics of the United States: Colonial Times to 1970. Bicentennial Edition.* Part I. Washington D.C.: Government Printing Office, 1975, p. 41.

[a]One parent with one or more unmarried children under 18 years old, living in a household and related to, but not including, the head of the household or his wife.

[b]A primary individual is a household head living alone or with nonrelatives only.

[c]A secondary individual in a household is a person such as a guest, lodger, or resident employee who is not related to any other person in the household p. 6-7.

adding up to 30 percent of families, have been discussed in several studies, including those of Ross and Sawhill (1975) and Hayghe (1975). The ideology of the 1970s was much more supportive of the independent woman than it had been in the 1930s and 1940s, and the Social Security Act and its amendments provided an economic base for some of these families. As we shall see in the following chapters, however, U.S. society has not been very willing to help individual women, or certain categories of husbandless women, either financially or in terms of services, especially when compared to other societies (see Kamerman and Kahn, 1978; Grønbjerg, Street, and Suttles, 1978).

Married women stayed out of the labor force, in response to the "cult of domesticity" and the structural and attitudinal barriers to their employment around the turn of the century, as is well documented in Table 3.1 (see Ehrenreich and English, 1979). Employers saw mainly unmarried workers since only 15 percent of the female labor force was married. By 1930, married women formed 29 percent of the female labor force but only 12 percent of the total labor force. In addition to single women (a category that contributed a consistently smaller fraction to the figures for employed women, due to the increase in married workers), a steady 14 to 18 percent of the female employees are widowed or divorced. Many women who are no longer married have stayed out of the labor force because of old-age and health problems, while others could not get a job. These distributions have changed again in recent years.

Although in 1948 few married women worked, whether they had any children or not, it is the presence of small children in the home that has most often prevented the employment of American females. However, even here there has been a great deal of change, especially among mothers of school-age children. One of the reasons may be that the number of children under age eighteen, and even under age six per household has dropped considerably. It is easier for women with fewer children to find mother-substitutes or to arrange alternative schedules in order to enter paid employment than it is for women with a larger family, even in the absence of a father or another adult from the home (Bird, 1979; Komarovsky, 1953; Lopata and Norr, 1980). In addition there have been ideological and economic changes.

Not only did the marital and parental distributions of women in the labor force change from the turn of the century to 1930 and then again before the 1970s, but so did their occupational involvement. The shift from agriculture reflects the change in the population as a whole. Involvement of women in manufacturing has decreased first with the entry of men, then with the whole movement of the economy from the smoke-stack industries (Brownlee and Brownlee, 1976; Coll, 1969; Degler, 1970; Rothman, 1978). Domestic and personal service dropped, with workers shifting from the domestic service to the public sector. The highest increase was in clerical occupations, as women took over from men and the typewriter expanded the market for such labor. As professional services expanded for women, they became increasingly sex-segregated, funneling women into teaching and nursing (Brownlee and Brownlee, 1976; Ehrenreich and English, 1979; Smuts, 1959/1971).

Children aged 10 to 15 were still employed as late as 1930. However, by 1930, the number of children aged 10 to 15 of both sexes who were in paid employment was down to about one-third the number in 1910. Of course, it was often hard for census takers or researchers to determine the exact numbers of working children once the tide of opinion as to the benefits of such employment shifted. Although children's wages continued to be an important part of family economics in the first half of the twentieth century, the value system changed definitions of the situation and the demand for their education decreased this source of family income (see Tattler, 1970). This means, however, that women were deprived of yet another source of maintenance, having themselves been discouraged from earning it directly.

AMERICA OF THE 1930s:
SOCIAL PROBLEMS AND SOCIAL POLICIES

By 1930 the United States was in the midst of a serious depression, with no idea of when it would end and no government policy or program to alleviate it. President Hoover did not initiate a recovery program, in spite of a report by the President's Research Committee on Social Trends, which he appointed in 1929, which warned of "the need for constructive social policy and initiative" (Sanders, 1973:52).

> President Hoover, who reflected the views of the conservative forces in the country, denied at the outset the need for any change or governmental intervention. In the 1928 presidential campaign, Herbert Hoover had acclaimed the solution of socioeconomic problems automatically by the business process as "our American experiment in human welfare" (Sanders, 1973:50).

President Hoover's refusal to institute programs to alleviate the increasing depression, create jobs, and help families was based on three sets of values and attitudes. In the first place he

> argued that federal aid would impair the credit and solvency of the government, that it would delay natural forces at work to restore prosperity, and that it was illegal—a violation of the age-old principles of local responsibility and states rights (Trattner, 1979:225).

In addition, Hoover was optimistic that the situation would vanish and prosperity would return soon without intervention. Finally,

> Hoover was trapped by his loyalty to the American folklore of self-help. For him, relief was a moral, not merely an economic matter; private charity was fine, but public aid, especially from the national government was a "dole." Thus, he rejected all proposals for federal aid.... Federal aid for the unemployed and needy was defined by the President as government mastery. (Trattner, 1979:225).

In spite of the popularity of the traditional stance toward poverty, the depth of the Great Depression, with the stock market crash, the bank failures, and dramatically expanding unemployment made it apparent to millions of people and social leaders that governmental action was needed. Although controversial throughout, Roosevelt's administration and policies of the New Deal succeeded in turning the nation "from poor law to welfare state" (Trattner, 1979). This does not mean that the value system changed completely, since there remains even to this day the feeling that there are "deserving poor" and "unfit poor," as evidenced in the Federal Aid to Dependent Children program, but the various programs of the 1930s, including the Social Security Act developed a base of human right to economic and social welfare (Cook, 1979). This means that, in the case of social security

> ....federal responsibility was assumed on the grounds that national crises could occur irrespective of individual enterprise; welfare became a matter of right for certain groups of the population who were unemployed for reasons acknowledged to be other than personal (Grónbjerg, Street, and Suttles, 1978).

The man who defined poverty as a national problem, and organized a team to develop policies and programs to deal with it, was Franklin D. Roosevelt. He began by encouraging the legislature of New York to pass a State Unemployment Relief Act (Trattner, 1979:226–227). "Placing unemployment in the same category as old age, widowhood, and industrial accidents, the chief executive asked the state's lawmakers for funds to help local authorities meet the needs of the unemployed."

Roosevelt's administration developed several programs to help solve unemployment, and it was this problem which drew the greatest amount of attention in those years. Existing programs, such as mother's pensions and some state help to the aged existed, but as the nation sank deeper into the depression and unemployment, many counties diverted funds originally directed to these programs to help the families of the unemployed. By the early 1930s laws "providing for mothers with dependent children" had been passed by all states but the District of Columbia,

Alaska, and Hawaii (Epstein, 1933/1968:269). Although very restricted originally as to the categories covered by the laws, the states expanded their coverage:

> ....the trend has been to grant allowances to broader and broader classes of dependent mothers. All states having mothers' aid legislation cover widows with dependent children. Aid may be granted to any needy mother under eleven acts. In the remaining states, the latest information supplied by the United States Children's Bureau shows that 30 laws specify that aid may also be given to mothers whose husbands are imprisoned; 36 grant pensions to mothers whose husbands are incapacitated either at home or in an institution; 26 provide for deserted mothers, while 12 laws also extend aid to divorced mothers. In addition, 20 acts allow aid to guardian or any other woman *in loco parentis*. Eight statutes grant aid to expectant mothers, and 5 included unmarried mothers (Epstein, 1933/1968:631).

All the laws have maximum age requirements, some allowing for an extension of age if the child is in school because of school laws or "good scholarship." Residence "requirements also vary in the different states" (Epstein, 1933/1968:631), but the greatest variation was in the amounts paid. Epstein (1933/1968:633) found the program inadequate because so many children were not covered, and the sums were so low and irregular when given. "It is plain from all studies that even today no more than half the number of children who need home care are receiving benefits." Both he and Grace Abbott (1938) commented on the cuts in appropriations for this program due to the depression. All these programs were based, as originated, on a needs test and were locally administered through several different mechanisms.

Another federal policy that affected women was the 1921 Sheppard–Towner Act, "the first federally funded health care program to be implemented in the United States" (Rothman, 1978:136). The purpose of the program was to decrease the "infant and maternal mortality rate" with the help of funds allocated to states for the formation of health centers. The program was a result of pressure by educated American women and social workers and was intended to provide preventive care through regular check-ups. Staffed mainly by female doctors and nurses, the centers functioned for nine years before the increasingly powerful and male-dominated American Medical Association and related lobby groups had them closed down. In fact, the medical profession took over much of the illness prevention and curing activity of women, and the 1930 White House Conference on Health and Protection of Children was monopolized by male medical specialists (Rothman 1978:152).

Women who worked in paid employment because of the absence of a male breadwinner or the need to add earnings to the family income suffered with the depression, employers preferring to give jobs, when they had them, to men, and unions definitely pushing in that direction (Rothman, 1978:226). On the other hand, many wives went into the labor force, in occupations shunned by men, when their husbands lost their jobs, so the effect of the depression on women's economic dependency was mixed. The dependence of men on union or state programs made the concept of dependency less gender oriented. In addition, there were in 1930 "4,700,000 widows in the United States of whom 40 percent were sixty-five years of age or over and 82 percent forty-five or over" (Burns, 1936:6). Burns, deeply involved in the Social Security Program, explained that "Such women have a slim chance of obtaining paid employment in a world that has little use for older and inexperienced people."

Measures of the Roosevelt administration were primarily concerned with unemployment: the Federal Emergency Relief Act in 1933, established the Federal Emergency Relief Administration and authorized it to assign money to states for people needing temporary relief; work relief projects were created, such as the Works Progress Administration (WPA) and the Public Works Administration (PWA). However, the plight of the elderly came increasingly to the attention of the government.

A large number of the elderly were on public relief, still organized along the principle of the poor law, including a provision for family responsibility. Edith Abott (1938) argued against this provision because of the enormous amount of family antagonism growing out of litigation to compel adult children to support their parents. The lawsuits were also expensive, reducing the savings from already minimal relief funds. In making her argument she used figures from Cook County's Court Service Division of the County Bureau of Public Welfare.

> Most of these cases are brought for parent against adult children, but in a few cases brothers and sisters, or grandparents are the defendents....A study of individuals whose relatives are asked to assist them has shown that they are, in general, elderly persons, about an equal number of men and women, more than half of them widowed, and about 90 percent over fifty years of age (E. Abott, 1938:607–608).

Abbott's argument was in favor of eliminating the family responsibility provision in any future laws dealing with welfare. The situation was particularily bad during the depression since so many families had restricted resources. A main impetus for the concern for the economic security of old people came from the Townsend movement, which was organized in 1934 and spread throughout the nation. Dr. Townsend proposed that each person over 60 years of age receive a flat pension of $200.00 a month to be obtained from sales taxes "on the sole provision that they retire from work and spend the money" (Trattner, 1979:232; see also Leiby, 1978; Witte, 1963).

> The Social Security Act, and specifically its old-age insurance provisions, were to a large extent a response to the pressure exerted by the Townsend Movement. Undoubtedly there were other factors that influenced policy decisions, such as the depression of the 1930s, the leadership of President Roosevelt and his advisers, the agitation of other social reformers and movements; but the influence of the Townsend Movement and the economic panacea that it held out were of notable importance. The Townsend Movement helped to crystallize popular feeling in support of old-age security. Its impact on policy decisions and changes was not restricted to the Act of 1935 (Sanders, 1973:136–137).

Pressure from charitable organizations, social workers, and other groups, plus the threat of the Townsend Movement and his own concerns all led President Roosevelt to appoint a Committee on Economic Security in 1934 whose function it was to study the economic situation of the United States, examine security programs in other countries, and make recommendations as to the policy the United States should develop. The committee, composed of top advisers, made its recommendations for a Social Security Act to President Roosevelt, who endorsed the plan with some changes, and sent it on to Congress. Altmeyer (1968:16) stated that

> The committee had in mind that social insurance should be the first line of defense against destitution and public assistance a second line to be relied upon to the extent the first line proved to be inadequate.

The Social Security Act of 1935 that finally emerged from Congress greatly modified the recommendations of the Committee on Economic Security; for example, it no longer had a provision for national health insurance (see Social Security Board 1937 and details of the history of the Act in Quadagno, 1984). In included two different approaches to public income maintenance within the various programs it established. The Old Age Benefits program, which later became Old-Age, Survivors, and Disability Insurance (OASDI), was used as a social insurance approach.* It

---

*Orloff and Skocpol (1984:728) note that the U.S. government specified age 62 as the cut-off point for old-age benefits in 1906 in connection with its Civil War Veterans:

In practice, old age alone became a sufficient disability, and in 1906 the law was further amended to state explicitly that "the age of sixty-two years and over shall be considered a permanent specific disability within the meaning of the pension laws."

was designed as a universal program available to all members of society who met prescribed criteria for eligibility not specifically tied to the economic circumstances of the beneficiary. While the eligibility criteria for benefits identify groups, such as those of retirement age or the disabled who are presumed to require income supports, there are no specific tests of need. To make this program more acceptable, it was conceived as an earned right based on contributions to the system from prior work in employment covered under the program, with benefits related to prior wages.

Aid to Dependent Children (later Aid to Families with Dependent Children) and Old-Age Assistance reflected an assistance or public welfare approach. These programs are income or means tested with specific financial status requirements.

Congress made changes in the definition of "dependent children" from a general statement by the Committee on Economic Security to one specifying that the child must be deprived of parental support due to absence or physical and mental incapacity. This change removed the possibility of giving Aid to Dependent Children in the presence of both parents in the home and has been a bone of contention with many reformers since. However, according to Witte (1963), the first executive director of the Committee on Economic Security, "Congress had little interest in children." While the House Ways and Means Committee was debating whether this aid should come under the Social Security Act or be assigned to the Federal Emergency Relief Administration or the Department of States Children's Bureau, the Congress realized that the bill did not set any maximum limit.

> It was then suggested by Congressman Vinson that the limitation should be the same amount as the maximum pension payable to children of servicemen who lost their lives in the [first] World War, namely, $18.00 per month for the first child and $12.00 for the second and additional children in the family. In making this suggestion, the congressman completely overlooked the fact that under the Veteran's Pension Act a grant of $30.00 per month is made to the widow, while in aid for dependent children the grant for the children must normally also provide for the mother who takes care of them (Witte, 1963:163).

The motion was adopted. Witte pointed out to Congressman Vinson and other members of the House committee that it would be impossible for a widow and small children to live on what it assigned.

> This was acknowledged to be a justified criticism, but there was so little interest on the part of any of the members in the aid to dependent children that no one thereafter made a motion to strike out the restriction (164).

Women were included in the 1935 Social Security Act directly in only one, but altogether in four ways. The first inclusion was as retired workers in occupations covered by the act, having met the same requirements as men. The second was as pregnant women or mothers of children eligible for the special "maternal and child health services." This replacement for the defunct Sheppard–Towner Act required the establishment of need for the health services and was administered by the state with federal help (President's Committee on Economic Security, 1937:540–542). The third form of benefit went to women whose husbands had been covered and who became widows, according to the following format:

> If a contributor dies before the age of sixty-five, 3½ percent of the total wages paid to him after December 31, 1936 will be paid to his estate. If he died after the age of sixty-five but before the total sum paid to him in annuities amounts to 3⅓ percent of the total wages on which he has paid contributions, the difference is paid to his estate. Finally, if by some mistake he received during his life less than the correct annuity to which he was entitled, and the correct annuity was more than 3½ percent of his total wages, the differences between what he received and what he would have obtained is paid to his estate (Burns, 1936:115–116).

In the fourth inclusion, younger widows were benefited, in principle at least, in that the federal government stepped into the mothers' pension system by offering "to share one-third of the cost of monthly pensions paid to relatives undertaking responsibility for bringing up needy children" (Burns, 1936:108). The act originally contained a definition of "needy" but it was struck down as "it wormed its way through Congress," as was a minimum below which the state could not offer payments so that "there is now no limit to the smallness of pensions that may be paid by the states" (Burns, 1936:109).

The attention of society and Congress was mainly on the elderly worker and the unemployed. Survivor's benefits within the social insurance program were discussed and dismissed.

> While a supplementary system of survivor's insurance paying regular monthly benefits to qualified dependents is socially far more desirable than the benefit here described, it was not deemed advisable to recommend such a system until further investigation was possible (President's Committee on Economic Security, 1937:204).

Interestingly enough, the President's committee had investigated the situation of dependents, looking into state policies on "mothers' pensions" to determine the extent and amounts of expenditures, the number of families receiving aid, and the number of children benefiting from them in order to build the argument for the need for regular payments with the assistance of federal funds. It also looked into the number of families and children who needed and received emergency relief because of the inadquacies of the mothers' pension programs. In analyzing the characteristics of the recipients of such relief, the researchers found that

> In 44 percent of the relief families included in this summary the mother was a widow (about half the proportion found among families receiving aid to dependent children in 1931), in 47 percent she was separated from her husband, and in 9 percent she was divorced (President's Committee on Economic Security, 1937:242).

Yet, the concern with men workers and fear of the Townsend program, which had numerous supporters even in Congress, and lack of interest in women and children, resulted in an inadequate protection of families of workers. A major stumbling block to their inclusion was the philosophy that saw "economic insurance" as an earned right rather than as a family protection system. The aid to dependent children program was not to protect women but children. Although there was some social recognition that women, once married, were discouraged from paid employment and that many women actually depended on the earnings of men, this awareness was not translated into a policy of inclusion of such women into a federal program until the Social Security Act of 1935 became the subject of much social criticism and pressure for modification.

Before going into the social movement for amending the Social Security Act, we can see how the program of 1935 actually worked in one of the states, Michigan. That state already had a mother's pension program when it adopted the federal Aid to Dependent Children grants (Dancey, 1939). The differences in the programs are interesting:

> Under the Social Security Act a much broader group of relatives than just the mother has been included to receive assistance if they are caring for dependent children. Also specific causes of dependency are not enumerated as was characteristic of the Mothers' Pension Act. Michigan also added two additional requirements: (1) that no mother receiving a pension from the probate court would be considered eligible for Aid to Dependent Children; (2) the moral suitability of the custodian of the child must be established, a requirement that undoubtedly was inherited from the mothers' pension plan, which required the mother to be a fit and proper guardian for her child or children (Dancey, 1939:637).

The Aid to Dependent Children program went into effect in Michigan in 1936 in all counties and the caseload for ADC was removed from the WPA rosters (Dancey, 1939:638–639). In the years following adoption of the ADC program, most counties transferred families from mothers' pension rolls to the new program. The former was administered through the probate court in each county, the latter through a special administration under supervision of the state. According to Dancey (1939:646), the statewide nature of the program insured a greater standardization of payment and procedures for establishing eligibility. In addition, the state commission developed procedures by which families denied benefits under ADC or otherwise dissatisfied with the program could petition for a hearing.

SOCIAL SECURITY ACT AMENDMENTS OF 1939

The next few years after the passage of the Social Security Act of 1935 witnessed a great deal of social and political agitation over its basic principles and inadequacies. This activity took many forms. Burns published a book in 1936 explaining the problems of elderly wives, widows, and dependent children, who were not covered adequately in the act. The president of the League of Women Voters (who had "served with the Advisory Council of President Roosevelt's Committee on Economic Security in 1934," but who had been unsuccessful in drawing attention to the problem of dependent women and children) and the League itself organized "mass meetings to familiarize the public with its provisions and policy issues" (Sanders, 1973:142). Other women's groups such as the National Consumers League, the Women's Trade Union League, and the Women's Joint Congressional Committee pushed for a liberalization of the Social Security Act. Organized labor, in the form of the American Federation of Labor, which had been slow to enter the scene, finally endorsed the recommendations of the advisory council and used a variety of methods of lobbying and public education at annual conventions and through press releases. The Townsendites continued their pressure while the American Association for Social Security under Abraham Epstein and the American Association of Social Workers pushed for the expansion of social security coverage. Other social work groups continued to oppose any blanket government insurance. President Roosevelt recommended the extension of benefits to the dependents of covered workers in April 28, 1939, while the Democratic platform of 1936 had already made "specific reference to the 'protection of the family and the home' " (Sanders, 1973:89).

The Advisory Council on Social Security of 1937–1938 considered a variety of ways of solving the problem of dependents and survivors of those covered under old-age insurance.

The council proposed that a 50 percent supplementary allowance be paid on behalf of an aged wife (65 or over) or an eligible aged beneficiary, based on his benefit. A plain indication that this was considered a dependent's allowance in the form of a guaranteed underwriting and not a true benefit was the proviso that should the wife, after attaining age 65, become sligible for a benefit in her own right larger than the wife's allowance payable to her husband on her behalf, the benefit payable to her in her own right should be substituted for the wife's allowance. In the light of subsequent developments, it is important to note that the supplementary allowance was to be paid to the husband on behalf of a wife. The Council thus distinguished between an individual benefit right and an allowance to protect a family unit (Brown, 1972;135).

The problems facing the Advisory Council and the arguments swirling around the Social Security Act are due to two different types of programs of social insurance. One is an insurance covering people who have directly contributed to the system through their own and their employer's taxes. The other is a family protection approach that includes dependents of workers. The recommendations for what became the 1939 amendments to the Social Security Act shifted the program base of individual protection in the Old-Age Benefit program to one of family protection in Old-Age and Survivors Insurance (later OASDI). This moved the program

> . . . .from a hybrid compromise between private savings and social insurance to a clearcut concept of social insurance. The new focus became adequacy and the protection of the family unit (Brown, 1972:196).

The proposed amendments to the Social Security Act were debated at length in Congress. Altmeyer, the chair of the Social Security Board, presented the suggested amendments to the House Committee on Ways and Means of the 76th Congress, which had to approve the changes (Social Security Administration, 1939):

> Under a social insurance system the primary purpose should be to pay benefits in accordance with the presumptive needs of the beneficiaries, rather than to make payments to the estate of a deceased employee regardless of whether or not he leaves dependents. The payment of monthly benefits to widows and orphans, who are the two chief classes of dependent survivors, would furnish much more significant protection than does the payment of lump-sum benefits (Social Security Administration, 1939:5–6). The Board has given much consideration to the feasibility and desirability of providing benefits for widows under 65 years of age who have not young children in their care. The Board believes that only a temporary monthly benefit, covering the period immediately following the husband's death, should be paid in such cases.

However, the Board does recommend that all widows of persons who would have qualified for old-age benefits, if they had lived to age 65, be entitled to a deferred monthly benefit payable at age 65. Such benefits should bear some reasonable relationship to that which the deceased husband would have received (Social Security Administration, 1939:6).

The final amendments passed by Congress did not include the provision for a "temporary monthly benefit" to the widow following the death of the husband. The lump-sum payment was redefined from a percentage of the man's benefits paid to the estate to one designed to help defray funeral costs for the person who claims to have covered these. It is interesting to note that the Social Security Board was fully aware of the fact that it left a major segment of the American population without coverage, the widow of a covered worker without dependent children in her care who had not reached the age of 65. The justification for not awarding such benefits during the "black-out" period of widowhood lay in the difficulty of defining the economic dependency of women.

Normally, young widows without children can be expected to enter gainful employment, but middle-aged widows frequently find it more difficult to become self-supporting. On the other hand, they are likely to have more savings than younger widows and many of them have children who are grown and able to help them until they reach 65 years of age, when they would be entitled to a widow's benefits under the plan proposed. Though their problems are fully recognized, provision for connecting benefits to widows under 65 with no children would present certain serious anomalies. Any age selected for benefits to begin would appear arbitrary, excluding some widows just below that age. Moreover, the question would arise as to discrimination against unmarried women, who would not receive benefits until they reached 65. Yet, if the retirement age for women generally were lowered, the effect would be to discriminate against men and at the same time substantially to increase the cost (Social Security Administration, 1939:6).

None of the amendments to the Social Security Act have covered widows not caring for the deceased worker's dependent children or who have not reached the age of retirement. There is no overall policy concerning widows in general; they are seen only as mothers and carers of surviving children or as older women deprived of the husband's earnings or social security benefits. This was an important change for widowed mothers, however, in that the 1939 amendments placed their situation additionally under the social insurance benefit program. This policy separated them from mothers lacking a male breadwinner for reasons other than the death of the husband, who are still under only the means-tested welfare system. Vestiges of the Elizabethan Poor Laws hang on.

PUBLIC CRITICISM OF THE SITUATION OF WOMEN UNDER SOCIAL SECURITY

The Social Security Act of 1935 thus was changed considerably in 1939 and has been subject to many modifications since then. Different groups have objected to aspects, and various government administrations have tried to "patch up" the holes or even change the base of the system. The following is a list of some of the areas covered by the bills that have been the subject of criticism:

1. Single women feel it is unfair to them because of the implied assumption that all women who marry can draw benefits from their husband's record. A married man's earnings, therefore, produce benefits not only for him as a worker, but for his wife and dependent children and, in case of his death, for his widow and dependent children. The single woman (and man also, for that matter) pays an equal amount into the system but can draw benefits only for herself.

2. Married women who work most or all of their married lives generally do not draw any more benefits than they would by receiving 50 percent of their husband's benefit as a dependent wife of a worker. This is because of the inferior wage position of women that results in a lower benefit available on their own record. Many feel that social security credits and benefits should be based on the joint earnings of married couples (Kutza, 1975).

3. Married women or widows who interrupt their working careers to stay home and care for small children (as encouraged, if not forced, to do so by American society) feel the system is unfair because this discontinuous work involvement results in lower benefits. Benefits are based on an average earnings, with only the lowest five years of earning discounted (Bixby, 1972).

4. Housewives feel discriminated against because their role in the home "is not considered employment for social security purposes" (Bixby, 1972:10; Kutza, 1975:9).

5. Widows entitled to old-age benefits, who form half of the women aged 65 and over, often receive very small monthly payments because the deceased husband had not received a sufficiently high wage or worked long enough in covered occupations or industries to qualify for a higher benefit (Kutza, 1975:9).

6. Divorced wives who had not been married to the dead or retired husband the required number of years may be totally ineligible for benefits.

7. Finally, the Social Security program, as all other programs in a democratic and socially complex society, operates on the assump-

tion that its members are aware of all the provisions that apply to their individual cases. The society has built complex resources to solve personal or family problems and assumes that these will be used by people most in need of them. As we shall see in the example of Chicago-area widows, the assumption is not supported by fact.

Pressure on the government to change its policies regarding all women has led to various attempts to improve the match between problem and program. The Ford administration requested that the 1975 Advisory Council on Social Security reexamine the program from all angles (Snee and Ross, 1978:4–5). President Carter developed a very specific set of recommendations to change benefit and financing bases. The Social Security amendments of 1977 were different from what the president advocated, but did change the financing and benefit structure. There had been an effort to remove "gender-based distinctions," but the situation is so complicated by the increased heterogeneity of the female population in the United States that any single solution is impossible. Executive branch publications as well as special House and Senate hearings, document the complexity and the range of solutions. The final set of Social Security amendments of 1977 reflect the lack of agreement on what should be done by ignoring some of the more difficult issues. Several of the amendments affect widows. "Spouse's and surviving spouse's benefits under the social security program will be reduced by the amount of any government (Federal, State or local) pension payable to the spouse based on his or her own earnings in noncovered employment" (Snee and Ross, 1978:15). This change will not affect many widows currently receiving benefits, as we shall see shortly. On the other hand, the provisions dealing with divorce and remarriage of women have eased the beneficiary eligibility requirements. "Effective with respect to benefits for months after December 1978, remarriage of a surviving spouse after age 60 will not reduce the amount of widow's or widower's benefits" (Snee and Ross, 1978:15). The government had previously equalized the situation of widowers with that of widows by accepting a widower who had been dependent economically on his wife as beneficiary of a woman's account. The complexity of the situation and alleged sex discrimination led the Department of Health, Education and Welfare to set up a task force to study all issues. As a partial result, the amount a retired beneficiary can earn without affecting benefits was increased. This provision also affects widows. Thus, our society continues to "tinker" with its Social Security program in order to better fit it to the situation of its members in modern times.

Robert Ball (1978:140) explains the U.S. Social Security system's insistence on family maximum benefit limits in similar terms, although

"...in 1971, 32 percent of the widows' families were poor when there were one or two children in the family, but the percentage increased to 49 percent when there were three children, and 70 percent when there were four or more children." The maximum, which he would like to see alleviated or at least examined, was so set that the total sum going to a family would not exceed the earnings of the deceased. In other words, if the family lived in poverty when the earner was alive, it should continue to do so. Ball (1978:149), who had been commissioner of the Social Security Administration for three U.S. presidents, has recommended the following changes for the program:

- a one-year training and readjustment allowance for a widow not eligible for benefits at the time of the death of the wage earner
- full-rate benefits to disabled widows and widowers at any age
- a raise in the dollar maximum on the lump-sum payment
- much more attention given to the survivorship features of the social security program in the informational efforts of the Social Security Administration
- further study on ways to increase benefits for families headed by widows even when there are a large number of children in the family and the family maximum cuts the benefit level back below the poverty line.

THE SOCIAL SECURITY SYSTEM IN RECENT YEARS

With the 1972 Social Security amendments a widow 65 and over receives 100 percent of her deceased insured husband's primary insurance amount (PIA.)* A benefit subject to actuarial reduction is available as early as age 60 (Research Institute of America, 1977:56). Additionally, she can receive reduced benefits at age 50 if she is disabled for any gainful activity. These provisions were incorporated in amendments passed in the 1960s. A widow of any age caring for her deceased husband's child under age 18 (this was changed to age 16 in the 1981 provisions) is entitled to a benefit equal to 75 percent of the deceased workers' PIA (Social Security Handbook, 1974). A survivor's benefit of 75 percent of the

---

*PIA is the amount from which almost all cash benefits are derived, including monthly benefits for the worker himself, his dependents, and his survivors. The worker's retirement insurance benefit rate is equal to the PIA, except for certain special situations. The PIA and, therefore, the related benefits are computed on the average indexed monthly earnings because cash benefits are intended as partial replacement of earnings lost due to retirement, disability, or death of the worker.

deceased's PIA is available for each child under age 18 (22 if a full-time student).* Various program limitations may reduce the benefits actually paid. There is a maximum family benefit that can be obtained based on any worker's social security earnings record. This amount ranges between 1.5 and 1.85 times the PIA and is fixed by a table of benefit amounts depending on the PIA. The program also includes an earnings test by which social security cash benefits are reduced $1.00 for each $2.00 of earnings above a set level, unless the beneficiary is age 70 or over (Research Institute of America, 1977:44). There are some additional conditions related to the widow's benefits. A widow must be unmarried at the time she applies for benefits, unless she remarried after age 60, in which case the remarriage does not affect entitlement or reduce benefits (for benefits payable after 1978; prior to 1979 remarriage after age 60 would have resulted in entitlement to a 50 percent benefit rate). A widow receiving mother's insurance benefits because she is caring for the deceased husband's children will not lose these benefits if she marries a man who is also a beneficiary of social security.

A *widow* who had been *divorced* prior to the death of the ex-husband is entitled to benefits if she is aged 60** or over (age 50 if disabled), and was married to him for at least ten years before the divorce (20 years for benefits payable before 1979). A divorced widow of such a long marriage who is caring for a dependent child of the deceased worker is also eligible for benefits (Research Institute of America, 1977:62). A *divorced wife* of a retired husband is entitled to benefits if the marriage lasted ten or more years and if she is age 62 or over. The family maximum is not used as a basis for reducing the divorced wife's or widow's benefits. It is used as a criterion for reducing the benefits to be paid to other dependents,

---

*As of the 1981 provisions, this is being phased out and benefits eventually will be available to age 19 for elementary and secondary school students only.

**In 1939, worker's retirement benefits, wife's benefits, and widow's benefits (except for those caring for an eligible child) were all based on being age 65 and over. In 1956, the age of eligibility for women for all three was reduced to 62 with an actuarial reduction in benefits. The ages for men were set at the same level in 1961. In 1965, widows became eligible for reduced benefits at age 60. The age for widowers was set at 60 in 1972. Because of the availability of widow's benefits at 60, a non-working widow may collect benefits at this earlier age and then switch to a higher benefit later based on her own work record. Similarly, because of the limitations in wife's benefits if the husband is still working, a woman who is old enough might collect retired worker's benefits based on her own work record and then receive a higher benefit as a dependent wife on her husband's work record when he retired. The combination of the two concepts of worker and dependent, and the varying ages of eligibility in specific program provisions would make it possible for a widow to collect reduced widow's benefits at age 60 and then move to reduced retirement benefits at age 62.

but the existence of the previously divorced widow or ex-wife of a living husband is not taken into account in reducing the benefits of other categories of beneficiaries.

A *dependent wife** aged 65 and over is entitled to a benefit equal to 50 percent of her husband's PIA; the benefit is available to her at age 62, subject to actuarial reduction. These benefits are payable only if the husband himself is entitled to retirement or disability benefits. They are subject to the same restrictions on family maximum and the wife's own earnings, as are widow's benefits. The wife of a retired or disabled worker can receive a benefit (50 percent of PIA) at any age if she is caring for the worker's eligible child. The child also can receive a benefit equal to 50 percent of the PIA, subject to the family maximum and the limitations discussed earlier.

Finally, there is a lump sum payment of $225.00 to help defray funeral costs paid to the widow or other dependents entitled to cash benefits.

FAMILY PROTECTION ISSUES: EQUITY VERSUS ADEQUACY

We have previously discussed some of the criticisms made of the various programs of the Social Security Act and its amendments. There is, however, a basic issue underlying the system as a solution to the problem of the economic dependency of women and children in U.S. society in the twentieth century. The issue is adequacy of replacement income for specific types of families versus equity of benefits in relation to the contribution made by the worker to the system out of his or her earnings. The 1935 version of the Social Security Act was an individual protection program. It did not include benefits for the survivors of a deceased employee, except that his estate received the difference between the actual amount of Federal Insurance Contributions Act (FICA) taxes paid by the worker and the benefits paid him while he lived. Nor was there any increase in retirement benefits paid to a worker because he had

---

*The concept of dependent wife as we are using in this book is broader than that used by the Social Security program's concept of entitlement to benefits of a retired or disabled worker or for a widow based on her husband's social security record. The program excludes many women we define as dependent since it deals only with wives or widows of workers entitled to benefits from their own record. This means that the "dependent wife" has not earned in her own right as a worker a benefit equal to, or larger than, the benefit she is entitled to as a wife or widow. While we use the term "wife" and "widow" in explaining the program because of our focus on women, the program language has been adjusted in recent years in an effort to eliminate sex bias in its various provisions.

a wife or other dependents. The 1939 amendments dramatically changed the program to one of family protection. From this point forward the program provided a worker with additional income in retirement for his wife and dependent children, subject to specified criteria. In the event of his death, benefits based on his work record became available to his widow if she were old enough or if she were caring for his surviving dependent children who were eligible for benefits.

Thus, the policy orientation at the inception of the family protection approach of the program was clearly toward the protection of the families of predominantly male breadwinners. This was an appropriate focus, given the composition of the labor force and the basic structure of families as they existed at that time. In more recent years, access to these benefits has been made independent of the sex of the worker or surviving spouse. However, even now, it is more common for the woman to receive benefits from her husband's work record as a dependent or survivor than the other way around. This reflects the continued differences in survivorship of males and females, the older age of the husband, and the divergence in labor force participation rates and resultant eligibility for, and level of, workers' benefits. It is the unmarried female head of a household and the divorced wife of a marriage that lasted less than ten years who have no claims to benefits at retirement age based on a prior work record of any previous partner or spouse.

This movement to a family protection approach created problems in the treatment of women and their income adequacy, especially when the general issue of equity of the program is discussed. The family maximum policy is irrelevant to the program of individual protection—people other than the wage earner are entitled to benefits only in the family protection program. What purpose is served by the limit imposed on the amount received by a family based on the earnings record of any one worker? It limits the benefits payable to dependents at the expense of the benefits payable to wage earners without dependents.

There is a trade-off between adequacy and equity. The more attention the program pays to assuring that all beneficiaries receive an adequate benefit regardless of what their prior earnings were (i.e., regardless of the benefit level "earned"), the less attention is paid to assuring that each person who worked under the program receives an equitable return for his or her contributions to the program. Family protection benefits for the dependent family of the worker attempt to provide an adequate level of benefits for a family. The family maximum limits the amount of benefits one wage earner's record can provide. Since paying family benefits reduces the benefits paid to retired workers without dependents (there is just so much money available with which to pay benefits) the more adequate the family benefit, the less equitable the benefit to the individual retired worker.

Using a formula that replaces more of the prior earnings of lower-paid workers than of those with higher past earnings is one way to provide benefit adequacy for the lower wage earners in the population. It results in lower-paid earners getting a greater return on their contribution to the program than higher-paid earners and obviously affects the equity of the program. Providing additional benefits because the wage earner has dependents or survivors is another way of assuring the adequacy of benefits for workers with family obligations. This affects the equity of the program in a different way. Providing benefit adequacy for low wage earners affects the equity of return to higher wage earners. Providing adequate family benefits for workers with dependents affects the equity of return for workers without dependents. Placing a limit on the family benefits payable on the record of any given worker moves toward protecting the equity of the benefits that workers without dependent family members can receive. The family maximum offers a balance between adequacy and equity on this issue. However, while such a compromise may be conceptually fair and appropriate, its impact is a separate issue. The family maximum negatively affects the incomes of women with larger numbers of children.

For a woman who worked along with her husband prior to his death there is also a negative effect of the program's design. While this is not directly related to the adequacy–equity issue, it is a direct result of the family versus individual protection issue. The family protection approach of the 1939 amendments provided benefits for the dependents or survivors of workers. But, this was not intended to result in a windfall for workers. The woman who was both a wife and a worker in her own right (if such were the case) was not to receive benefits as both a dependent and a worker. The benefits were not to be additive. There was no extra benefit to be derived by a woman as a dependent wife if she had also worked long enough at a high enough rate to earn higher benefits. As an accounting matter, the benefit paid her shows up as partly based on her own prior work and partly on a dependent benefit under the husband's wage record. However, the total benefit cannot exceed what the woman would have received as either a worker or a dependent.

As in the case of program specification for retired workers, dependents and survivors have limitations on their own earnings after which their benefits are affected. Applying this rationale as whole cloth to the situation of the two-worker family results in what appears, from one perspective, to be an inequity. Assuming she was working and earning at a reasonable level, the widow will have no benefit payable to her because of her husband's death despite the loss of the major breadwinner. However, her earnings cannot offset the loss of her husband's earnings as they might if she had gone to work only after his death. No distinction is made for benefit purposes in terms of the relationship between a husband and a wife as either co-workers or worker and dependent. Workers are not paid benefits. The benefits are paid to offset the deceased worker's lost wages but not to current workers earning above the program's limit standards. Applying these rules results in no benefits for women in previously two-worker families based on the husband's death. This is a consequence of the program's family protection policy as contrasted to the individual protection policy with some controls over the level of benefits payable on a given account. As with the family maximum, it has identifiable negative, or potentially inequitable, implications in certain situations.

But recognition of the situation did not lead to immediate solutions. Steps that might be taken to increase the benefits paid on an individual's account for his family could increase the family maximum or pay full benefits for every dependent without regard to number. Another solution could acknowledge the "rights" to benefits of widows who worked along with their husbands. Such action would affect the ability to provide an equitable benefit relative to contributions to the program for those workers of either sex who never married or never had any or many dependents. The program was originally conceptualized as an earned right, contributory, wage-related social insurance. It has taken on many additional aspects. Obviously, a formula can be specified for computing the payment of benefits to dependents or survivors based on a worker's earnings. Because this benefit is built into the program it can be thought of as an appropriate earned benefit based on the worker's contributions. However, this does not mean the individual receiving the benefit has earned it by prior work under the system. The fact that such benefits are not directly an earned right based on contributions by the individual does not make them inappropriate under the system. It does make them an extension of the original concept which results in some distortions within the program.

From the policy perspective of insuring benefits in old age based on workers' prior contributions to the system, unequal rates of replacement of past earnings and payments to dependents and survivors are an aberration. From the perspective of the income needs of dependents and survivors, some of the program elements discussed are an aberration in the other direction. Viewed as an effort to accommodate different policy purposes in one program, these contrasting elements are more understandable, but are possibly in need of modification to reflect changes in male–female relationships, family structure, and family labor force participation.

What is the appropriate response if we identify program elements that are not consonant with current family realities? Do we accept possibly undesirable results of the program's design for some dependents and survivors since to correct them would result in inequities for workers without such dependents and survivors? Or, do we change the program to pay benefits based on the current needs of dependents and survivors and consider the equity issue secondary? As an alternate approach, do we accept that combining these separate policies into one program may well fit with the social realities of the late 1930s, but not the circumstances of the 1980s? In this latter case, it might be appropriate to consider a modified version of the 1935 model for the basic program design: to include a survivors' program and pay benefits to men and women based only on their own work records. Dependents could be considered under a separate program unrelated to the contributory, earned-right social insurance program and any forthcoming benefits paid out of general revenues based on need. But how would this affect a significant proportion of women, who still have histories of economic dependency on their male partners and labor force participation patterns similar to the common pattern of the 1930s?

SUMMARY AND IMPLICATIONS

One of the issues in assessing the match between problem and policy in dealing with widows and dependent wives is that the definitional perspective of the 1930s accepted certain "realities" despite the absence of consistent data and did not face other "realities" despite data indicating problem existence. The history of male–female and family relationships does not indicate a consistent pattern of the working man financially supporting the housekeeping woman who cared for the minor, non-economically productive children that the husband also supported. The 1930s showed this basic pattern, and this concept of the family and male–female relationships was built into the policy orientation toward dependents and survivors in the social insurance aspects of the Social Security Act in 1939.

With the 1935 version of the act, there was no identification of the problem as regards survivors or dependents of wage earners in the social insurance provisions; the focus was on wage earners. Since these were predominantly male—78 percent of the labor force was male in 1930, with 12 percent of married women in the labor force—the focus was primarily male. Women were eligible to receive benefits as workers in their own right, but discussions of possible benefit extensions for survivors and dependents centered around the notion of the male head of household/breadwinner and the need to replace his lost earnings on death or retirement. The motivation for the 1935 act itself was not solely a concern for the fate of the older wage earner, but also for the need to remove older workers from the labor force so that they did not compete with younger workers for jobs. At the same time, the act was to prevent the economic dislocation due to the presence of too many older people without earnings or other income.

When the individual wage-earner protection approach of the 1935 act was transformed to a family protection approach by the 1939 amendments, a limited definition of the problem of dependents and survivors was applied. The family protection approach defined the problem as the protection of the children of breadwinners, and included the economic needs of elderly women who had been the wives of wage earners. Younger women were included only if they were caring for the breadwinner's minor children. The problem was not defined from the perspective of the population of dependent women potentially in need, but from the perspective of the major responsibility of the predominantly male wage earner. As a result, the basic fact of female economic dependency in the marital-familial relationship was not the perspective of problem definition. There was no overall policy focus on dependent women, regardless of whether the husband was still alive in retirement or had died. Given the general social expectation in the 1930s for women to marry (indeed, fewer than one of ten women did not marry) and that in 1930 only 12 percent of married women and 34 percent of widowed or divorced women were in the labor force, most adult women were economically dependent on their husbands. Was it reasonable to expect a woman to work to support herself in the event her husband retired, became unable to work, or died? While undoubtedly self-support could be forced by the situation, the policy ignored the reality of the married woman and therefore ignored the problem of poverty if the husband's earnings were lost and in need of replacement on retirement or death. And, yet, this is what was done when the problem was defined for policy purposes in establishing a family protection approach. As indicated, the "black-out" period for widows was not defined within the problem target. Nor was this time period between the youngest child reaching legal adult status and the woman reaching the age for old-age benefits for the wives of retired workers. Here again, was it reasonable to expect these women to enter the labor force at all, let alone without some assistance and temporary support? If the woman was economically dependent on her husband and did not work, as was generally the case, did her age influence the need for a dependent benefit in the event of his retirement? The same point obviously holds in the event of his death. Whether widowhood (the more serious situation) or a wife's dependency on a retired worker is considered part of the problem must rest on the issue of equity with the small percentage of never married women, the difficulty of defining such dependency, or the more pragmatic priority of values for the use of limited resources. However, none of the reasons for not including these women's situations as part of the problem alters the lack of conceptual consistency in problem definition, stemming from the nature of the familial and economic relationships between men and women at the time. A minimum policy inclusion that would have reflected a more appropriate definition of the problem and led to a better match between the underlying problem and policy (even from the perspective of the breadwinner's responsibility as contrasted to the needs of dependent women) would have been the provision of some transitional support for the women in between (i.e., the "black out" years). This was considered, but not included.

Our focus now turns to the program in its latter-day effect on the lives of women. How well did the program and its effect fit with the intended policy and the underlying problem as it was and could have been defined? How well do the policy and program fit with changes in the social and economic situation, family concepts, and the behavior of and relationships between men and women as we enter the 1980s?

REFERENCES

Abbott, Edith. 1913. *Women in Industry: A Study in American Economic History*. New York: D. Appleton and Co.

——. 1938. Poor law provision for family responsibility. *The Social Service Review* 12: 598–618.

Abbott, Grace. 1938. *The Child and the State*. Vol. 2 of *The Dependent and the Delinquent Child*. Chicago, IL: University of Chicago Press.

——. 1934. Recent trends in mothers' aid. *The Social Service Review* 8, no. 2 (June): 191–209.

Achenbaum, Andrew W. 1978. *Old Age in the New Land: The American Experience Since 1790*. Baltimore, MD: Johns Hopkins University Press.

Altmeyer, Arthur J. 1968. *The Formative Years of Social Security*. Madison, WI: University of Wisconsin Press.

Anderson, Michael. 1977. The impact on the family relationships of the elderly of changes since victorian times in government income-maintenance provision. In *Family, Bureaucracy and the Elderly: An Organizational/Linkage Perspective*, edited by Ethel Shanas and Marvin B. Sussman, pp. 36–59. Durham, NC: Duke University Press.

Aries, Philippe. 1962. *Centuries of Childhood*. New York: Random House, Vintage Books.

Babcock, Barbara Allen, Ann Freedman, Eleanor Holmes Norton, and Susan C. Ross. 1979. *Sex Discrimination and the Law: Causes and Remedies*. Boston, MA: Little, Brown.

Ball, Robert M. 1978. *Social Security Today and Tomorrow*. New York: Columbia University Press.

Bird, Caroline. 1979. *The Two-Paycheck Marriage: How Women at Work are Changing Life in America*. New York: Rawson, Wade Publishers.

Bixby, Lenore E. 1972. Women and social security in the United States. *Social Security Bulletin* 35, no. 9 (September): 3–11. Department of Health, Education, & Welfare, publication no. (SSA) 73-11700.

Bloch, Ruth H. 1978. Untangling the roots of modern sex roles: A survey of four centuries of change. *SIGNS: Journal of Women in Culture and Society* 4, no. 2 (Winter): 237–252.

Boardman, F.W. 1970. *America and the Progressive Era, 1900–1917.* New York: Henry Z. Walck.

Boorstin, Daniel J. 1973. *The Americans: The Democratic Experience.* New York: Random House.

——. 1965. *The Americans: The National Experience.* New York: Random House.

——. 1958. *The Americans: The Colonial Experience.* New York: Random House.

Bowlby, John. 1951/1966. *Maternal care and mental health.* In series, *Deprivation of Maternal Care.* New York: Schocken Books.

Brinker, Paul, and Joseph J. Klos. 1976. *Poverty, Manpower and Social Security.* Austin, TX: Austin Press.

Brody, David. 1968. The rise and decline of welfare capitalism. In *Change and Continuity in Twentieth Century America, the 1920s,* edited by John Braeman, Robert H. Bremner, and David Brody. Columbus, OH: Ohio State University.

Brown, J. Douglas. 1972. *An American Philosophy of Social Security: Evolution and Issues.* Princeton, NJ: Princeton University Press.

Brownlee, W. Elliott, and Mary M. Brownlee. 1976. *Women in the American Economy: A Documentary History, 1675 to 1929.* New Haven, CT: Yale University Press.

Bucklin, Dorothy R. 1939. Public aid for the care of dependent children in their homes, 1932–1938. *Social Security Bulletin* 2, no. 4 (April): 24–35.

Burns, Eveline M. 1954. Significant contemporary issues in the expansion and consolidation of government social security programs. In *Economic Security for Americans: An Appraisal of the Past Half-Century, 1900–1953,* pp. 65-77. Assembly's National Policy Board (no city, no publisher given).

——. 1936. *Toward Social Security: An Explanation of the Social Security Act and a Survey of the Larger Issues.* New York: Whittlesey House.

Chafe, William H. 1972. *The American Woman: Her Changing Social, Economic and Political Roles, 1920–1970.* New York: Oxford University Press.

Chambers, Clarke. 1963. *Seedtime of Reform: American Social Services and Social Action, 1919–1933.* Minneapolis, MN: University of Minnesota Press.

Chapman, Rane Roberts, and Margaret Gates, eds. 1977. *Women Into Wives: The Legal and Economic Impact of Marriage.* Beverly Hills, CA: Sage Publications.

Coll, Blance D. 1969. *Perspective in Public Welfare: A History.* Washington, D.C.: U.S. Department of Health, Education and Welfare.

Cook, Fay Lomax. 1979. *Who Should be Helped: Public Support for Social Services.* Beverly Hills, CA: Sage Publications.

Costin, Lela B. 1972. *Child Welfare: Policies and Practice.* New York: McGraw-Hill.

Cott, Nancy F. 1977. *The Bonds of Womanhood: Women's Sphere in New England, 1780–1885.* New Haven, CT: Yale University Press.

Dancey, Maria H. 1939. Mother's pensions and the aid to dependent children program in Michigan. *The Social Service Review* 13:634–651.

Davidson, Marshall. 1951/1974. *Life in America: Bicentennial Edition.* Boston, MA: Houghton Mifflin.

Degler, Carl N. 1970. *Out of Our Past: The Forces that Shaped Modern America,* rev. ed. New York: Harper Colophon Books.

de Mause, Lloyd. 1974a. *The History of Childhood.* New York: Psychohistory Press.

——. 1974b. *The Evolution of Childhood*. In *The History of Childhood*, edited by Lloyd de Mause, pp. 1–73. New York: Psychohistory Press.

Demos, John. 1973. *A Little Commonwealth: Family Life in Plymouth Colony*. New York: Oxford University Press.

Douglas, Ann. 1977. *The Feminization of American Culture*. New York: Avon Books.

Drake, St. Clair, and Horace Cayton. 1945. *Black Metropolis*. New York: Harcourt, Brace and Co.

Dulles, Foster Rhea. 1965. *A History of Recreation: America Learns to Play*. New York: Appleton-Century-Crofts.

Easton, Barbara L. 1976. Industrialization and femininity: A case study of nineteenth century New England. *Social Problems* 23, no. 4 (April): 389–401.

Ehrenreich, Barbara, and Deirdre English. 1979. *For Her Own Good: 150 years of the Experts' Advice to Women*. Garden City, NY: Anchor Press.

Eichler, Margrit. 1973. Women as personal dependents. In *Women in Canada*, edited by Marylee Stephenson, pp. 36–55. Toronto: New Press.

Ekirch, Arthur A. 1969. *Ideologies and Utopias: The Impact of the New Deal on American Thought*. Chicago, IL: Quadrangle Books.

Elder, Glen. 1974. *Children of the Great Depression*. Chicago, IL: University of Chicago Press.

Epstein, Abraham. 1933/1968. *Insecurity: A Challenge to America*. New York: Agathon Press.

Fredericksen, Hazel. 1950. *The Child and His Welfare*. San Francisco, CA: W.H. Freeman and Company.

Friedan, Betty. 1963. *The Feminine Mystique*. New York: Norton.

Glazer, Nona. 1980. Everyone needs three hands: Doing unpaid and paid work. In *Women and Household Labor*, edited by Sarah Fenstermaker Berk, pp. 249–273. Beverly Hills, CA: Sage Publications.

Glazer-Malbin, Nona. 1977. Housework. *SIGNS: Journal of Women in Culture and Society* 1, no. 4 (Summer): 905–921.

Grønbjerg, Kirsten. 1977. *Mass Society and the Extension of Welfare, 1960–1970*. Chicago, IL: University of Chicago Press.

Grønbjerg, Kirsten, David Street, and Gerald D. Suttles. 1978. *Poverty and Social Change*. Chicago, IL: University of Chicago Press.

Hareven, Tamara K., ed. 1977. *Family and Kin in Urban Communities, 1700–1930*. New York: New Viewpoints.

Hareven, Tamara K., and Randolph Langenbach. 1978. *Amoskeag: Life and Work in an American Factory City*. New York: Pantheon Books.

Harris, Barbara. 1979. Careers, conflict and children: The legacy of the cult of domesticity. In *Career and Motherhood: Struggles for a New Identity*, edited by Alan Roland and Barbara Harris, pp. 55–84. New York: Human Sciences Press.

Hartman, Mary S., and Lois Banner, eds. 1974. *Clio's Consciousness Raised: New Perspectives on the History of Women*. New York: Harper & Row.

Hayghe, Howard. 1975. Marital and family characteristics of the labor force, March, 1974. *Monthly Labor Review* 98: 173.

Howards, Irving, Henry Brehm, and Saad Z. Nagi. 1980. *Disability: From Social Problem to Federal Program*. New York: Praeger.

Illick, Joseph. 1974. Child-rearing in seventeenth century England and America.

In *The History of Childhood*, edited by Lloyd de Mause, pp. 303–350. New York: Psychohistory Press.

Kamerman, Shella, and Alfred J. Kahn. 1978. *Family Policy: Government and Families in Fourteen Countries*. New York: Columbia University Press.

Keyssar, Alexander. 1974. Widowhood in eighteenth century Massachusetts: A problem in the history of the family. *Perspectives in American History* 8: 83–119.

Kleinberg, Susan. 1973. Technology's stepdaughters, the impact of industrialization upon working class women, Pittsburgh, 1865–1890. Unpublished dissertation, University of Pittsburgh, Department of History.

Komarovsky, Mirra. 1953. *Women in the Modern World: Their Education and their Dilemmas*. Boston, MA: Little, Brown and Co.

Krauskopf, Joan M. 1977. Partnership Marriage: Legal Reform Needed. In *Women Into Wives: The Legal and Economic Impact of Marriage*, edited by Jane Roberts Chapman and Margaret Gates, pp. 93–121. Beverly Hills, CA: Sage Publications.

Kreps, Juanita M. 1977. Intergenerational transfers and the bureaucracy. In *Family, Bureaucracy and Elderly: An Organizational/Linkage Perspective*, edited by Ethel Shanas and Marvin B. Sussman, pp. 21–34. Durham, NC: Duke University Press.

Kutza, Elizabeth Ann. 1975. *Policy Lag: Its Impact on Income Security for Older Women*. University of Chicago School of Social Service Administration, occasional paper no. 6, June 1975.

Lantz, Herman R., Margaret Britton, Raymond L. Schmitt, and Eloise C. Snyder. 1968. Preindustrial pattern in the colonial family in America: A content analysis of colonial magazines. *American Sociological Review* 33 (June): 413–426.

Lantz, Herman R., Jane Keyes, and Martin Schultz. 1975. The American Family in the preindustrial period: From baselines in history to change. *American Sociological Review* 40 (February): 21–38.

Lantz, Herman R., Raymond Schmitt, and Richard Herman. 1973. The preindustrial family in America: A further examination of early magazines. *American Journal of Sociology* 79 (November): 566–589.

LaPierre, Richard. 1959. *The Freudian Ethic*. New York: Duell, Sloan and Pearce.

Laslett, Barbara. 1978. Family membership, past and present. *Social Problems* 25, no. 5 (June): 476–491.

———. 1973. The family as a public and private institution: An historical perspective. *Journal of Marriage and the Family* 35, no. 3 (August): 480–492.

Leff, Mark H. 1973. Consensus for reform: The mothers' pension movement in the progressive era. *Social Service Review* 47 (September): 397–417.

Leiby, James. 1978. *History of Social Welfare and Social Work in the United States*. New York: Columbia University Press.

Lerner, Gerda. 1969. The lady and the mill girl: Changes in the status of women in the age of Jackson. *American Studies Journal* 10, no. 1 (Spring): 5–15.

Lopata, Helena Z. 1984. Social construction of social problems over time. *Social Problems* (February): 249–272.

———. 1976. *Polish Americans: Status Competition in an Ethnic Community*. Englewood Cliffs, NJ: Prentice-Hall.

———. 1979. *Women as Widows: Support Systems*. New York: Elsevier.

Lopata, Helena Znaniecka, with Cheryl Allyn Miller and Debra Barnewolt. 1984

City Women: Work, Jobs, Occupations, Careers. Vol. 1: America. New York: Praeger.

Lopata, Helena Znaniecka, Debra Barnewolt, and Cheryl Allyn Miller. 1985. *City Women: Work, Jobs, Occupations, Careers. Vol. 2: Chicago.* New York: Praeger.

Lopata, Helena Znaniecka and Kathleen Norr. 1980. *Changing Commitments of American Women to Work and Family Roles.* Social Security Bulletin 43: 3–14.

Lubove, Roy. 1968. *The Struggle for Social Security, 1900–1935.* Cambridge, MA: Harvard University Press.

Mayhew, Henry. 1861. *London Labor and the London Poor.* New York: Harper & Brothers.

Mills, C. Wright. 1956. *White Collar.* New York: Oxford University Press.

Modell, John, and Tamara K. Hareven. 1973. Urbanization and the malleable household: An examination of boarding and lodging in American families. *Journal of Marriage and the Family* 35 (August): 467–479.

Morgan, Myfanwy, and Hilda H. Golden. 1979. Immigrant families in an industrial city: A study of households of Holyoke, 1880. *Journal of Family History* 1 (Spring): 59–68.

Murstein, Bernard I. 1974. *Love, Sex and Marriage Through the Ages.* New York: Springer Publishing.

Nilson, Linda Burzotta. 1978. The social standing of a housewife. *Journal of Marriage and the Family* 40, no. 3: 541–548.

Norton, Mary Beth. 1979. American history review essay. *SIGNS: Journal of Women in Culture and Society* 5 (Winter): 324–333.

Platt, Anthony M. 1970. The rise of the child-saving movement: A study in social policy and correctional reform. In *Crisis in American Institutions*, edited by Jerome H. Skolnick and Elliot Currie, pp. 442–463. Boston, MA: Little, Brown.

President's Committee on Economic Security. 1937. *Social Security in America: The Factual Background of the Social Security Act as Summarized from Staff Reports to the Committee on Economic Security.* Washington, D.C.: Government Printing Office.

Quadagno, Jill S. 1984. Welfare capitalism and the Social Security Act of 1935. *American Sociological Review* 49, no. 5 (October): 632–647.

Ramey, James W. 1977. Legal regulation of personal and family life styles. *The Family Coordinator* 26, no. 4 (October): 349–360.

Research Institute of America. 1977. *What You Should Know About Your Social Security Now.* New York: Research Institute of America.

Riegel, Robert F. 1975. *American Women: A Story of Social Change.* Madison, NJ: Fairleigh-Dickinson University Press.

Riesman, David, Nathan Glaser, and Reuel Denney. 1950. *The Lonely Crowd.* New Haven, CT: Yale University Press (also by Doubleday Anchor Books, 1956).

Rosaldo, Michelle Zimbalist. 1974. Women, culture and society: A theoretical overview. In *Women, Culture and Society*, edited by Michelle Zimbalist Rosaldo and Louise Lamphere, pp. 17–42. Stanford, CA: Stanford University Press.

Ross, H.L., and I.V. Sawhill. 1975. *Time of Transition: Growth of Families Headed by Women.* Washington, D.C.: Urban Institute.

Rossi, Alice S. 1965. Equality between the sexes: An immodest proposal. In *The Woman in America*, edited by Robert Jay Lifton, pp. 98–143. Boston, MA: Houghton Mifflin Co.

Rothman, Sheila M. 1978. *Woman's Proper Place: A History of Changing Ideals and Practices*. New York: Basic Books.

Rutledge, Wiley. 1933. The federal government and child labor. *The Social Service Review 7*, no. 4 (December): 555–571.

Ryan, Mary. 1979. *Womanhood in America: From Colonial Times to the Present*. New York: New Viewpoints.

Sanders, Daniel S. 1973. *The Impact of Reform Movements on Social Policy Change: The Case of Social Insurance*. Fair Lawn, NJ: R.W. Burdick.

Schulz, James H. 1976. *The Economics of Aging*. Belmont, CA: Wadsworth Publishing.

Shorter, Edward. 1975. *The Making of the Modern Family*. New York: Basic Books.

Social Security Handbook, July, 1973, fifth edition. U.S. Department of HEW, Washington D.C. Social Security Administration, Publication SSA73-10135, 1974.

Smuts, Robert W. 1959/1971. *Women and Work in America*. New York: Schocken Books.

Snee, John, and Mary Ross. 1978. Social Security Amendments of 1977: Legislative history and summary of provisions. *Social Security Bulletin 41*, no. 3 (March): 3–21.

Snowman, Daniel. 1977. *Britain and America: An Interpretation of their Culture, 1945–1975*. New York: Harper & Row.

Social Security Administration. 1939. Hearings relative to the Social Security Act Amendments of 1939 before the U.S. Congress, House Committee on Ways and Means, House of Representatives, 76th Congress. Washington, D.C.: Government Printing Office.

Social Security Board. 1937. *Social Security in America: The Factual Background of the Social Security Act as Summarized from Staff Reports to the Committee on Economic Security*. Washington, D.C.: Government Printing Office.

State of Minnesota. 1980. House File 408 2135. *Session Review* (May): 11.

Sussman, Marvin B., Judith N. Cates, and David T. Smith. 1970. *The Family and Inheritance*. New York: Russell Sage Foundation.

Tattler, Walter I. 1970. *Crusade for the Children: A History of the National Child Labor Committee and the Child. Labor Reform in America*. Chicago, IL: Quadrangle Books.

Thomas, W.I. and Florian Znaniecki. 1918–1920. *The Polish Peasant in Europe and America*. New York: Alfred A. Knopf.

Tocqueville, Alexis de. 1876/1969. *Democracy in America*. Edited by J.P. Meyer. Garden City, NY: Doubleday and Co.

Trattner, Walter I. 1979. *From Poor Law to Welfare State: A History of Social Welfare in America*. New York: The Free Press.

U.S. Bureau of the Census. 1975. *Historical Statistics of the United States*. Washington, D.C.: U.S. Printing Office.

Vinovskis, Maris A. 1978. Marriage patterns in mid-nineteenth century New York state: A multivariate analysis. *Journal of Family History 3*, no. 1 (Spring): 51–61.

Vogel, Lise. 1977. Hearts to feel and tongues to speak: New England mill women in the early nineteenth century. In *Class, Sex and the Woman Worker*, edited by Milton Cantor and Bruce Laurie, pp. 64–82. Westport, CT: Greenwood Press.

Walzer, John. 1974. A period of ambivalence: Eighteenth century American childhood. In *The History of Childhood*, edited by Lloyd de Mause, pp. 351–382. New York: Psychohistory Press.

Ware, Caroline. 1977. Introduction. In *Class, Sex and the Women Worker*, edited by Milton Cantor and Bruce Laure, pp. 3–19. Westport, CT: Greenwood Press.

Welter, Barbara. 1966. The cult of true womanhood: 1820–1860. *American Quarterly* 18, no. 2 (Summer): 151–160.

Witte, Edwin E. 1963. *The Development of the Social Security Act*. Madison, WI: University of Wisconsin Press.

Wittner, Judith. 1977. Households of strangers: Career patterns of foster children and other wards of the state. Unpublished dissertation, Northwestern University, Department of Sociology.

4
Old-Age and Survivors' Insurance and its Impact on Widows

Reviewing the effects of the current social insurance policy and program on widows and dependent wives involves looking at various pieces of data. Most of the data we will consider come from two specific studies in which the authors were involved. Additional data come from Social Security program and research sources.

The logic of human concern has women first as wives, whether dependent or not, and then as widows. However, from a variety of perspectives it is easier to discuss the situation of these women and to review the available data on them, starting with widows, since they represent a more clearly defined category. When a married women should be considered a dependent wife and when she should be considered a worker is a complicated question since most women have at least some history of past employment. Widowhood is easier to determine even with program exclusions, legal definitions, and remarriages. Widows as a group are older than dependent wives and in worse economic circumstances. From a policy perspective, it may be possible to justify regarding the dependent wife as the husband's responsibility whenever the program does not measure up. But to whom do we refer the widow? We will start our review with the situation of widows and work backwards into the situation of dependent wives.

The study of Chicago-area widows drew its sample from current and past Social Security survivor beneficiaries and from widows who were entitled to the lump-sum burial benefit only. Five categories of widows were studied (a) widowed mothers—those entitled to benefits because they had the deceased worker's minor child or children in care; (b) aged widows—those entitled to benefits because they were age 60 or over (or between 50 and 60 and disabled); (c) lump-sum beneficiaries—those widows entitled to receive the lump-sum burial benefit only; (d) remarried widows—those who had previously been survivor beneficiaries but lost entitlement because of remarriage; and (e) widows with adult children—those who had previously been widowed mother beneficiaries but lost entitlement because their youngest child in care had reached age 18* (no disabled child in care). The categories of widows in the sample do not include women whose husbands left them outside of the social security survivors benefit program permanently. That group constitutes a relatively small segment of all widows in the United States. Within the sample, the current beneficiary categories are (a) and (b), the past beneficiary categories are (d) and (e), and the potential future beneficiaries are in category (c). The last category includes widows with no children in care under age 18 who are themselves not yet age 60 (or age 50 and disabled).

While the data for the Chicago-area widows study was collected in 1974, the general review it provides of the circumstances of widows is relatively current since the absolute as well as relative income positions of widows in the United States did not change appreciably between 1974 and 1985, nor did the Social Security program of benefits for these survivors change significantly. As a result, there is no major reason to consider the Chicago-area widows study out of date for use in this assessment.

Our analyses focus on the five categories of widows listed above and on the combined sample when appropriate. Each subsample was drawn in different ratios, so that the weighted total is 82,085. The number of widows in the Chicago Standard Metropolitan Statistical Area in 1970 was 324,925, and an additional 54,465 women are known to have been widowed in the past (Lopata, 1979:56). Six of ten widows represented by our sample were 65 years of age or older when we interviewed them, although only one-fourth had been that age at the time of the death of the husband. The average number of years they have been living as widows is ten. As typical of older women in American society, few (13 percent) had any college education and 38 percent achieved only eight grades of schooling or less. Most of their parents had been born outside of Chicago, often in another country or state, so that the homes in which they grew up were ones of "urban villagers" (Gans, 1962). It is not surprising, in view of these limitations, that many have very restricted knowledge of the city and its resources beyond the few blocks with which they are familiar. The most likely to be employed are the widows in the age 45 to 54 cohort, with 65 percent in the labor force. The younger women are apt to have children still in the home and the older ones are less likely to have the skills and the desire to be employed.

---

*This was the cut-off age for widowed mothers' benefits at the time of the Chicago study; it was later changed to 16.

A prior study of older widows found that the higher the education and the more middle-class a life style a woman developed with her husband when he was well, the more disorganized her life and identity became when he died. Less educated women are less involved with their husband in social roles and less apt to consciously reconstruct their identities both at marriage and at widowhood (Lopata, 1973). On the other hand, the more education a woman has, and the more middle-class her life style, the more personal resources are available to her for rebuilding her support systems and life once the period of heavy grief is over. American urban centers require voluntary social engagement, replacing roles and relations when previous ones are lost. Many older widows, socialized into passivity vis-à-vis the world outside the home, simply lack the self-confidence and knowledge needed for such re-engagement.

Widows are a heterogeneous subgroup, with varied social life and support systems. What they have in common, of course, is the experience of a prior marriage, the death of the husband, and current status as widows. Few have remarried, younger ones are often tied down at home with small children, and the statistical disproportion between men and women in older age makes contact and development of relations rare. In addition, many widows do not wish to remarry, often idealizing the late husband to a point of "sanctification" (Lopata, 1981). They also do not wish to repeat the experience of the illness and death of a husband.

Widows often face common problems, such as a lack of opportunity to grieve, lack of emotional supports after the official mourning period ends, bad advice, a lack of supports for the children when they are grieving, loneliness, absence of self-help groups, inadequate knowledge of community resources, and lack of familiarity with the world of work which could enable job training and employment. Financial problems exist for many, as we shall see. Problems of younger widows include isolation in the home with small children, lack of inexpensive daycare centers, a feeling of being stigmatized, and strain in relations with married friends. Problems peculiar to older widows include the inability to earn an income, agism, contact with others, fear of rejection, inadequate housing, and health or nutritional problems. At the same time, many widows are quite satisfied with their life, are active, obtain supports from others, and feel quite independent. They do not want to give up this independence, even if it often leaves them lonely (Lopata, 1979: 381–383). They especially do not want to give up their homes to move in with married children. They prefer to live alone, wanting to manage their own time and activities, to avoid conflict or irritation, helping with homemaking or baby sitting only on their own terms and only occasionally.

The economic, service, social, and support systems we asked about proved very interesting. The respondents were given 195 chances to list someone as providing or receiving such supports, and they varied considerably in the complexity and diversity of their support networks. The average number of times someone was listed by our respondents is only one-fourth of the total chances. The less educated and lower-class widows are likely to be dependent on very few people. Relations with children living outside the home are asymmetrical, for example, one daughter is contributing more support than the other offspring. Many of the widows have remained in their own homes in changing neighborhoods; in these cases they are relatively isolated from neighbors who speak a different language or are of a different race. Churches and clubs also change, so that these sources of supports vanish. Many women think that friendships can be made only in childhood and do not know how to develop relationships later in life. One-fourth of the respondents never mentioned a friend as a supplier or recipient of supports. We were surprised at the infrequency with which the women use a sister or a brother as a source of supports. Sibling groups often disperse in metropolitan centers (Lopata, 1978a). Community resources in the form of churches or organizations are infrequently mentioned (Lopata, 1978b). Many widows are invisible to such groups. Only initiative on their part builds up a support network after such a dramatic event as the death of the husband, and many of the older, less educated women simply cannot do that, depending on already established relations.

THE ECONOMIC SITUATION OF CHICAGO WIDOWS

The death of the head of a household almost inevitably introduces changes in the amount and sources of income for survivors. Few widows live with their married children or in circumstances requiring no expenditure on food, rent, clothing, and so on.

The original old-age and survivors' insurance program and subsequent changes to it were based on certain assumptions. The program was intended to eliminate poverty and dependency on public welfare on the part of survivors of deceased family breadwinners. However, one of the basic assumptions of the program was that social security beneficiaries would have income from other sources. The study of Chicago-area widows examined the validity of this assumption. The interview provided information as to other sources of income available to these women, which was analyzed by the categories of widows in the sample.

Amount of Income

The interview contained two measures of income, one in a precoded question on the total income the year prior to the husband's fatal illness or accident and in 1973, the other a detailed set of questions on income from specified sources. These source categories were: wages and salaries; rent from property, sales, and special money making projects; interest on savings, dividends, stocks, and bonds; benefits from old-age, survivors, or disability insurance or from supplementary security income (Social Security Administration administered benefits); veteran widow's pension; employee pensions; private insurance; other assistance or welfare, public or private; and other sources, public or private. In follow-up questions widows were asked who in the family received the income and how much was received.

Table 4.1 shows aggregate income as the total of specific sources by characteristics of the widows. The median amount for all widows indicates that half of them lived on a total family income of less than $3,500. The consistently higher mean amounts reflects the presence of some women with substantially higher incomes than most of the others in each category. About 18 percent of the total had incomes of more than $10,000, with 5 percent receiving more than $20,000. The highest amount of reported income was over $80,000. At the other end of the scale, about one in six (16 percent) of the widows was living on $1,000 or less. This includes about 10 percent who claimed not to be receiving any income from any source or stated that income came to them or to some other member of the family living in the household but that they did not know how much money was involved.

Income figures by Social Security beneficiary status group seem to reflect the effect of other variables. Remarried widows had the highest amount of income; they had a male head for the family and, probably, were also younger. Aged widows, of course, had the least amount of income: they were the oldest and most probably lived in households they headed themselves. Widowed mothers, widows with adult children, and lump-sum beneficiaries fell between the two extremes.

As expected, families with male heads had more income than families with female heads, and white widows had more than did non-white widows. However, the sex of the head of the household apparently made a greater difference for family income than did race.

Age and education also effect family income—education is positively related to mean and median income. However, about one-fifth of those with more than a high school education reported having annual incomes of less than $1,000 compared to only 12 percent of grade school gradu-

Table 4.1 Aggregate Income in 1973 for Chicago-Area Widows

	Base		Amount ($)								
	K	I	Under 1000	1000–2499	2500–3999	4000–6999	7000–9999	10000 + over	Total	Mean	Median
Total	82,085	100.0	16.1	17.4	21.4	18.3	8.4	18.3	99.9	5,853	3,436
Race											
White	70,164	85.5	15.8	17.6	20.8	17.5	8.5	19.8	100.0	6,091	3,480
Black	11,922	14.5	18.1	16.7	24.5	23.3	7.7	9.7	100.0	4,453	2,820
Sex of family head											
Male	11,695	14.2	14.5	22.7	10.8	10.6	8.3	33.1	100.0	8,460	5,420
Female	70,390	85.8	16.4	16.4	23.2	19.6	8.5	15.9	100.0	4,596	3,399
Age											
Under 31	1,064	.3	1.4	11.3	8.9	32.7	18.9	26.8	99.9	7,883	6,499
31-40	3,293	4.0	8.5	5.2	2.9	23.9	16.7	42.8	100.0	10,601	8,959
41-50	8,961	11.0	8.0	2.7	6.9	16.0	23.2	43.3	99.9	11,383	8,900
51-60	12,988	15.9	11.6	13.5	8.6	18.1	17.1	31.1	99.8	7,979	6,609
61-70	23,340	28.6	15.7	19.5	19.0	23.8	4.6	17.4	99.9	5,576	3,215
71+	31,856	39.1	21.9	22.5	35.2	14.4	1.7	4.3	100.0	3,088	2,542
Age											
Under 45	6,241	7.7	7.9	4.9	4.7	23.5	18.0	40.9	99.9	10,891	8,729
45-54	11,040	13.5	8.1	7.1	6.3	15.9	20.4	42.2	100.0	10,266	8,559
55-64	15,345	18.8	11.6	14.4	11.4	25.4	14.0	23.3	100.1	6,898	5,320
65+	43,873	60.0	20.5	21.9	30.4	16.3	2.3	8.7	100.1	3,893	2,639

Education											
0-7	14,717	18.7	19.5	18.2	31.4	22.3	4.8	3.8	100.0	3,426	2,646
8	15,653	19.9	12.3	23.6	36.2	14.6	6.3	6.9	99.9	3,883	2,842
9-11	15,915	20.2	15.6	17.7	14.9	23.6	9.3	18.5	99.9	5,886	4,032
12	21,661	27.5	14.9	18.0	8.9	17.9	12.5	27.9	100.1	7,438	5,377
13+	10,874	13.8	21.7	7.2	12.7	15.5	7.0	35.9	100.0	8,945	6,180
Number of earners											
0	55,516	67.6	23.6	25.1	28.3	16.2	3.1	3.7	100.0	3,119	2,500
1	21,264	25.9	.5	1.4	8.7	26.1	22.9	40.6	100.2	10,029	8,501
2	4,887	6.0	0.0	.3	0.0	11.7	7.0	80.9	99.9	16,936	15,500
3+	419	.5	0.0	0.0	0.0	0.0	0.0	99.5	100.0	26,958	24,789
Number of dependent children (under 18)											
0	68,056	82.9	17.8	20.2	24.5	17.9	6.2	13.4	100.0	4,900	2,837
1	6,227	7.6	9.4	6.4	6.6	16.2	16.6	44.8	100.0	10,197	9,001
2	3,596	4.4	5.6	1.3	8.3	17.4	29.3	38.0	99.9	10,096	8,601
3	2,065	2.5	8.3	0.0	4.6	31.3	14.5	41.0	99.7	10,480	8,500
4+	2,141	2.6	6.5	2.9	5.0	27.8	14.0	43.8	100.1	11,916	8,447
Beneficiary status											
Widowed mother	15,832	19.3	7.8	4.8	9.3	21.6	19.5	37.1	100.1	9,275	8,200
Aged widow	54,079	65.9	19.5	22.9	27.8	17.6	3.4	8.8	100.0	3,976	2,634
Lump sum beneficiary	3,010	3.7	12.9	16.3	12.5	19.3	20.8	18.2	100.0	6,290	5,600
Remarried widow	2,497	3.0	10.5	7.6	4.1	8.2	9.4	60.2	100.0	14,636	13,245
Widow with adult children	6,669	8.1	11.8	6.7	8.7	20.5	16.9	35.4	100.0	9,463	7,299

Source: Chicago area widowhood study, compiled by G. Kim.

ates. Thus, although the increase in mean and median income as education increases is seen for the highest income group, the pattern is not consistent. However, the question must be raised whether some better educated women are more hesitant to report income or live under circumstances where they are less aware of the size and sources of income.

There is a negative relationship between age and income when the four categories of age are used (see Table 4.1); in general, the older the widow the less income she has.

The number of children under 18 years of age seems to make no difference for family income, although the presence of at least one dependent child clearly makes a difference. Widows without any dependent children had the lowest incomes; however, the widows without dependent children are also the older widows.

The more wage earners in the family the higher the family income. Two-thirds of the widows had no earnings and no other earners; their mean and median incomes were substantially lower than those for all other widows.

In-Kind Economic Suppports

A question that must be addressed is whether some widows are receiving in-kind economic supports, particularly if they live with someone else, or are receiving help with the payment of their expenses.

Table 4.2 presents the distribution of receipt of each type of in-kind financial support. Three-quarters of the women were not recipients of any of these forms of support. Overall, help in the form of food or assistance in the payment for food was given most often. This was received by aged widows in the largest percentage, as reflected also in distribution by age, education, and number of dependent children. It was not necessarily as predominently received by those widows who were the poorest and the most in need, as seen in distribution by income and race. This may relate to the ability of others in the environment of those most in need to provide these supports. In general aged widows received more of all these forms of help, with the exception of rent, which was received by a large percentage of the widows with adult children.

Sources of Income

Three-fourths of the widows reported that they or another family member received income from social insurance, defined for this data source as either the Old-Age, Survivors, or Disability Insurance program or the Supplemental Security Income program administered by the Social Security Administration (Title II or XVI of the Social Security Act). This was the single most frequently reported source of income (Table

Table 4.2 Non-Income Financial Supports

Variable	Kind (percentage received)					
	Gift	Rent	Food	Clothing	Bills	Other
Total	8.8	8.8	11.2	5.7	7.9	1.0
Race						
White	9.2	8.7	11.8	5.5	7.6	1.1
Black	7.0	9.7	8.0	7.1	9.9	0.5
Age (1973)						
Under 31	14.6	5.6	5.6	0.0	1.4	0.0
31–40	5.2	4.3	2.9	0.4	6.2	1.9
41–50	4.0	6.4	7.4	1.4	2.9	0.7
51–60	6.6	9.5	9.3	1.9	5.8	1.4
61–70	10.8	11.0	11.6	4.9	11.0	1.2
71+	10.1	8.4	14.2	10.0	8.5	0.8
Age (1974)						
Under 45	7.3	5.2	5.9	1.0	5.5	1.0
45–54	2.5	6.1	6.6	1.8	3.8	0.5
55–64	7.7	14.1	12.2	3.0	7.1	1.3
65+	11.0	8.4	12.9	8.2	9.5	1.1
Education						
0–7	10.4	15.8	25.0	18.5	11.6	0.3
8	16.8	7.1	15.5	7.7	9.9	3.7
9–11	10.9	10.3	8.1	2.5	9.0	0.7
12	4.7	6.2	6.3	1.8	4.7	0.4
13+	3.2	3.7	3.4	0.0	7.0	0.1
Number of dependent children						
0	9.7	9.7	12.5	6.8	8.8	1.1
1	1.7	5.1	7.1	0.0	2.8	1.0
2	9.6	7.0	5.3	1.3	2.6	1.6
3	2.3	4.6	2.3	0.0	7.6	0.0
4+	6.5	0.0	0.44	0.7	3.6	0.7
Income (dollars)						
Under 1,000	5.8	11.4	13.4	8.4	7.3	0.5
1,000–2,499	8.3	4.3	8.8	2.4	8.8	0.1
2,500–3,999	12.9	9.4	13.8	11.3	6.9	0.1
4,000–6,999	12.1	10.5	10.0	1.8	7.2	3.8
7,000–9,999	7.6	6.7	5.1	5.5	11.8	1.7
10,000+	4.6	9.7	13.1	4.3	7.7	0.4
Beneficiary status						
WM	4.5	6.6	7.5	0.9	5.4	0.6
AW	10.8	9.4	12.8	7.9	9.4	1.0
LS	8.4	7.6	10.6	4.6	6.1	1.9
R	4.1	1.2	1.8	0.6	3.5	1.2
WA	5.1	13.3	11.8	2.6	4.6	2.1

Gift, gifts; rent, payment or help on payment of your rent or mortgage; food, food or payment for food; clothing, clothing or payment for clothing; bills, payment or help in payment of other bills such as medical or vacation expenses; other, any other financial help.

Source: Chicago area widowhood study, compiled by G. Kim.

4.3). The second most frequently reported source was earnings, with about one-third of all widows showing such income contributed by at least one family member, and one-fourth having earned income from their own work. The category "interest on savings, dividends, stocks, bonds" helps about 30 percent of the women. However, for most the amounts are small. Other sources of income are generally available to few of these women.

Within the social insurance category, social security survivors' benefits were the source most frequently reported. Over half the widows and/or their children had such income. One in six widows received old age benefits; slightly over one in twenty received supplementary security income.

Even when encouraged to list different sources of family income most widows were unable to list more than social security, their own or another family member's earnings, or interest on savings. Any assumption that widows are wealthy because they have a variety of income sources is incorrect for most of the women studied for two reasons. First, most are not receiving much income. Second, most of them are dependent on one of three sources, with a heavy reliance on social security.

Looking at income sources by beneficiary status, widows with dependent children (widowed mother) and aged widows were the most apt to report social security benefits. Some aged widows, in particular, may not be aware they are receiving benefits. Many of the widowed mothers also either were working themselves or had income from another earner in the family. Relatively few aged widows reported this source of income. Widows with adult children were more likely to have earnings of their own than any of the other groups. They had the lowest percentage receiving social insurance, with the exception of those eligible for lump-sum burial benefits only. Their children are beyond the age of entitlement, and they are not old enough for aged widow benefits. Remarried widows, that is, widows who lost benefits because of remarriage, are less likely to be working than all other groups except aged widows, but are among the most likely to have a worker in the household, probably the new husband. They are just below widowed mothers and aged widows in the percentage reporting social insurance benefits paid to the family. These are predominantly survivors' benefits, most probably paid to the children of the deceased husband.

There were large differences by race in the percentage receiving interest income and public assistance. While about one-third of the whites had interest income from savings of one form or another, only about 7 percent of the non-whites had such income. On the other hand, about 19 percent of the non-whites but only 2 percent of the whites had income from public assistance.

The proportion having earnings from their own work is closely related to the age of the widow. There is a downward trend in the percentage having their own earnings on either end of the mid-forties to mid-fifties range. Younger widows are more limited in their ability to work, probably because of child-rearing responsibilities; older widows are in the labor force in the smallest percentages.

Middle-aged widows are somewhat more likely to have their own earnings; they also more probably have grown children and cannot receive social insurance based on their own ages. For the oldest widows, the most commonly reported income source was social insurance.

The number of dependent children affected the probability of a widow having her own earnings. Only 20 percent of the widows with no dependent children had earnings, probably because they were older women. Among widows with dependent children, the proportion with their own earnings decreases as the number of dependent children increases. This pattern is similar to the findings of some other investigators. Mallan (1975:7), using 1971 Current Population Survey data, found that the median earnings for widows with one or two dependent children was about the same and declined if there were more children. She noted that ''. . . it is a well-known fact that mothers work less as the number of their children increases'' (Mallan, 1975:7). In our sample, mothers of one or two dependent children were more likely to be employed than were mothers of three or more offspring.

The family maximum provision of social security (1.5 to 1.85 times the PIA) sets a limit of benefits paid to a widow with dependent children based on the deceased worker's earnings record. The cut-off point of no further benefit amount for an additional dependent child is affected by whether the widow is working or eligible for benefits for herself. If the widow is not working, as may be the case with three or more dependent children at home, there is no additional benefit amount paid beyond that for the widow herself and approximately one dependent child.*

NUMBER AND PATTERNS OF INCOME SOURCE UTILIZATION

About three-fourths of Chicago-area widows had two or fewer income sources in 1973 (Table 4.4).

---

*The widowed ''surviving mother'' is entitled to 75% of PIA as is each dependent child. At most the ''family maximum'' is 1.85 times the PIA. At this level, additional benefits are payable only partially for a second dependent child if the mother receives benefits. At the 1.5 PIA level, benefit amounts are limited to what would be paid for the mother and one child. Administratively, the benefit amount is distributed over all dependents if there are more dependent children. However, each gets a smaller benefit amount paid on his or her basis, since the ''family maximum'' cannot be exceeded. The multiple of PIA for the family maximum is determined by the PIA amount.

Table 4.3 Utilization of Income Sources by Chicago-Area Widows, by Race, Age, Education, Dependent Children, and Beneficiary Status

Variable	Base	None	SW	TW	RS	SI	IS	VP	EP	PI	PA	O
						Income source (percentage use)						
Total	82,084	12.8	25.3	32.5	11.7	74.3	29.6	9.0	10.4	1.8	4.2	4.1
Race												
White	70,163	13.5	25.3	33.3	10.7	73.8	33.5	9.4	11.0	2.0	1.7	4.3
Black	11,922	8.6	25.4	27.9	17.5	76.8	6.8	6.6	6.6	.9	18.7	2.9
Age												
Under 31	1,064	1.4	38.3	49.6	1.4	85.0	20.3	12.1	0.0	1.1	6.9	13.4
31–40	3,293	8.1	45.5	61.0	8.4	88.6	22.3	18.6	2.6	5.6	13.4	6.1
41–50	8,961	7.3	57.4	69.7	12.3	70.9	32.0	27.7	7.7	2.4	6.2	6.8
51–60	12,987	10.3	53.6	62.8	16.4	49.8	33.4	10.4	10.1	1.9	3.9	6.0
61–70	23,339	14.5	24.3	34.1	8.0	75.5	30.2	2.8	13.9	1.4	5.1	3.7
71+	31,855	15.2	3.3	5.5	12.5	82.2	28.5	6.8	10.0	1.7	2.1	2.5
Age												
Under 45	6,241	7.6	43.0	59.0	9.9	85.4	25.5	19.4	3.6	3.4	10.0	7.4
45–54	11,041	7.4	59.6	69.4	12.7	66.7	30.7	23.8	8.6	2.4	4.6	7.2
55–64	15,345	10.6	44.4	54.2	14.4	55.3	34.6	4.8	15.7	1.2	5.5	6.7
65+	48,873	15.5	9.5	14.3	10.5	80.3	28.6	5.8	10.1	1.7	3.0	2.3

Education

		SW	TW	RS	SI	IS	VP	EP	PI	PA	O	
0-7	14,717	13.8	13.4	18.4	19.7	81.4	12.0	3.3	13.5	.1	7.0	1.0
8	15,653	7.2	15.2	20.3	8.7	81.5	35.2	7.2	11.4	.3	4.6	7.3
9-11	15,914	11.7	27.4	33.1	7.9	75.5	31.1	9.4	9.6	.8	6.1	5.7
12	21,660	13.5	33.8	46.3	11.7	67.7	29.5	11.8	10.0	3.0	1.5	3.9
13+	10,874	20.5	38.3	45.3	8.9	64.4	43.9	12.7	9.7	6.3	3.5	3.0

Number of dependent children (under 18)

0	68,056	13.9	20.6	26.5	11.8	71.7	29.7	6.0	10.9	1.7	3.6	3.2
1	6,227	8.6	55.6	67.3	9.9	81.8	30.4	20.1	10.3	1.2	.5	6.8
2	3,596	5.6	53.2	60.8	12.6	93.6	24.6	30.9	7.4	4.8	9.5	13.5
3	2,065	8.3	34.1	53.5	14.5	88.6	24.2	26.0	4.6	3.7	1.7	9.2
4+	2,141	6.5	30.7	53.8	10.9	86.2	36.4	19.6	5.8	2.9	25.6	4.3

Beneficiary status

Widowed mother	15,831	7.2	52.1	61.7	11.1	83.8	29.9	22.8	8.1	2.7	6.3	7.8
Aged widow	54,078	15.1	10.7	15.6	11.2	80.0	28.8	4.9	11.2	1.5	3.4	2.9
Lump-sum beneficiary	3,010	9.1	54.2	59.5	10.6	24.6	38.3	8.7	16.7	2.7	4.9	3.0
Remarried widow	2,497	10.5	35.7	72.5	12.9	68.4	25.7	14.0	4.7	4.7	4.1	7.0
Widow with adult children	6,669	10.3	62.6	72.8	17.4	29.7	32.8	8.2	8.2	1.5	5.1	4.6

SW, own wages; TW, total wages; RS, rent, sales; SI, social insurance; IS, interest, savings; VP, veteran's widow pension; EP, employee pension; PI, private insurance; PA, public assistance; O, other.

Source: Chicago area widowhood study, compiled by G. Kim.

Table 4.4 Number of Utilized Income Sources by Race, Age, Education, Dependent Children, and Beneficiary Status

	Base		Number of income sources utilized					
Variable	n	%	0	1	2	3	4+	Total
Total	82,078	100.0	12.9	24.4	37.4	14.8	10.5	100.0
Race								
White	70,163	85.5	13.6	22.1	37.1	16.0	11.2	100.0
Black	11,922	14.5	8.6	37.6	39.6	7.8	6.3	99.9
Age (1973)								
0–30	1,064	1.3	1.4	36.7	34.5	23.0	4.5	100.1
31–40	3,293	4.0	9.6	12.1	31.5	25.1	21.7	100.0
41–50	8,961	11.0	7.3	15.6	26.2	21.4	29.5	100.0
51–60	12,988	15.9	10.2	22.5	33.2	16.5	17.6	100.0
61–70	23,339	28.6	14.5	22.8	38.9	12.7	11.1	100.0
71+	31,856	39.1	15.2	28.5	42.6	12.8	1.0	100.1
Age (1974)								
0–44	6,241	7.7	8.3	18.0	28.4	23.6	21.6	99.9
45–54	11,041	13.5	7.4	17.5	28.2	18.1	28.8	100.0
55–64	15,345	18.8	10.5	21.5	36.3	18.2	13.5	100.0
65+	48,874	60.0	15.5	26.9	41.5	12.1	4.1	100.1
Education								
0–7	14,717	18.7	14.2	25.4	49.2	9.9	1.3	100.0
8	15,653	19.9	7.2	30.2	40.0	19.0	3.6	100.0
9–11	15,915	20.2	11.7	27.2	32.1	16.7	12.2	99.9
12	21,661	27.5	13.5	22.9	33.7	14.3	15.5	99.9
13+	10,874	13.8	20.4	11.9	27.8	17.5	22.4	100.0
Dependent children								
0	68,056	82.9	13.9	26.3	39.8	13.4	6.7	100.1
1	6,227	2.6	8.6	17.3	22.7	21.1	30.2	99.9
2	3,596	4.4	5.6	12.2	24.9	28.8	28.5	100.0
3	2,065	2.5	8.3	16.8	34.1	19.6	21.2	100.0
4+	2,141	2.6	8.7	13.1	29.8	15.0	33.4	100.0
Beneficiary status								
WM	15,832	19.3	7.5	15.6	27.8	21.3	27.8	100.0
AW	54,079	65.9	15.1	26.8	41.5	11.7	4.9	100.0
LS	3,010	3.7	9.1	29.2	42.0	13.3	6.4	100.0
R	2,497	3.0	9.9	15.8	27.5	19.9	26.9	100.0
WA	6,669	8.1	10.3	26.7	29.2	23.6	10.3	100.1
Mean income			22.8*	3,020	5,892	8,866	15,216	5,853

*It deviates from the expected 0 because wrong transformation of some data on which number of income sources utilized is based.

Source: Chicago area widowhood study, compiled by G. Kim.

The proportions of aged widow beneficiaries, blacks, older widows, widows with less education, and those with no dependent children with three or more sources of income was lower than for other groups. These characteristics describe the lowest-income widows. In general, the higher-income women reported more sources of income.

Table 4.5 shows the patterns of combination of income sources. In addition to being the most frequently reported income source (three of four widows), social insurance was also the single source on which more widows were totally dependent than any other. About one of five widows was in this situation. As indicated previously, 13 percent reported a total absence of income from any source. Beyond that, the next most frequently reported single or combination of income sources was social insurance along with savings that brought in income. This combination was reported as the source of income by one of ten widows.

Amount and Relative Share of Income Sources

The frequency of use of different income sources and patterns of source combinations does not reflect the amount of income derived from each source. The importance of an income source can be assessed by the amount of income it provided for those who received it, and by the relative shares of recipients' total income that came from the source.

Social insurance is very important for widows because it is the most frequently mentioned source of income. In terms of the median income received from each source, social insurance was second in importance to earnings income of the widow herself or her family (see Table 4.6). Thus, though the largest proportion of widows received social insurance income, it did not provide the largest amount of income to recipients.

Earnings were far more important than any other source of income in the amounts they provided recipients, particularly if there were other earners in the family besides the widow herself. The median earnings of widows with their own earnings was $5,000; the median for total earnings was $6,999, indicating the importance of other family members' earnings. The median income from social insurance for beneficiaries was $2,292.

Widows whose only income came from social insurance had lower mean incomes than widows who had multiple sources of income. To have social insurance as the only source of income means these widows had not accumulated assets from which they could receive income, did not have employee pension or private insurance income, were not working themselves, and had no other workers in the family. It seems plau-

Table 4.5 Most Frequently Reported Patterns of
Income Source Utilization among Chicago-Area Widows

	Frequencies		Mean income (dollars)
Income sources used	n	%	
Social insurance	16,561	20.2	2,423
No sources reported	10,536	12.8	0
Social insurance + interest or savings	8,161	9.9	4,201
Own wages + total wages + social insurance	5,460	6.7	9,061
Rent or sales + social insurance	3,651	4.4	4,050
Social insurance + employee pension	2,918	3.6	4,437
Own wages + total wages + social insurance + interest or savings	2,880	3.5	11,326
Own wages + total wages	2,825	3.4	7,608
Own wages + total wages + interest or savings	2,421	2.9	12,620
Social insurance + public assistance	2,340	2.9	3,298
Total wages + social insurance	2,142	2.6	13,563
Social insurance + interest or savings + employee pension	1,668	2.0	5,729
Social insurance + veteran's widow pension	1,660	2.0	3,387

Source: Chicago area widowhood study, compiled by G. Kim.

Table 4.6 Median Amount Received from Income Sources
Reported by Chicago-Area Widows

Income source	Percentage receiving	Median amount received
Base (all widows)	100.0	3,436
Own wages (SW)	25.3	5,000
Total wages (TW)	32.5	6,999
Rent, sales (RS)	11.7	1,018
Interest, savings (IS)	29.6	599
Social insurance (SI)	74.3	2,292
Old age	16.7	2,063
Disability	3.3	1,919
Survivor	54.1	2,300
Supplementary	5.6	2,279
Veteran's widows pension (VP)	9.0	684
Employee Pension (EP)	10.4	1,752
Private Insurance (PI)	1.8	1,887
Public Assistance (PA)	4.2	911
Other (O)	4.1	798
Total with any reported income	87.2	4,100

Source: Chicago area widowhood study, compiled by G. Kim.

sible that the husbands of these widows had work histories that resulted in relatively low PIAs. If this was the case, such widows would have low benefits and no other income sources.

Table 4.7 shows the relative share of income from seven major sources.* On the whole, the median relative share of income from social insurance was about two-thirds of the income for those with this income source. Earnings of the family, when present, provided three-quarters of total income for the average widow. Rental, employee pension, and public assistance had a median share of income between one-fourth and one-third of total income for recipients. Income from interest provided a relatively low share of total income for those with such income.

Measured in terms of the relative share of total income provided by a source, social insurance and earnings are clearly the most important sources. Combining the percentage with income from the source, and the amount and relative share of total income they received from it, we have a picture of the overall importance of different income sources for widows. When earnings were available, they provided the largest amount and share of income for widows. However, only about one in three of the widows had such income. Social insurance, primarily Social Security survivors' or old-age benefits, were received by three of four widows, and were a close second to earnings in relative share of income when received. For one in five widows, this was the only source of income. However, the median amount received was about one-third what earnings provided. Obviously, widows with earnings in the family were in far better shape financially. Other sources of income were either infrequently used or provided relatively little income to recipients. When they were relied on for a major share of income, the widow had limited income.

Earnings were not a significant source of income for aged widows (receiving old-age benefits). This was apparently a major factor in their more limited total incomes. However, it was a major source of income for remarried widows, who also had the highest median income. With reference to the age of the widow, the median relative share of income provided by earnings was highest among middle-aged widows (55–64), whereas social insurance provided the highest median proportion of total income for older widows (Table 4.8). Almost half of the 80 percent of the oldest widows who said they received social insurance had 80% or more of their income from this source.

Aged widow beneficiaries show a median relative share of income

---

*While Public Assistance (PA) was received by few widows it is included because of its role as a public program for the financially needy.

Table 4.7 Relative Share of Each Income Source of Chicago-Area Widows

Percentage share	Source						
	SI	TW	SW	IS	RS	EP	PA
Use	74	33	26	30	12	10	4
1–10	4	1	4	46	19	9	29
11–20	12	2	9	21	23	21	28
21–30	11	6	9	9	25	23	25
31–40	8	5	9	10	14	12	1
41–50	4	7	11	3	5	5	0
51–60	4	10	11	3	1	8	4
61–70	10	12	11	2	6	8	0
71–80	11	13	8	4	3	10	9
81–90	6	18	8	1	0	3	0
91–100	31	27	20	1	3	2	4
Total	100	100	100	100	100	100	100
Median	68	76	58	14	27	30	33

See Table 4.3 for meaning of income source abbreviations.
Source: Chicago area widowhood study, compiled by G. Kim.

from social insurance of 74 percent; widows with adult children received such income less frequently, and among those that did, the median relative share of total income was 21 percent (Table 4.9).

The reverse situation is seen on earnings for these two categories. Few aged widow beneficiaries, as with the general category of older widows, had their own earnings or other earners in the family. When these earnings were present, they contributed a large share of total income. Widows with adult children were the most likely to be working themselves (63 percent), with this income source contributing 79 percent of total income on the average. However, among lump-sum beneficiaries wages contributed the greatest median share of income (86 percent), while they were somewhat less likely to have been working than widows with adult children (54 percent).

A comparatively small percentage of remarried widows earn their own income, and this makes up a small percentage of their total income for those with such earnings. As might be expected, these widows show a high percentage with family earnings (73 percent), and these earnings contributed a median 80 percent share of total earnings. Unlike the other categories of widows where family earnings contributed a major share of total income, the family earnings for remarried widows was not based on their own work and earnings. Presumably, it was the new husband who worked and contributed earnings. The widows with adult children could count less on such support from their children to supplement their own earnings.

Table 4.8 Relative Share of Each Income Source of Chicago-Area Widows by Age, 1974

Source and age	Base		Share						
	n	%	1–20	20–40	40–60	60–80	80–100	Total	Median
SI									
Below 45	5,333	85.4	20.8	26.9	15.9	11.2	25.1	99.9	42.8
45–54	7,367	66.7	32.9	27.7	11.9	11.6	16.9	100.1	29.6
55–64	8,491	55.3	20.9	26.2	14.7	16.3	21.9	100.0	44.9
65+	39,249	80.3	8.0	13.1	8.5	23.3	47.1	100.0	77.9
Total	60,440	74.2	13.9	17.9	10.4	19.8	37.9	99.9	68.2
SW:									
Below 45	3,681	59.0	12.4	13.1	25.5	28.8	20.3	100.1	59.9
45–54	7,665	69.4	2.8	10.0	17.6	28.7	40.8	99.9	76.3
55–64	8,313	54.2	3.8	7.3	14.9	19.6	54.4	100.0	82.1
65+	6,992	14.3	4.5	16.4	16.9	21.2	41.0	100.1	67.6
Total	26,651	32.7	4.9	11.3	17.7	23.9	42.3	100.1	75.7
SW:									
Below 45	2,684	43.0	28.9	19.6	25.6	17.2	8.2	100.1	41.8
45–54	6,580	59.6	7.8	22.0	23.4	23.3	23.5	100.0	58.4
55–64	6,818	44.4	4.4	14.5	21.3	16.7	43.2	100.1	73.3
65+	4,663	9.5	22.6	19.0	20.7	13.3	24.4	100.0	45.4
Total	20,744	25.5	12.7	18.6	22.4	18.1	28.3	100.1	50.0
PA:									
Below 45	624	10.0	27.5	38.0	9.4	17.5	7.6	100.0	32.0
45–54	504	4.6	33.0	9.1	32.7	11.7	13.6	100.1	47.7
55–64	545	5.5	1.7	79.2	15.0	0	4.0	99.9	31.7
65+	1,461	3.0	39.4	21.3	39.4	0	0	100.1	35.0
Total	3,343	4.2	27.0	36.8	27.0	4.9	4.4	100.1	32.6

Source: Chicago area widowhood study, compiled by G. Kim.

Table 4.9 Relative Share of Each Income Source of Chicago-Area Widows by Social Security Beneficiary Status

Source and beneficiary status	Base		Share						
	n	%	1–20	20–40	40–60	60–80	80–100	Total	Median
SI									
Widowed mother	13,272	83.8	21.4	29.3	15.4	11.8	22.1	100.0	39.7
Aged widow	43,263	80.0	8.5	14.6	8.5	23.2	45.1	99.9	73.6
Lump-sum beneficiary	741	24.6	20.0	24.6	12.3	10.8	32.3	100.0	45.9
Remarried widow	1,700	68.4	46.2	18.8	10.3	6.3	17.9	99.5	21.4
Widow with adult children	1,984	29.7	48.3	19.0	15.5	10.3	6.9	100.0	21.0
Total	60,968	74.3	13.8	18.2	10.3	19.7	38.0	100.0	68.2
SW									
Widowed mother	9,764	61.7	9.2	12.1	24.8	34.0	19.9	100.0	61.8
Aged widow	8,442	15.6	3.1	15.6	18.8	15.6	46.9	100.0	77.8
Lump-sum beneficiary	1,790	59.5	3.2	6.4	5.1	17.8	67.5	100.0	91.2
Remarried widow	1,810	72.5	2.4	8.1	9.7	27.4	52.4	100.0	81.1

Widow with adult children	4,856	72.8	.7	4.9	9.2	19.0	66.2	100.0	90.6
Total	26,663	32.5	4.9	11.3	17.7	23.9	42.3	100.1	75.7
SW									
Widowed mother	8,248	52.1	12.6	20.7	28.2	27.0	11.5	100.0	52.2
Aged widow	5,804	10.7	18.2	18.2	22.7	9.1	31.8	100.0	53.8
Lump-sum beneficiary	1,630	54.2	4.9	9.8	9.1	18.9	57.3	100.0	85.9
Remarried widow	891	35.7	32.8	31.1	14.8	11.5	9.8	100.0	28.6
Widow with adult children	4,172	62.6	4.1	15.6	17.2	13.9	49.2	100.0	79.4
Total	20,744	25.3	12.7	18.6	22.4	18.1	28.3	100.1	58.0
PA									
Widowed mother	995	6.3	28.6	33.3	19.0	14.3	4.9	100.0	35.6
Aged widow	1,847	3.4	28.6	42.9	28.6	0	0	100.1	31.7
Lump-sum beneficiary	148	4.9	15.4	15.4	38.5	7.7	22.1	100.1	50.8
Remarried widow	102	4.1	57.1	14.3	14.3	14.3	0	100.0	16.0
Widow with adult children	342	5.1	10.0	30.0	40.0	0	20.0	100.0	56.5
Total	3,434	4.2	27.0	36.8	27.0	4.9	4.4	100.1	32.6

Source: Chicago area widowhood study, compiled by G. Kim.

What emerges as the most effective way for a widow to obtain the highest income level possible was for her to remarry and to a working man. Working herself or having some other family member working was the next most effective way for a widow to maximize income. Unfortunately, demographic reality is against the widow's potential for remarriage. Working, or having another family member who works, among the widows who have not remarried, is most characteristic of those with adult children still in the household. The bulk of widows are older and do not have much prospect for remarriage, or potential for employment or for having other workers in the family.

Social Insurance Benefits and Earnings

The present Social Security system of this country operates as a wage replacement mechanism. There is no limit on the amount of income a beneficiary may obtain from non-work sources, but in 1973 the retirement test set limits on the earnings the widow could obtain from her own work and still receive benefits, unless she was over 72. The supplemental security income program operates differently in that it is means tested and not wage related.

How much income did those households reporting benefits for 1973 obtain from social insurance and earnings only? Table 4.10 shows that the median income in 1973 from earnings and benefits among the beneficiary households was $2,536. Beneficiary status, age, education, and the presence of a dependent child all impact on the amount of income received from social insurance and work; race makes little difference. The factors are interrelated. Younger widows had more income from social insurance and earnings than older widows; educated widows had more of such income than the less-educated widows. Widows without a dependent child had basically the aged widow beneficiaries, but older widows in general also had less income from social insurance and earnings than widows with dependent children; and remarried widows had much more of such income than widows in other beneficiary status groups.

What proportion of total 1973 income came from social insurance and/or earnings among the beneficiary households? Table 4.11 shows that, for 1973 beneficiaries, the median relative share of income from social insurance and earnings was more than nine-tenths (91.7 percent) of their total income. Although beneficiary status, race, age, education, and number of dependent children made some difference, the variations were minor. For all the categories of widows, income from social insurance and/or earnings formed a large proportion of the total amount of 1973 income for those who reported benefits.

RELATIVE AMOUNT OF INCOME

In addition to information on the incomes widows have to live on and the sources of those incomes, we need to consider how widowhood has affected their income situation. A fuller understanding of the impact of the death of the husband on the financial condition of his widow necessitates examination of her relative income using three separate bases of comparison.

First, how does the income of widows compare to the income of the general population? This addresses the issue of how much income widows have to live on relative to non-widows at the same point in time. The second basis for comparison looks at the effect on income of becoming a widow by comparing income in 1973 to the income in the year before the husband's illness or accident that resulted in his death. These are incomes at two different points in time. The comparison is complicated by differences within the group of widows in the span of time between the two years.

The third comparison used is of 1973 income to the poverty level as a measure of the amount needed for a minimal living standard.

Comparisons to National Income

Table 4.12 presents comparative incomes for the total U.S. population, the metropolitan population, and the widows of this study. Chicago-area widows had incomes less than those of the population as a whole. While the 1973 median family income in the United States was $12,051, the income of the widows in our study was between one-third and one-fourth of that amount ($3,436). If we eliminate the widows who reported no income the median goes up to $4,100, which is still only slightly over one-third of the total population's income. While half of metropolitan Americans lived on less than $13,626, half of Chicago-area widows lived on $3,436.

Table 4.13 compares the income of the widows in our study with the income of the United States total population in female-headed households, controlling for race. The median income of the widows is less than that of female-headed households in the total population for both whites and non-whites. The difference among whites is greater than the difference among non-whites.

It has been repeatedly observed that male-headed families have more income than female-headed families. Table 4.14 compares the income of Chicago-area widows with the income of the total U.S. population, controlling for the sex of the family head in both cases. The widows have less income than the general population, regardless of the sex of family

Table 4.10 Income from Earnings and Social Insurance among Widowed Chicago-Area Social Insurance Beneficiaries

Variables	Base		Amount						Median
	n	%	1	2,500	5,000	7,500	10,000	Total	
Total	60,967	74.3	48.3	24.0	8.4	4.9	14.4	100.0	2,536
Race									
White	51,815	73.8	48.0	23.7	7.8	4.8	15.6	99.9	2,543
Non-white	9,152	76.8	49.7	25.7	11.6	5.1	7.9	100.0	2,520
Age (1973)									
30 and less	905	85.0	10.5	21.0	35.9	15.7	16.9	100.0	6,518
31-40	2,917	88.6	11.2	15.1	20.0	15.6	38.0	99.9	7,799
41-50	6,355	70.9	7.7	14.8	20.3	14.9	42.3	100.0	8,700
51-60	6,471	49.8	26.3	17.8	13.2	13.9	28.8	100.0	6,201
61-70	17,620	75.5	51.0	23.6	10.2	3.0	12.1	99.9	2,483
71+	26,172	82.0	67.1	28.7	1.1	0.0	3.2	100.1	2,399
Age (1974)									
Less than 45	5,333	85.4	10.0	18.1	20.6	14.2	37.2	100.1	7,644
45-54	7,367	66.7	11.6	13.0	18.6	15.6	41.3	100.1	8,599
55-64	8,491	55.3	43.7	21.9	11.1	9.5	13.8	100.0	3,401
65+	39,249	80.3	61.3	27.0	4.4	0.7	6.6	100.0	2,400

Education									
0–7	11,976	81.4	61.8	27.8	3.0	3.3	4.1	100.0	2,300
8	12,753	81.5	62.5	26.1	4.1	1.2	6.1	100.0	2,399
9–11	12,010	75.5	44.7	19.2	15.2	6.0	14.9	100.0	3,000
12	14,660	67.7	37.0	22.3	8.0	8.4	24.1	99.8	3,402
13+	6,999	64.4	24.9	22.5	16.7	6.4	29.4	99.9	5,750
Dependent children									
0	48,830	71.7	58.2	25.2	5.4	2.4	8.8	100.0	2,400
1	5,094	81.8	10.7	20.8	12.3	13.9	42.4	100.1	8,440
2	3,367	93.6	6.1	17.8	25.2	19.1	31.8	100.0	7,601
3	1,831	88.6	0.0	22.3	27.5	18.9	31.3	100.0	8,099
4+	1,846	86.2	14.2	16.2	27.3	5.1	37.2	100.0	6,549
Beneficiary status									
Widowed mother	13,272	83.8	11.1	20.7	19.6	15.7	32.9	100.0	5,838
Aged widow	43,263	80.0	62.2	26.2	4.3	1.2	6.1	100.0	2,399
Lump-sum beneficiary	741	24.6	49.2	16.9	13.8	7.7	12.3	99.9	2,520
Remarried widow	1,708	68.4	12.0	9.4	11.1	7.7	59.8	100.0	12,636
Widow with adult children	1,984	29.7	24.1	13.8	19.0	8.6	34.5	100.0	6,341

Source: Chicago area widowhood study, compiled by G. Kim.

Table 4.11 Relative Share of Income of Chicago-Area Widows from Earnings and Social Insurance among Social Insurance Beneficiaries

Variable	Base		Relative Share						Mean	Median
	n	%	1-20	20-40	40-60	60-80	80-100	Total		
Total	60,967	74.3	1.4	10.1	5.8	21.0	61.7	100.0	80.5	91.7
Race										
White	51,815	73.8	1.3	11.1	4.3	21.3	62.0	100.0	80.4	91.2
Non-white	9,152	76.8	1.9	4.6	14.3	19.5	59.5	100.0	81.1	99.9
Age (1973)										
30 and under	905	85.0	0.0	0.0	5.2	15.7	79.0	99.9	91.1	99.8
31-40	2,917	88.6	3.2	3.7	5.4	15.6	72.0	99.9	84.2	96.4
41-50	6,355	70.9	1.5	4.9	7.3	12.4	73.9	100.0	84.6	93.3
51-60	6,471	49.8	1.2	2.0	7.8	24.1	64.8	99.9	83.8	90.4
61-70	17,620	75.5	0.0	15.3	7.5	18.5	58.7	100.0	78.4	91.8
71+	26,172	82.0	2.2	10.1	4.0	25.2	58.4	99.9	79.6	91.1
Age (1974)										
Less than 45	5,333	85.4	1.8	6.8	4.7	14.2	72.6	100.1	84.7	96.9
45-54	7,367	66.7	1.3	1.0	7.4	16.6	73.7	100.0	85.9	93.6
55-64	8,491	55.3	0.9	14.5	6.4	23.3	54.9	100.0	76.9	83.4
65+	39,249	80.3	1.5	10.8	5.7	22.6	59.6	100.2	79.9	91.5

Education									
0–7	11,976	81.4	2.6	9.5	7.7	26.3	53.9	100.0	77.5	83.5
8	12,753	81.5	0.0	8.7	4.1	23.6	63.6	100.0	82.7	92.3
9–11	12,010	75.5	0.4	11.3	4.7	20.5	63.1	100.0	81.7	96.4
12	14,659	67.7	2.9	7.5	6.8	18.5	64.3	100.0	81.5	93.2
13+	6,999	64.4	0.9	16.8	7.8	12.8	61.7	100.0	77.0	89.5
Dependent children									
0	48,830	71.7	1.4	11.7	5.3	22.6	59.0	100.0	79.4	91.5
1	5,094	81.8	0.9	3.7	5.6	13.0	76.8	100.0	87.3	97.4
2	3,367	93.6	0.0	1.8	11.3	17.2	69.6	99.9	84.6	90.1
3	1,831	88.6	0.8	0.0	8.6	10.4	80.3	100.1	87.9	94.9
4+	1,846	86.2	5.1	11.1	9.1	17.8	56.9	100.0	75.1	87.6
Beneficiary status									
Widowed mother	13,272	83.8	1.4	3.6	7.9	16.1	71.1	100.0	84.6	93.3
Aged widow	43,263	80.0	1.2	12.8	4.9	23.2	57.9	100.0	78.9	90.7
Lump-sum beneficiary	741	24.6	1.5	9.2	12.3	13.8	63.1	99.9	80.1	93.3
Remarried widow	1,708	68.4	0.9	1.7	4.3	8.5	84.6	100.0	90.1	99.3
Widow with adult children	1,984	29.7	5.2	1.7	12.1	20.7	60.3	100.0	79.7	91.0

Source: Chicago area widowhood study, compiled by G. Kim.

Table 4.12 Income Comparison between the
Total U.S. Population and Chicago-Area Widows

Amount (dollars)	Current Population Report[a]		Widowhood Study[b]	
	U.S.	Metropolitan areas[d]	Widows reporting an income	
n[c]	5,440	2,646	71,549	82,078
Percentage	100.0	100.0	87.2	100.0
Under 1,000	1.1	0.9	3.3	16.1
1,000–1,499	0.7	0.4	2.7	2.7
1,500–1,999	1.1	0.7	5.1	5.1
2,000–2,499	1.4	1.2	9.6	9.6
2,500–2,999	1.7	1.3	12.8	12.8
3,000–3,499	2.0	1.8	4.7	4.7
3,500–3,999	2.1	1.8	3.9	3.9
4,000–4,999	4.5	4.2	6.8	6.8
5,000–5,999	4.6	3.9	5.2	5.2
6,000–6,999	4.8	3.9	6.3	6.3
7,000–7,999	4.9	4.3	2.5	2.5
8,000–8,999	5.1	4.3	3.5	3.5
9,000–9,999	4.9	4.0	2.4	2.4
10,000–11,999	10.7	9.5	4.0	4.0
12,000–14,999	14.8	14.5	4.7	4.7
15,000–24,999	26.2	30.5	8.0	8.0
25,000–49,999	8.3	11.4	1.5	1.5
50,000 and over	1.0	1.4	0.1	0.1
Median income (dollars)	12,051	13,626	4,100	3,436
Mean income (dollars)	13,622	15,236	6,714	5,853

[a]*Source:* Bureau of the Census, Current Population Report, P-60, no. 97, "Money income in 1973 of families and persons in the United States." January 1975, Table 24.

[b]Chicago area widowhood study, compiled by G. Kim.

[c]All CPR n in thousands.

[d]Metropolitan areas with 1,000,000 or more population.

head, also reflecting in part the effect of age. The difference is greater among male-headed than among female-headed households. When comparisons are made after controlling for age of the family head, the Chicago-area widows (male- and female-headed households) have more family income than female-headed households in the total U.S. population only if they are under 55 years of age. If they are over 55, as are more than 75 percent of these widows, their income is less than that of female-headed households in the population (Table 4.15). The more positive relative income situation for younger widows diminishes with age,

Table 4.13 Income Comparisons between the Total U.S. Female-Headed Household Population and Chicago-Area Widows, by Race

Amount (dollars)	White		Non-white[d]	
	CPR[a]	Widows[b]	CPR	Widows
n[c]	4,835	70,164	1,849	11,922
Percentage	100.0	—	100.0	—
Under 1,000	4.1	15.8	4.8	18.1
1,000–1,499	2.2	3.0	4.6	1.2
1,500–1,999	3.4	4.3	6.5	9.9
2,000–2,499	4.4	10.3	8.0	5.6
2,500–2,999	4.8	12.0	7.4	17.4
3,000–3,499	5.2	4.8	8.0	4.0
3,500–3,999	4.5	4.0	8.1	3.1
4,000–4,999	8.9	6.6	11.7	8.0
5,000–5,999	8.2	4.7	9.2	8.2
6,000–6,999	8.1	6.2	7.6	7.1
7,000–7,999	7.0	2.5	7.0	2.0
8,000–8,999	5.8	3.4	4.0	4.3
9,000–9,999	5.8	2.6	3.2	1.4
10,000–11,999	8.4	4.1	3.7	4.0
12,000–14,999	8.4	5.2	3.2	1.7
15,000–24,999	9.3	8.7	2.9	3.6
25,000–49,999	1.6	1.7	0.2	0.4
50,000 and over	0.2	0.1	—	—
Median income (dollars)	6,560	3,480	4,226	2,820
Mean income (dollars)	8,003	6,091	5,236	4,453

[a]*Source:* Bureau of the Census, Current Population Report, P-60, no. 97, "Money income in 1973 of families and persons in the United States." January, 1975, Table 25.

[b]Chicago area widowhood study, compiled by G. Kim.

[c]All CPR n in thousands.

[d]"Negro" for CPR and "non-white" for widowhood study.

and probably reflects the effect of male household head earnings and widows' benefits.

In summary, widows in this study have less income than the general U.S. population and less than both male- and female-headed households in the United States, unless certain unusual circumstances are present (e.g., households of widows under age 55 have more income than households headed by a woman under age 55, because there is more likely to be a male earner in the widow's household). However, conditions of this type are not frequent. The widows in the Chicago area who fall into our sample are in an income-disadvantaged situation compared to the U.S.

Table 4.14 Income Comparison between the Total U.S. Population and Chicago-Area Widows, by Sex of Head of Household

Amount	Male head		Female head	
	CPR[a]	Widows[b]	CPR	Widows
n[c]	48,249	11,695	6,804	70,390
Percentage	100.0	100.0	100.0	100.0
Under 1,000	0.7	14.2	4.2	16.4
1,000–1,499	0.4	4.7	2.8	2.4
1,500–1,999	0.6	7.4	4.3	4.7
2,000–2,499	0.9	10.6	5.3	9.4
2,500–2,999	1.2	9.7	5.5	13.4
3,000–3,999	1.6	0.3	5.4	4.5
4,000–4,999	3.8	0.29	9.7	7.5
5,000–5,999	4.1	1.4	8.4	5.8
6,000–6,999	4.3	6.3	8.1	6.3
7,000–7,999	4.6	0.4	7.0	2.8
8,000–8,999	5.1	4.6	5.3	3.4
9,000–9,999	4.9	3.3	5.1	2.3
10,000–11,999	11.2	5.0	7.2	3.9
12,000–14,999	15.9	9.5	6.9	3.9
15,000–24,999	28.8	13.3	7.5	7.1
25,000–49,999	9.3	5.1	1.2	0.9
50,000 and over	1.1	0.2	0.2	0.1
Median income (dollars)	12,965	4,596	5,797	3,399
Mean income (dollars)	14,524	8,460	7,228	5,420

[a]*Source:* Bureau of the Census, Current Population Report, P-60, no. 97, "Money income in 1973 for families and persons in the United States." January 1975, Table 2.
[b]All CPR n are in thousands.
[c]Chicago area widowhood study, compiled by G. Kim.

population in general. Compared to other women, they are better off only if they are young; they are worse off if they are old. They are better off if they have income from earnings, but worse off if they do not.

Comparisons to the Past

How does the present income of widows compare to their income prior to the husband's fatal illness or accident? Table 4.16 shows clearly that the widows are worse off compared to their past. On the average, they are living on about half the income they had in the past.

Table 4.17 shows the percentage gaining and losing income after

Table 4.15 Income Comparison of the Total U.S. Population of Female-Headed Households and Chicago-Area Widows (female- and male-headed households), by Age

Amount (dollars)	Age 18–24 CPR[a]	Widows[b]	25–34 CPR	Widows	35–44 CPR	Widows	45–54 CPR	Widows	55–64 CPR	Widows	65+ CPR	Widows
n[c]	606	385	1,485	1,613	1,419	5,089	1,256	11,779	902	16,501	1,136	46,134
Percentage	100.0	100.0	100.0	100.0	100.0	100.0	100.0	100.0	100.0	100.0	100.0	100.0
Under 1,000	12.9	3.8	6.4	—	3.4	11.6	2.8	7.6	2.2	11.9	0.8	21.0
1,000–1,499	6.7	—	3.8	0.9	2.4	—	1.0	1.6	2.1	2.6	2.6	3.4
1,500–1,999	11.1	3.0	4.4	0.9	4.1	1.5	3.1	1.8	2.7	7.1	3.6	5.8
2,000–2,499	9.9	12.3	8.0	3.8	4.5	1.9	3.8	3.6	2.7	7.1	4.3	12.6
2,500–2,999	11.0	—	6.2	—	4.5	2.1	4.4	2.1	4.0	8.2	5.5	19.1
3,000–3,499	11.1	12.3	6.5	2.9	6.0	1.9	3.9	2.7	3.3	2.3	6.6	6.4
3,500–3,999	7.6	—	7.9	—	4.7	0.9	2.9	1.5	3.6	3.0	6.2	5.3
4,000–4,999	8.5	3.0	11.9	2.9	9.5	7.0	9.4	7.6	6.5	6.6	10.7	7.0
5,000–5,999	6.0	3.0	8.8	9.7	8.6	2.8	7.7	5.6	9.5	11.3	8.9	3.1
6,000–6,999	8.4	39.9	9.8	13.6	8.4	9.6	7.5	5.1	7.5	7.8	6.4	5.3
7,000–7,999	2.2	12.3	8.7	11.8	8.5	3.0	6.8	5.4	6.7	4.0	5.7	0.7
8,000–8,999	1.6	—	3.9	6.6	6.9	8.6	6.2	9.4	6.2	4.3	5.2	0.6
9,000–9,999	0.5	—	4.1	6.8	6.2	4.9	6.5	6.2	6.1	2.2	5.1	1.1
10,000–11,999	2.1	3.0	4.8	16.3	7.4	6.4	8.6	7.5	10.9	4.4	8.2	2.4
12,000–14,999	—	—	3.1	6.8	7.7	10.6	10.7	11.3	9.2	6.0	8.6	1.9
15,000–24,999	0.2	7.6	1.6	11.3	6.2	19.5	12.5	16.3	14.6	9.3	9.6	4.1
25,000–49,999	—	—	0.1	5.7	0.8	7.1	2.0	4.3	2.0	1.6	2.1	0.1
50,000 and over	—	—	0.1	—	0.2	0.6	0.2	0.3	0.2	0.1	0.1	—
Median income	2,927	6,032	4,570	8,501	6,276	8,900	7,515	8,440	7,870	5,063	6,149	2,640
Mean income	3,349	5,965	5,295	10,611	7,286	11,393	9,030	9,943	9,264	6,505	8,142	3,806

Source: [a]Bureau of the Census, Current Population Report, P-60, no. 97, "Money income in 1973 of families and persons in the United States," January 1975, from "female head" columns of Table 35.
[b]Chicago area widowhood study, compiled by G. Kim.
[c]All CPR n are in thousands

123

Table 4.16 Income of Chicago-Area Widows Prior to the
Husband's Fatal Illness or Accident and in 1973

	Time (1973 constant dollar value)			
	Before widowhood[a]		1973	
Amount	Precode[b]	Precode	I>0[c]	Total
Base n (%)	60,345 (73.5)	60,407 (86.3)	71,589	820,178 (100)
Missing (%)	21,733 (26.5)	21,671 (13.7)	87.2	0 (0)
Under 1,000	2.5	1.4	3.7	16.0
1,000–1,999	1.0	9.5	9.0	7.8
2,000–2,999	3.5	22.1	25.7	22.4
3,000–3,999	7.0	13.1	9.8	8.6
4,000–4,999	3.5	7.1	7.8	6.8
5,000–5,999	7.1	9.6	6.0	5.2
6,000–6,999	6.3	4.8	7.2	6.3
7,000–7,999	7.3	4.8	2.8	2.5
8,000–8,999	7.6	5.7	4.1	3.5
9,000–9,999	7.3	3.4	2.8	2.4
10,000–14,999	18.3	9.2	10.0	8.7
15,000–19,999	14.3	5.1	5.7	4.9
20,000 and over	14.4	4.2	5.4	4.7
Total	100.0	100.0	100.0	100.0
Mean income	11,862	6,371[d]	4,100	3,436
Median income	9,580	4,553	6,714	5,853

[a]The year before the husband's fatal illness or accident that led to his death.

[b]Amount of income before widowhood was precoded into the amount categories used herein. Transformation to the constant dollar value (1973) is made by taking the middle value of each range.

[c]Amounts of those whose income is greater than zero.

[d]Mean and median are obtained by taking the mid-value of each range.

Source: Chicago area widowhood study, compiled by G. Kim.

widowhood and the median figures involved, listed by characteristics of the widow. Beneficiary status made a difference. More than half of the remarried widows had more income in 1973 than prior to the husband's illness or accident. This was the only category to show a higher percentage gaining than losing. Only 16 percent of the aged widows had some gain in income from the period before widowhood; lump-sum beneficiaries were the least likely to gain (13 percent), and gained the least on average when they did gain. Widowed mothers and widows with adult children showed less than one-third gaining in income after widowhood. The range of loss was relatively narrow, between $5,500 and $7,400.

In terms of the general characteristics of the widows, whites more

Table 4.17 Percentage of Women Experiencing a Gain or Loss of Income from Pre- to Post-Widowhood and the Median Gain or Loss, by Race, Age, Education, Number of Dependent Children, and Beneficiary Status

	Base	Gain		Loss	
Amount	n	%	Median	%	Median
Total	60,344	22.3	2,267	77.7	5,675
Race					
White	49,868	21.4	2,711	78.6	6,000
Non-white	10,477	26.9	1,870	73.1	3,747
Age					
30 and under	922	30.6	3,457	69.4	3,677
31–40	2,917	49.9	4,969	50.1	6,012
41–50	8,043	38.1	4,442	61.9	6,515
51–60	10,614	23.2	3,184	76.8	6,501
61–70	18,585	15.9	4,071	84.1	5,962
71+	18,976	15.9	753	84.1	5,164
Age					
44 and under	5,516	43.1	4,969	56.9	5,863
45–54	9,754	33.8	4,227	66.2	6,516
55–64	12,535	16.2	3,775	83.8	7,478
65+	32,253	17.1	1,175	82.9	5,310
Dependent children					
0	47,770	18.6	1,588	81.4	5,675
1	5,553	32.6	4,341	67.4	6,513
2	3,234	28.5	5,510	71.5	5,619
3	1,879	43.2	6,089	56.8	5,982
4+	1,908	55.8	4,442	44.2	8,881
Beneficiary status					
Widowed mother	13,793	31.6	3,701	68.4	5,838
Aged Widow	36,404	15.9	1,180	84.1	5,543
Lump-sum beneficiary	2,588	12.8	996	87.2	7,240
Remarried widow	2,088	58.0	7,320	42.0	7,411
Widow with adult children	5,472	32.5	3,936	67.5	6,493

Figures in 1973 constant dollars.

Source: Chicago area widowhead study, compiled by G. Kim.

often lost income and lost more than non-whites because they had higher income to begin with. The widows aged 55–64 were the hardest hit financially; they were least likely to gain, most likely to lose, and gained the least and lost the most on the average when these events occurred. The oldest widows infrequently gained income, and when they did it was in relatively small amounts. These widows lost income as frequently as those aged 55–64, but in lower amounts. They had less income to start with. Income gain, in percentage gained and amount, basically decreased with age; for income loss, the reverse was true.

The number of dependent children makes some difference in the income mobility of widows, probably because of its relationship to age, work status, beneficiary status, and family maximum benefit. Those with no dependent children, primarily the aged widows, tended to have a higher probability of loss. The relatively few women with larger numbers of dependent children fared best in terms of percentage showing a gain. However, as other data indicate, they were still more likely to be poor because of the size of the household supported.

In sum, about three-fourths of the Chicago-area widows studied had less income in 1973. Furthermore, those widows who lost income after widowhood experienced losses that were much greater than the amount gained by those women who gained. Most women were worse off financially at the time of the survey than they were when the husband was alive and well. Their situation is worst if they are older, without dependent children, and not remarried. These characteristics undoubtedly are clustered.

Comparisons to a Poverty or "Survival" Standard

Our analysis compared the income of widows to an accepted measure of relative "poverty" income created by the Social Security Administration for the total population. The measure is comprehensive in the sense that it takes into account the multiple factors affecting income needs. It has been used on many studies conducted and/or sponsored by the Social Security Administration and other agencies. The low-income index is used as the measure of relative amounts of income in this analysis.

On the whole, more than two-fifths (43 percent) of the Chicago-area widows were poor, as measured by the SSA low-income index (Table 4.18). Among widows who live alone, 41 percent were poor, and this figure covers half of the total number of widows represented by our sample. The percentage living below the poverty line increases to half for widows living in two-person households but then drops considerably for three-and four-person households. Beyond that size, the percentage continues to increase dramatically. Fortunately, there were few widows in such large households in the study.

Table 4.19 shows the pattern of percentage in poverty by category of widow. Half of the aged widow beneficiaries were poor, a larger share in poverty than among any of the other beneficiary groups. Those with many dependent children, whose incomes had to support more family members, and those with no dependent children, who are primarily older widows, had the highest percentages in poverty. Non-white widows were more likely to be poor than white widows; and, the less-educated were more often poor than the better-educated.

Table 4.18 Mean Amount of Income Needed for SSA Low-Income Index
and Percentage of Chicago-Area Widows Living below the Low-Income Level

Aggregate size of household	Base (widows in study)		Living in poverty	
	n	%	%	Mean
1	40,555	49.4	41.2	2,501
2	22,479	27.4	50.2	3,602
3	9,369	11.4	37.3	4,438
4	4,268	5.2	27.2	5,805
5	2,628	3.2	43.1	6,729
6	1,500	1.8	48.4	7,779
7	509	0.6	58.4	8,853
8	277	0.3	56.6	10,467
9	408	0.5	96.4	11,613
10	77	0.1	80.9	12,813
11	15	—	0.0	15,200
Total	82,085	99.9	43.2	3,551

Source: Chicago area widowhood study, compiled by G. Kim.

There is, of course, a direct relationship between the income category of the widow and poverty status. We showed earlier that a large proportion of widows had less income in 1973 than before they became widows. However, what was their poverty status in 1973 relative to what it was before they became widows? The income of widows in comparison to the SSA low-income index was greater prior to widowhood than at the time of the survey. It went from a mean of 2.38 times the low-income index to a mean of 1.11 times the index. Becoming widowed resulted in the reduction of both the absolute amount of income and the relative value of this income compared to the poverty measure (Table 4.20).

When the income situation of widows is compared to the general U.S. population in terms of relative poverty status rather than absolute amount of income,* widows in this study were in about the same circumstances as female-headed, non-farm families (Table 4.21). However, as expected, Chicago-area widows were definitely worse off than per-

---

*The poverty status of Chicago-area women prior to widowhood was compared relative to the situation in 1973 by using the ratio of income to the SSA low-income index. However, the 1970 census poverty cut-offs were used for this comparison because the 1970 census and Current Population Survey used this measure as a basis for assessing poverty. For these purposes the ratio of income for the 1970 census poverty cut-offs was divided into "poor" (0 through 0.99) and "not poor" (1.00 +).

Table 4.19 Income Deficit for SSA Low-Income Index: Total Income

Variable	Base					Amount				
	n	%	1000	1000–2000	2000–3000	3000+	Total	Mean	Median
Total	35,426	43.2	36.7	18.7	28.0	16.6	100.0	1,858	1,572
Race									
White	28,709	40.9	36.0	20.1	28.2	15.7	100.0	1,806	1,461
Non-white	6,717	56.3	39.7	12.7	27.1	20.4	99.9	2,082	1,955
Age									
19-30	292	27.5	21.2	20.1	21.2	37.4	99.9	2,185	2,152
31-40	1,285	39.0	22.1	14.8	17.0	46.1	100.0	3,346	2,929
41-50	2,393	26.7	29.6	12.7	9.1	48.6	100.0	3,050	2,842
51-60	4,315	33.2	23.1	27.1	24.8	24.9	99.9	2,275	1,892
61-70	9,661	41.4	43.6	14.9	28.6	13.0	100.1	1,639	1,159
71+	17,170	53.9	37.7	20.2	32.4	9.6	99.9	1,616	1,409
Age									
20-44	2,079	33.3	21.2	14.2	16.3	48.2	99.9	3,366	2,934
45-54	3,093	28.0	23.3	24.8	10.1	41.8	100.0	2,798	2,412
55-64	5,159	33.6	25.8	30.4	29.3	14.5	100.0	1,908	1,884
65+	24,785	50.7	41.4	16.2	31.2	11.3	100.1	1,620	1,334
Education									
0-7	7,011	47.6	33.3	19.1	24.0	23.7	100.1	1,966	1,954
8	7,842	50.1	42.9	32.1	15.7	9.3	100.0	1,427	1,191

9–11	6,916	43.5	41.0	15.7	32.1	11.1	99.9	1,709	1,279
12	8,766	40.5	38.3	14.9	31.8	15.1	100.1	1,870	1,572
12+	3,779	34.8	12.3	9.7	42.4	35.6	100.0	2,914	2,492
Dependent children									
0	30,910	45.4	38.8	19.2	29.8	12.3	100.1	1,663	1,409
1	1,790	28.7	22.0	10.6	24.5	42.9	100.0	2,849	2,732
2	813	22.6	23.3	19.3	21.1	36.3	100.0	2,945	2,605
3	723	35.0	8.6	36.8	6.6	48.1	100.1	3,415	2,044
4+	1,189	55.5	31.9	8.0	4.0	56.2	100.1	3,745	3,494
Income (dollars)									
Less than 1,000	13,221	100.0	—	4.8	59.7	35.5	100.0	3,056	2,492
1,000–2,499	14,236	99.7	55.3	33.9	8.5	2.3	100.0	1,004	823
2,500–3,999	5,599	31.9	72.8	11.9	8.6	6.8	100.0	1,220	839
4,000–6,999	1,990	13.2	43.2	21.3	13.3	22.2	100.0	1,831	1,211
7,000–9,999	284	4.1	33.3	33.3	16.7	16.7	100.0	2,025	1,755
10,000+	95	0.6	100.0	—	—	—	100.0	647	647
Beneficiary status									
Widowed mother	5,072	32.0	26.2	22.4	13.1	38.3	100.0	2,749	2,070
Aged Widow	27,171	50.2	40.8	18.4	31.1	9.7	100.0	1,580	1,328
Lump-sum beneficiary	992	33.0	21.8	23.0	33.3	21.8	99.9	2,197	2,159
Remarried widow	686	27.5	10.6	12.8	23.4	53.2	100.0	3,602	3,055
Mother with adult children	1,505	22.6	20.5	11.4	20.5	47.7	100.1	2,865	2,713

Source: Chicago area widowhood study, compiled by G. Kim.

Table 4.20 Relative Amount of Income of Chicago-Area Widows
before Widowhood and in 1973

		1973	
Relative amount	Before*	Total	Income greater than zero
Base n	60,054	82,078	71,545
%	73.2	100	87.2
Less than 0.25	2.2	15.3	21.7
0.25–0.49	3.4	5.1	5.8
0.50–0.74	6.6	9.5	10.6
0.75–0.99	6.6	13.3	15.7
1.00–1.49	16.6	20.6	23.5
1.50–1.99	14.2	8.7	10.1
2.00–2.99	33.1	13.0	14.8
3.00+	27.2	14.6	16.8
Mean	2.38	1.11	1.27
Median	2.02	1.27	1.86

*Relative amount of income prior to widowhood is computed on the basis of household income and mean amount of SSA low-income index for 1973. Income prior to widowhood has been standardized (1973 value).

Source: Chicago area widowhood study, compiled by G. Kim.

sons in male-headed families in the non-farm population, regardless of household size. Since there was a three-year time lag between the 1970 census and this study, and since there was a consistent decrease in the incidence of poverty in the nation in that period, the comparisons between the U.S. non-farm population and the widows of this study were reexamined in an effort to avoid the effects of this time lag. Table 4.22 shows data on the percentage below the 1970 census poverty cut-offs for the U.S. population in 1970 and in 1973 as well as for the widows of this study in 1973, by race and number of dependent children. The same basic findings of relative poverty compared to female-headed families and all families can be seen. When compared to the female-headed families in the U.S. population, the Chicago-area widows are very much disadvantaged if they have no dependent child living with them. While only 9 percent of the female-headed families in the United States without any dependent children were poor, one-third of the study widows with no dependent child were poor. On the other hand, study widows were better off than female-headed families if they had dependent children.

An interesting effect of race can be seen in this table. When compared to female-headed families, white widows were not significantly different from white, female-headed families in the total population. For

Table 4.21 Percentage of Male- and Female-Headed Households in the U.S. and the Households of Chicago-Area Widows with Incomes below the Poverty Measure, Using 1970 Census Cut-Off by Size of Household

	Percentage below measure		
	1970 census[a]		1973[b]
Size of household	Male head	Female head	Widows study
Total	—	32.5	30.7
1*	29.3	41.7	31.8
2	9.5	23.0	31.6
3	5.0	28.0	27.0
4	4.6	40.5	21.3
5	6.0	49.1	23.6
6	8.4	54.1	35.8
7	17.1	66.5	58.4
8	19.3	67.3	22.4
9	21.7	67.2	38.4
10	24.9	62.9	80.9
11	27.2	62.5	0.0

Source: [a] Census of Population Subject report: Low Income Population, Table 1, p. 88, PC(2)-9A; Table 11: "Families by size, number of related children under 18 years old, poverty status in 1969 and sex and race of head and unrelated individuals by poverty status in 1969, sex, and age in 1970 (non-farm residents).

[b] Chicago area widowhood study, compiled by G. Kim.

* Unrelated individuals

the non-white group, widows in the Chicago area were significantly less likely to be poor than female-headed families in the U.S. population. Non-whites covered by social insurance, and many of the non-white widows in this study, were receiving benefits, and are probably better off financially and occupationally than non-covered non-whites. The white widows in the study may better typify the case for white women in female-headed families in the general population than that for non-white widows. Non-white study widows were worse off than both white study widows and white female-headed families in the U.S. population, but were better off than non-white, female-headed families in the total population.

Overall, the comparison of income to the poverty level for Chicago-area widows and the U.S. population results in the following observations: study widows were worse off than the U.S. population on the whole, but not worse off than female-headed families; non-white study widows were better off than non-white, female-headed families in the general population; and white study widows were better off than white, female-headed families in the general population if they were working

Table 4.22 Percentage with Incomes below the Poverty Cut-Offs for U.S. Population in 1970 and 1973 and for Chicago-Area Widows, by Race and Number of Dependent Children

	1970 census[a]		1973 CPR[b]		1973 widows study[d]	
	Total	Female head	Total	Female head	Total	Female head
Families	11.6	38.3	8.8	32.2	30.7	29.9
Persons	13.6	39.5	11.1	34.9	30.2	26.8
Race						
White	—	—	6.6	24.5	29.3	28.3
Non-white	—	—	28.1	52.7	38.7	39.1
Number of dependent children						
0	9.2	14.4		9.3	32.5	31.6
1	8.6	29.6		31.3	20.9	20.1
2	8.8	38.9		37.5	16.9	15.7
3	11.8	51.7		54.7	23.7	22.3
4	16.8	62.8		65.8	23.3	24.5
5	26.0	70.5		76.4[c]	32.0	32.2
6	33.5	80.0			27.0	34.9
7	34.6	80.1			100.0	100.0
8	38.2	77.8			0	0
9 +	39.8	74.7			—	—

[a]*Source:* 1970 Census of Population, subject report: Low-income population, Table 11, p. 89, ''Type of residence of persons by poverty status in 1969, family status and sex, race, and Spanish origin of head: 1970.''

[b]*Source:* 1973 CPR, Table 1: ''Persons below the low-income level by family status and sex and race of head: 1959 to 1973.'' Table D: ''Percent of families below the low-income level in 1973 by number of related children under 18 years and sex and race of head.''

[c]5 and more.

[d]Chicago area widowhood study compiled by G. Kim.

for wages or salaries or on public assistance, but not if they were receiving Social Security (Table 4.23).

SOCIAL INSURANCE FOR WIDOWS

As previously observed, three-fourths of the households of Chicago-area widows studied received an income from social insurance benefits in 1973; 57 percent of the widows received these benefits themselves (Table 4.24). Widowed mothers received more benefits than others because they had dependent children. Aged widows had a much lower median benefit; they had no dependent children. The number of dependent chil-

Table 4.23 Percentage of U.S. Population and Chicago-Area Widows with Incomes below the 1970 Census Poverty Cut-Offs by Sources of Income, Sex, and Race of Family Head

	Percentage below poverty cut-offs					
	CPR[a]			1973 widows study[b]		
Source of Income	Total	White	Negro	Total	White	Non-white
All families	8.8	6.6	28.1	30.7	29.3	38.7
Wages or salaries	5.6	4.0	20.0	3.7	3.3	6.7
Social security	10.4	8.2	29.6	20.6	19.0	29.2
Public assistance	51.5	45.0	62.6	25.3	11.7	32.6
Families with female head	32.2	24.5	52.7	29.9	28.3	39.1
Wages or salaries	21.5	16.0	38.0	3.9	3.3	7.2
Social security	16.8	11.7	38.2	19.1	17.3	28.2
Public assistance	64.4	58.6	70.9	26.3	11.7	33.9

Source: [a]CPR: "Characteristics of the low-income population: 1973," Table 42: "Type of income in 1973: number and mean income of families and unrelated individuals by low-income status in 1973 and sex and race of family head."
[b]Chicago area widowhood study, compiled by G. Kim.

133

Table 4.24 Income of Chicago-Area Widows from Social Insurance by Race, Age, Education, Dependent Children, Wages, Income, and Beneficiary Status

Variable	Base n	Base %	144–500	504–983	1000–1500	1512–1992	2000–2500	2511–3000	3010–3500	3510–4500	4536–10310	Total	Median
Total	60,957	74.3	3.1	4.1	9.2	17.0	33.7	14.0	4.0	4.2	10.8	100.1	2,292
Race													
White	51,815	73.8	3.1	2.5	9.1	15.0	38.2	14.1	4.4	3.1	10.4	99.9	2,314
Non-white	9,152	76.8	3.6	5.5	11.0	26.6	15.0	15.0	1.7	10.6	13.0	100.0	2,159
Age (1973)													
30 and under	905	85.0	1.3	0.0	5.2	0.0	22.6	12.1	5.2	3.2	50.4	100.0	4,710
31–40	2,917	88.6	1.6	2.1	1.5	7.4	16.6	5.4	5.3	15.5	44.6	100.0	4,191
41–50	6,355	70.9	1.1	2.5	9.8	11.4	13.6	5.9	3.2	16.0	36.5	100.0	3,756
51–60	6,471	49.8	3.4	2.0	6.2	31.8	22.4	7.3	2.1	8.7	16.2	100.1	2,167
61–70	17,620	75.5	4.6	2.0	9.3	19.9	43.2	9.6	4.9	3.0	5.7	100.2	2,196
71+	26,172	82.2	3.0	4.2	11.3	14.2	39.4	20.8	4.0	0.0	3.0	99.9	2,399
Age (1974)													
Less than 45	5,333	85.4	1.3	1.2	4.9	5.4	16.8	7.0	5.8	11.1	46.5	100.0	4,319
45–54	7,367	66.7	2.4	2.8	9.5	18.0	13.3	6.2	1.9	15.9	29.9	99.9	2,723
55–64	8,491	55.3	4.3	4.6	5.1	37.1	29.4	3.9	1.4	5.4	8.7	99.9	1,939
65+	39,249	80.3	3.4	2.9	11.0	13.9	42.2	18.0	4.8	0.9	2.9	100.0	2,240
Education													
0–7	11,976	81.4	2.3	7.9	11.5	22.2	31.7	16.7	2.2	1.6	3.9	100.0	2,106
8	12,753	81.5	4.2	2.1	14.8	18.2	34.0	18.5	2.2	2.8	3.2	100.0	2,279
9–11	12,010	75.5	2.9	0.6	7.9	16.7	35.9	6.7	7.9	6.0	15.4	100.0	2,399

12	14,660	67.7	2.9	3.1	7.3	13.2	38.2	10.5	3.1	4.8	16.9	100.0	2,399
13+	6,999	64.4	4.6	0.9	5.6	9.5	30.4	18.3	3.4	8.7	18.7	100.1	2,500
Dependent children													
0	48,830	71.7	3.7	3.3	10.3	18.7	39.4	15.8	4.0	1.4	3.3	99.9	2,231
1	5,094	81.8	1.9	0.9	5.8	13.5	28.3	9.9	3.7	17.3	18.9	100.1	2,300
2	3,367	93.6	0.0	0.0	5.6	4.5	8.9	4.7	5.1	18.0	53.3	100.1	4,579
3	1,831	88.6	0.0	2.6	3.4	7.6	4.2	0.0	2.6	11.2	60.5	100.1	1,530
4+	1,846	86.2	2.6	4.1	5.8	5.9	5.9	6.7	5.7	11.7	51.6	100.0	6,801
SW													
none	42,869	77.3	2.7	3.0	9.8	17.5	34.7	17.9	4.0	2.1	0.3	100.0	2,299
less than 2500	4,123	82.2	1.1	2.3	12.4	4.5	40.3	4.0	0.0	10.7	24.7	100.0	2,375
2500+	13,971	64.6	5.3	3.1	7.1	18.3	33.2	4.7	5.4	8.8	14.2	100.1	2,291
Income													
less than 1000	1,642	12.4	65.0	32.1	2.9	0.0	0.0	0.0	0.0	0.0	0.0	100.0	214
1,000–2,499	13,538	94.8	0.4	0.4	22.7	28.2	48.3	0.0	0.0	0.0	0.0	100.0	1,955
2,500–3,999	16,775	95.5	0.0	2.2	4.2	14.7	40.2	33.7	3.5	1.5	0.0	100.0	2,400
4,000–6,999	12,456	82.7	2.3	3.5	7.5	13.6	27.0	11.0	9.0	7.8	18.2	100.0	2,400
7,000–9,999	47,620	68.8	2.0	1.0	4.9	21.1	28.7	7.8	1.0	6.3	27.2	100.0	2,400
10,000+	11,795	78.4	3.8	3.0	6.1	10.5	26.8	9.5	6.0	8.8	25.5	100.0	2,500
Beneficiary status													
Widowed mother	13,272	83.8	1.4	2.1	5.4	11.4	18.6	7.5	3.2	14.6	35.7	99.9	3,510
Aged widow	43,263	80.0	3.7	3.0	10.4	17.7	40.9	16.5	4.3	0.6	3.0	100.1	3,232
Lump-sum beneficiary	741	24.6	12.3	6.2	13.8	20.0	27.7	13.8	1.5	0.0	4.6	99.9	1,834
Remarried widow	1,708	68.4	0.9	2.6	7.7	17.1	17.1	6.8	6.0	17.0	23.9	100.0	2,809
Widow with adult children	1,984	29.7	3.4	3.2	13.8	31.0	27.6	8.6	3.4	3.2	3.4	99.8	1,942

Source: Chicago area widowhood study, compiled by G. Kim.

135

dren was positively related to the amount of benefits received. Younger widows received higher median benefit amounts than older widows because they had more dependent children. However, there was a drop in median benefit for those with four or more dependent children, reflecting the combined effect of the maximum family benefit (1.5 to 1.85 times the PIA) and the effect of larger numbers of children on the ability of the widow to be in the paid labor force.

As was discussed earlier, the family maximum limit provides no additional benefits for more than two to three children, depending on the PIA and whether the widow is working. Additionally, it may be recalled that widows with one or two dependent children work for earnings more often than widows with more children. The combination of these factors affects the differences in the median amount of benefits received by widows with different numbers of dependent children. Race made little difference in the percentage who were beneficiaries or in the median amount of benefits.

The most frequently received type of social insurance in the study of widows' households was survivors' insurance under social security. However as Table 4.25 shows, the proportion of widows receiving old-age benefits increased with age. Because of the effect of age, both education and the number of dependent children also show relationships to the receipt of old-age benefits. A small percentage of the widows' households also received disability benefits and/or Supplemental Security Income (SSI). In total, only about 2 percent of the widows themselves received benefits of more than one type, and this was most often SSI in combination with a Social Security benefit. There was little receipt of multiple benefits within their households in general.

INCOME ADEQUACY AND SOCIAL CHARACTERISTICS

Having reviewed the income of Chicago-area widows, in terms of amount, sources, and adequacy, we can now look at a few background and life situation characteristics of these widows that are associated with the relative amount of income they had at the time of the study. The ratio to poverty level based on the SSA low-income index is used as the measure of income comfort. Widows whose incomes were above the poverty level we are calling ''comfortable,'' although this was clearly only true relative to poorer widows for most of the study population. Those whose incomes were below the poverty level we are calling ''poor.''

Table 4.26 summarizes the characteristics of the different types of widows who reported having income organized by ratio to the poverty level (poor or comfortable). Remarried widows, although few in number, were more apt to be comfortable than those who were still living

Table 4.25 Utilization of Social Insurance by Chicago-Area Widows by Race, Age, Education, Dependent Children, and Beneficiary Status

	SI Benefits*					
	Total					Suppl.
Characteristics of widows	%	Median	Old age	Disability	Survivor	income
Total	74.3	2292	16.7	3.3	54.1	5.6
Race						
White	73.8	2314	17.8	3.1	53.8	4.5
Non-white	76.8	2159	10.7	4.6	55.7	11.9
Age (1973)						
19–30	85.0	4710	0.0	0.0	80.6	4.5
31–40	88.6	4101	0.0	0.0	77.6	19.6
41–50	49.8	2147	2.2	8.6	37.4	6.5
51–60	75.5	2184	17.8	3.2	55.0	6.1
61–70	82.2	2399	27.8	2.5	54.2	1.8
Age (1974)						
20–44	85.4	4319	0.8	0.0	78.1	13.4
45–54	66.7	2723	2.3	4.4	57.4	9.4
55–64	55.3	1939	5.4	7.3	46.2	3.4
65 +	80.3	2280	25.2	2.4	53.4	3.9
Education						
0–7	81.4	2104	26.4	4.6	49.9	6.6
8	81.5	2279	18.0	0.6	61.5	4.6
9–11	75.5	2399	18.1	5.1	52.8	5.8
12	67.7	2399	18.1	5.1	52.8	5.8
13 +	64.4	2500	11.2	3.1	49.9	8.3
Dependent children						
0	71.7	2231	19.9	3.8	48.8	3.8
1	81.8	2500	1.0	1.8	74.6	16.2
2	93.6	4679	0.4	1.3	88.0	8.3
3	88.6	5500	2.3	0.0	83.5	8.1
4 +	86.2	4801	2.9	0.0	77.3	22.0
Beneficiary status						
Widowed mother	83.8	3510	2.7	2.1	76.6	12.6
Aged widow	80.0	2232	23.4	3.4	54.1	3.9
Lump-sum beneficiary	24.6	1824	4.9	6.1	12.9	3.8
Remarried widow	68.4	2808	4.7	1.8	57.9	7.0
Widow with adult children	29.7	1942	5.6	5.1	16.9	2.6
Median			2,063	1,919	2,300	227

*Percentage receiving the given benefit.

Source: Chicago area widowhood study, compiled by G. King.

Table 4.26 Percentage of Chicago-Area Widows with Selected Characteristics in Relative Income Categories

Characteristic	Base[a] n	Base[a] %	Total	Percentage Poor	Percentage Comfortable
Language[b]					
English	57,517	80	100	31	69
Other	13,768	20	100	47	53
Marital status					
Remarried	4,059	6	99	15	84
Widowed	67,490	94	100	36	64
Others in the household[c]					
Yes	7,247	10	99	60	39
No	69,302	90	99	31	68
Total			71,538	24,890	46,648
n%			100	35	66

[a]Respondents who have no income are excluded.
[b]Language mentioned first as most often spoken in home during childhood.
[c]Individuals other than husband and children living with widow.
Source: Chicago area widowhood study, compiled by G. Kim.

as widows, a finding that reflects prior comments. Widows who had someone other than a husband or children living with them were more likely to be poor than those who had no others in the household. This probably reflects problems in maintaining themselves without the assistance. Widows who spoke English at home as children were more often above the poverty line than were the non–English-speaking childhood widows, suggesting those who were themselves or whose parents were foreign born had a higher probability of being poor.

Table 4.27 indicates some differences between the comfortable (above the index) and the poor (below the index) widows in their income sources. The comfortable widows were about seven times as likely to earn an income themselves as were the poor widows (40.0 to 5.9 percent), and over twice as likely to receive benefits from social security or income from interest and savings. The poor widows, on the other hand, were twice as apt to receive veterans' widow pensions and 20 times as apt to receive public assistance as were the comfortable widows.

Another consideration is whether the financial situation of the widow relates to social, emotional, and service supports flowing to her. Were poor widows more or less likely to receive such supports from others around them than were widows who were more comfortable financially? Among those widows reporting income, there is some suggestion in our interview data that the poor widows also received less in the way of so-

Table 4.27 Percentage of Widows by Income Category with Income from Various Sources and Median Income from each Source

Source	Total		Above the index		Below the index	
	Percentage with income from source	Median	Percentage with income from source	Median	Percentage with income from source	Median
SW	25.3	5,000	40.0	5,499	5.9	1,799
TW	32.5	6,999	51.9	7,363	9.1	1,729
Rent	11.7	1,018	17.7	1,020	14.0	747
IS	29.6	599	43.1	799	17.2	400
VP	9.0	684	11.5	721	27.5	501
EP	10.4	1,752	16.2	1,800	11.1	861
PI	1.8	1,897	3.2	1,897	0.8	1,800
PA	4.2	911	3.0	897	59.3	914
SI	74.3	2,292	83.2	2,400	36.4	2,040

See Table 4.3 for income source abbreviations.
Source: Chicago area widowhood study, compiled by G. Kim.

cial and emotional supports than the more financially comfortable widows. There was no difference between the two in the receipt of services, but the poor received slightly more financial aid, in terms of number of providers of such aid. However, most widows received no financial aid regardless of their circumstances. Not surprisingly, those widows who were more comfortable financially also were more apt to be giving financial help to others; these widows also were more likely than their poorer counterparts to give service supports. Being more comfortable financially is somewhat related to being richer in all types of supports from those around the widow. However, the relationships are weak individually, although they tend to point consistently to the same pattern.

The Importance of Economic Matters

How salient are financial matters for widows? Do they think first of money when asked about their lives—about matters such as: problems faced after widowhood, desired but absent help after widowhood, reasons for no longer seeing old friends, reasons for changes in organizational involvement, reasons for working, reasons for not receiving training or retraining, and any other questions for which financial matters could be a potential answer. Saliency of financial matters was defined by the number of times finances was given as an answer to such questions. We are concerned here with whether the poor widows gave financial answers more often than the others did.

Among those reporting income, the more financially comfortable widows were more apt to mention finances, but the total number of such references indicates that the widows were not very concerned with economic matters. However, the relationship is not a very strong one. The frequency of mentioning financial matters is positively related to the number of dependent children (0.248) and negatively related to the age of the widow (-0.442). There seems to be no reason to believe that poor widows were overly cognizant of their financial matters in the sense that they responded to various questions by giving a financial matter as the answer.

The Earnings Test

Under Social Security's annual earnings test, as of 1973, deductions could be made from the retirement or survivors' benefits of a person under age 72 (and from the benefits of his or her dependents) if he or she had earnings in excess of the monthly and yearly exempt amounts. Basically, this was in line with the main purpose of the social security monthly benefits, to replace some of the earnings from work lost because of the retirement or death of a worker.

The earnings test under which these deductions could be made was specified by age, employment, and amount of earnings. The test applied only to beneficiaries under age 72; only to income earned from gainful employment; and only if these earnings exceeded the yearly exempted amount, which in 1973 was $2,400. Beneficiaries with annual earnings in excess of $2,400 had their benefits reduced by one dollar for every two dollars of earnings over this exempt amount.

This $1 for $2 provision was designed as a work-incentive measure, to avoid the deterrent to work of a $1 for $1 benefit loss based on earnings. However, in order to function as a motivator to paid employment, the measure had to be known in specific detail to a beneficiary.

The study of Chicago-area widows who were current or former beneficiaries of Social Security in 1973 suggests that assumptions about such knowledge were not valid at that time and that, as a result, the earnings test could not motivate beneficiaries to seek paid employment. The interview contained a set of questions aimed at determining the knowledge base. As a general introductory question, the respondents were asked, "Do you know about the earnings test which determines how much money a social security beneficiary can earn in wages or salaries without affecting the amount he or she receives in social security benefits?" Only about two in five of the widows said "yes" to the question, although all of these women had received benefits within the last 12 years, and three-fourths were in current beneficiary households (Table 4.28).

There is some suggestion that those with the least likelihood of working or being affected by the earnings test were the least likely to know about it (i.e., aged widows, lump-sum-only beneficiaries, non-whites, those with three or more dependent children, those with less income and/or education).

In addition to knowledge as to the existence of an earnings test, beneficiaries must be aware of the conditions under which it could affect them. In order to test this knowledge the widows were asked: "What is the yearly amount a woman of your age and family situation can earn in wages or salaries without affecting the amount of her social security benefits?" The correct answer varies by whether the widow is over age 72 or not and by family composition because of the application of the family maximum benefit and the possible redistribution of benefits within the maximum to dependent children if the widow works over the earnings limit. As a result, there were two possible answers that could be correct: "No limit," and the annual earnings test amount, $2,400.

Table 4.28 Responses to Questions as to the Amount of Earnings without Reduction of Social Security Benefits among Chicago-Area Widows (in percentages)

| | Did not know about earnings test | Answers by those who claimed knowledge | | |
		Did not know amount/No answer	Wrong answer	Right answer
Total (base = 82,070)	58.3	9.4	17.5	14.8
Race				
White	56.1	9.4	18.1	16.3
Non-white	70.8	9.9	13.6	5.7
Age				
0–44	46.9	9.5	31.3	12.3
45–54	46.9	13.6	23.3	16.2
55–64	47.6	10.1	24.2	18.1
65+	65.2	8.4	12.5	13.9
Education				
0–7	77.3	4.5	10.8	7.4
8	66.9	18.3	7.3	7.5
9–11	54.3	11.6	21.5	12.6
12	52.0	9.4	20.4	18.2
13+	38.3	17.7	23.8	20.2

142

Dependent children				
0	62.2	8.8	14.8	14.2
1	32.6	11.9	30.9	24.6
2	39.4	12.1	34.0	14.5
3	51.3	10.0	25.8	12.9
4+	47.9	15.8	29.0	7.3
Beneficiary status				
Widowed mother	41.0	12.0	31.1	16.8
Aged widow	63.9	8.3	13.1	14.7
Lump-sum beneficiary	66.7	10.6	12.5	10.2
Remarried widow	50.0	16.7	22.7	10.6
Widow with adult children	52.8	9.8	22.1	15.3
Income (dollars)				
Less than 1,000	63.4	8.2	13.7	14.7
1,000–2,499	62.4	12.3	12.4	12.9
2,500–3,999	73.6	5.9	8.1	12.4
4,000–6,999	53.1	7.0	25.0	14.9
7,000–9,999	47.2	6.1	24.6	22.1
10,000 +	42.2	16.1	26.6	16.1

Source: Chicago area widowhood study, compiled by G. Kim.

Both answers were considered correct, even for categories of widows where one or the other answer was obviously the only correct one. This would tend to inflate somewhat the percentage with the right answer.

Only a small percentage of the widows knew how much they were allowed to earn without losing any benefits. Of the total only 15 percent knew either correct amount; 18 percent gave a wrong amount, and 9 percent said they did not know the amount. The rest had said earlier they did not know about the test (58 percent). Fully 85 percent of Chicago-area widows did not know the correct answer on the annual earnings test's limitations.

Were there variations in proportions of widows knowledgeable about the earnings test? Beneficiary status did not show a consistent effect. The two categories of beneficiary with the lowest percentages with correct answers, the remarrieds and the lump-sum beneficiaries, were those least affected by it. However, the other categories of widows were not much more informed. Younger widowed mothers of one or two dependent children were among those who said they knew about the test the most frequently, but they were also among those who most often gave the wrong sum. Education made the greatest difference in such knowledge. However, even for those with some college, only about one in five of the widows knew the correct answer. Data on the number of dependent children indicates that widows for whom there would be the least impact from the earnings test also had the lowest percentage with correct answers (i.e., those with three or more dependent children). Widows with one dependent child were the most knowledgeable (one in four). Overall, the level of correct knowledge was quite low, in spite of Social Security Administration publicity on the subject.

Another aspect of the earnings test is that income from sources other than employment does not affect benefits. As long as the income is from sources such as pensions, private insurance, investment, or gifts, a beneficiary may receive any amount without reducing her benefits. How many of the study widows knew that fact? When asked "What additional income, other than wages and salaries, affects the amount a beneficiary can receive from social security?" the respondent should have said "Nothing." Only about one in 14 (7 percent) of the widows knew that no unearned income affected benefits. As discussed previously almost three of five did not know about the test; almost a third said they knew about it but did not know what additional non-work income affected social security benefits. A small percentage indicated other factors affected benefits. Accurate knowledge of this aspect of the earnings test appears to have been a rarity. Those widows with higher education and/or income were the best informed, but fewer than one in five of the widows with some college were correctly aware that other income did not affect benefits.

Historically seen, social security was conceived in the depression, when many workers were affected by factors beyond their individual control for the risk of unemployment, or economic deprivation because of old age or the death of the family breadwinner. At the same time, the U.S. Social Security system was never supposed to be an American version of the Elizabethan Poor Laws. The first principle underlying the program was that security for the worker and his family grew out of his own work; people who did not work in "covered employment" had no part in the program. Since benefits are an earned statutory right, they are to be paid regardless of the need for benefits. The individual is supposed to build up additional protection through his own initiative and effort.

What happens when a large proportion of the beneficiary or potential beneficiary population does not know the policies based on this principle? If only 7 percent of the study widows knew that non-work income did not affect their social security benefits, how well can we assume they planned for their economic futures and took the receipt of social security benefits into consideration in that planning?

SUMMARY AND CONCLUSIONS

This chapter has focused on the amount of income widows reported having had in 1973, the sources of income and relative contribution to total income from each source, the incidence and extent of poverty, and the characteristics of widows affecting these items.

The main topics were analyzed in terms of social insurance beneficiary status, age, and number of dependent children.

The Effects of Beneficiary Status

The different categories of beneficiary status, the basis on which our sample was drawn, show different patterns of economic circumstance in widowhood and the effect of becoming widowed. Widowed mothers showed a median total income second only to remarried widows. Their social insurance benefits were higher than for the aged widows because they had dependent children. However, the median share of income from social insurance among widowed mother beneficiaries was 40 percent compared to 74 percent for aged widow beneficiaries. The widowed mothers were younger and over half had their own earnings; over 60 percent had some household earnings. They shared with the remarried widows the tendency to have more income sources than other categories of beneficiaries. Still, over two-thirds lost income in widowhood, and one-third had incomes below the poverty line.

The aged widows are in the worst financial condition. They have the least income. They are older, unlikely to be working or to have another person in the household working. Social insurance is the main source of income and accounts for a median 74 percent of income among beneficiaries. More than eight of ten lost income in widowhood and over half lived in poverty.

The two most important sources of income for all widows were earnings and social insurance. However, only one-third of the widows had household earnings, while three-quarters had social insurance income. When available, earnings were the largest income source. Those with incomes from social insurance only had the lowest incomes.

Lump-sum-only beneficiaries had the next lowest incomes to aged widows. The greatest share of their incomes came from earnings. Six of ten had household earnings, with most in this group having their own earnings. They were the least likely to have household earnings of any category except aged widows. However, they were more likely to work themselves than were widowed mothers or remarried widows. Almost nine of ten lump-sum-only beneficiaries lost income in widowhood, and one-third were living on incomes below the poverty line.

Widows with adult children were the most likely to have their own earnings and, with remarried widows, the most likely to have household earnings. They had more total income than aged widows and lump-sum-only beneficiaries, but less than widowed mothers and remarried widows. Over two-thirds lost income in widowhood; over one-fifth were living in poverty.

The best off financially were remarried widows. They had the highest median income, based on having another person in the family with earnings, presumably the new husband. However, these widows were less likely to have their own earnings than any category of widow except the aged widows. They matched widowed mothers in having the most income sources; they were comparable to widows with adult children in being most likely to have household earnings. More than half of the remarried widows gained income in widowhood. Despite this favorable situation, almost three of ten were living on incomes below the poverty line.

General Findings

The analysis indicates that over 40 percent of Chicago-area widows were poor, in that their incomes fell below the low-income index (the poverty line). Lack of adequate income is not offset by economic supports of other kinds or by service supports from other people or groups.

One-quarter of the widows had only one income source, in addition to the over 10 percent who reported no income at all. Three-quarters of the women received social security benefits or had someone in their household who received benefits. However, social security by itself was not always sufficient to bring older widows or widows with four or more dependent children out of poverty.

Among the aged widows, social insurance provided a high median relative share of income. Black widows and those with large families also got help from public assistance, but overall fewer than 5 percent of the widows received income from that source. Best off economically were women who had a combination of one or more wage earners in the family and social security. Working or being remarried with a working husband provided the best economic security.

The median income derived by the families of widows in 1973 from social insurance was $2,292. Family wages provided a median of $6,999 for the one-third of the women who reported having this source and the one-fourth of widows who worked themselves contributed a median of $5,000 in earnings. The median total income for all the widows was $3,436. This figure includes the women who reported not receiving any income at all.

The income on which the widows were living in 1973 was considerably lower for three-fourths of the families than had been available the year before the husband's fatal illness or accident. White women suffered a greater drop in income than did the black women. When compared to the U.S. population in general, the income of Chicago-area widows resembled that of female-headed households, but it was much lower than that of households in which the head was a man. The poorer widows received lower levels of non-financial support from society than those who were more comfortable financially.

There was no indication from their interview responses that the study widows saw financial problems at the base of their difficulties in general. They did not give finances as the reason in answers to questions on their life changes and problems.

The level of awareness of the annual earnings test and the limitations it imposes was low, although it tended to be somewhat higher among those with a higher probability of being affected. This latter group had more awareness, but also more misinformation.

In general, there is little to suggest most of these widows are in other than poor shape financially. However, it would be inappropriate to expect they could rise above that situation by their own devices. Their program knowledge does not suggest a base for their own financial planning. The best routes out of poverty, earnings from work or remarriage, are closed avenues for most of them.

REFERENCES

Gans, Herbert. 1962. *The Urban Villagers: Group and Class in the Life of Italian-Americans.* New York: Free Press.

Lopata, Helena Z. 1981. Widowhood and husband sanctification. *Journal of Marriage and the Family* 43 (May): 439–450.

———. 1979. *Women as Widows: Support Systems.* New York: Elsevier-North Holland.

———. 1978a. Contributions of extended families to the support systems of metropolitan area widows: Limitations of the modified kin network. *Journal of Marriage and the Family* 40 (May): 355–364.

———. 1978b. The absence of community resources in support systems of urban widows. *The Family Coordinator* 27, no. 4 (October): 383–388.

———. 1973. *Widowhood in an American City.* Cambridge, MA: Shenkman.

Lopata, Helena Z., Henry Brehm, Frank Steinhart, and Gertrude Kim. 1977. Support systems involving widows in a metropolitan area of the United States. Report to the Social Security Administration (no. SSA74-3411).

Mallan, Lucy, B. 1975. Young widows and their children: A comparative report. *Social Security Bulletin* 38, no. 5 (May): 3–21.

5

America and Its Women
in the 1970s

U.S. society has experienced and undertaken enormous changes since the 1930s. World War II ended the Great Depression and sent men into military service and women to replace them in the labor force. It then provided the G.I. Bill to veterans, offering educational and housing advantages unavailable to many of their predecessors. Returning veterans resumed their family life or married, went to school, or went to work. Their wives withdrew from their jobs in the factory, often involuntarily (Anderson, 1947/1981), and stayed home, influenced by the strengthening "feminine mystique" so vividly described by Betty Friedan (1963). If they were employed outside the home, it was often to help the husband go through school:

> ...an adjustment has evolved in society which enables men to marry young while continuing their education. This involves the wife's working and providing support, which means, of course, that she drops out of school, thus deferring to his educational need (Davis, 1972:247).

Davis was describing this situation for 1968, and it was even more frequent in the early post–World War II years. He foretells some of the consequences of this arrangement:

> If she remains in the labor force, or returns to it, in later years, it will generally be in a dead-end job that requires little education and which can be taken up or dropped as the husband's career demands (Davis, 1972:247).

What Davis does not mention are the negative consequences to the woman if she and the husband she helped through school obtain a divorce and she must now depend on only her earnings to maintain herself and, often, the children. Few fathers continue the economic support of their children after divorce, even when ordered by the courts to do so (Pearce and McAdoo, 1984; U.S. Department of Commerce, Bureau of the Census 1978). He also does not refer to the women who become widows at a time or in circumstances that do not guarantee social security benefits (see Chapter 4).

Those women who did not have to help their husbands through school but continued working until the birth of the first child used earnings in place of a dowry to furnish a new home or apartment (Davis, 1972). The post–World War II young marrieds, often only one or two generations away from poor immigrant ancestors, used the advantages of the G.I. Bill to move out of the central cities in great waves to the newly constructed suburbs. Black immigrants took their places in the cities, especially in the north, and started the slower move upward, hindered by visible physical differences from the dominant whites and a history of subjugation as well as the "benign neglect" of public agencies. They were later joined by Puerto Rican and Mexican immigrants (Lopata, 1984).

The new white suburbanites created a completely new life style different from that in which they grew up, a revolution as great as that undertaken by their ancestors who left behind village life in Europe (Lopata, 1971a; Riesman et al., 1950). The new home and garden and the babies kept the women busy, and the new affluence, compared to the economic resources of their parents, allowed for a definition of life better than that visualized in youth (Lopata, 1971a; Skolnick, 1983). However, the excitement of creating a new subculture wore off somewhat as life became established away from the diversity of the city. Unnoticed at first, there grew a reconstruction of reality on the part of the suburban women that questioned the dominant themes of the 1950s and 1960s (see also Skolnick, 1983). The competent middle-aged women started looking at broader horizons, often helped by Friedan's (1963) clarification of the "problem that has no name."

Initial returns to employment outside of the home were explained in economic terms—to buy a major appliance needed by the family or to put the kids through college—but the increased independence of the earning woman drew notice of neighbors who began contemplating similar action. Women deprived of a completed education by past events returned to schools and special job training programs—not for basketweaving, although creative courses drew many women wishing to develop their talents. Medical and law schools enrolled only small numbers of women at that time, the professional flood not beginning until the late 1970s and 1980s. If not the mother, then the daughter began reexamining the situation of her gender in this society. By the 1970s, the public image and the frame of reference of women were changing, as dramatic undercurrent changes surfaced. The mass media drew attention to the "successful woman," no longer as the one who maintains a perfect home for a perfect husband and children, but as a business manager, lawyer, doctor, and so on. However, most women were not in such positions, taking instead easy entry and exit jobs with short or no career lines and low pay (Lopata, Barnewolt, and Miller, 1985). Still, the life patterns of American urban women were decrystallizing as far as involvement in major roles was concerned. A wider choice became institutionalized. Feminism as a movement to change the very base of the culture to make it less sexist fought for the expansion of such choice. Even the age cohort born prior to World War II, which was socialized into the feminine mystique, contributed to what Bird (1979) calls a revolution of American life through reentry into the labor force and involvement in *The Two-Paycheck Marriage*. Its girl children are much more apt to decide early in life (at least earlier than the mothers) to prepare for extensive, if not necessarily continuous, involvement in the labor force and in occupations that provide greater rewards than the traditional female-intensive ones of the past. They anticipate the need to support themselves financially in case of broken marriages, and even to avoid a dependency relation by earning money even in the presence of a husband, or by not marrying at all. They have definitely been postponing marriage, and/or motherhood and having fewer children, if they have any. The social pressure to decrease fertility because of the population explosion is encouraging the move to fewer or no children (Keller, 1972; Skolnick, 1983).

Many questions are being raised by the two-pronged situation of change and persistence. Has the movement of American women back into school and/or the labor force decreased their economic dependence on husbands in adult years? How are women in different marital situations doing in terms of the annual income on which they must maintain themselves and, often, the children. What are the age cohort differences in the way women relate to the various sources of economic support? Are any of them organizing their lives in a way that will best utilize the social security system in their older years? What do they know about the program? What sources of income do they expect in retirement? How many are now dependent on welfare programs that have isolated the women and children of men who never marry, who desert, or who are divorced. How many are beneficiaries of social security because of the death of an insured husband? What is the attitude of women toward the social security system and its "fairness" to different categories of women? We can draw on a study of American women in metropolitan Chicago for answers to these questions.

THE CHICAGO WOMAN: DEPENDENCE AND CHANGE

The study to which we referred above was of changing commitments and economic situations of women, and focused on their histories, role involvements, and construction of reality. Almost a thousand (996) women aged 24 to 54 were interviewed in the winter of 1977–1978 with an oversampling of those currently unmarried, so that the weighted sample numbers 1,877. Their changing commitments were analyzed elsewhere, in preliminary and final reports (see Lopata and Norr, 1978, 1979, 1980). Their background and school, work and occupational histories, their construction of reality as to the job and self, and their role clusters are described in the two volume *City Women: Work, Jobs, Occupations, Careers Volume I: America* (Lopata) *Volume II: Chicago* (Lopata, Barnewolt, Miller). In this book we concentrate on those characteristics of the women that are related to our basic theme: the economic dependence of American women and the extent to which the societal solution to their economic problems through social security or their personal solutions actually meets their economic needs. We have already established that the social problem, from the vantage point of the 1930s, was the economic dependence of women on the earnings of a husband which they were subsequently deprived of due to his being disabled, retired, absent, or dead. In the previous chapter we found that many widows are not covered at all by the social security system or receive inadequate funds while being unable to earn income on their own. Now we look at younger women of all marital situations to see if they are acting in relation to paid employment in a way that makes them economically independent, whatever their marital situation, and which will ensure adequate coverage in the event of retirement or the absence of a husband as a wage earner. The assumption behind the 1939 provisions of the Social Security Act, we must remember, was that most women will not have a sufficiently strong and long attachment to the labor force to receive benefits on their own that are higher than those they can obtain as dependents of the husband, under specified conditions. Let us then see what their current economic situation is and whether there are differences in role involvements among women of different age cohorts.

The Sample

Seventy-eight percent of the women are white; the vast majority of the others are black, with a few Asians and native Americans included. The proportion of non-whites is higher than that of the nation as a whole, but is representative of metropolitan Chicago, where blacks and Hispanic Americans are numerous, though concentrated in highly segregated areas of the city and in some suburbs. The strong ethnic character of Chicago is also reflected in our sample. Only 20 percent of the women identified their background as "American," and most were able to trace themselves to a single main nationality or ethnic group. Almost half state that their family was "very closely identifed" with their ethnic group, and only 32 percent said that the identification was weak. On the other hand, the families have been in the United States over two generations, since only 18 percent of the mothers and 21 percent of the fathers were born in other countries. These younger women are less frequently first- or second-generation Americans that were the widows. However, our earlier comments about the urbanization of the United States are supported by the fact that less than a third of the women's mothers or fathers grew up in large cities; many spent the majority of their early years on a farm or in a rural area. Most of the respondents themselves grew up in a large city or its suburbs, so it was the parents who migrated. This indicates that many of the respondents were undoubtedly reared by "urban villagers" not sophisticated in the resources of urban centers (see chapter 4 and Gans, 1962). This supposition is reinforced by the finding that about half of the mothers and fathers had not even finished high school, and that around 13 percent of the daughters do not know how much education the parents had completed. Of course, this is partly due to the absence of one or both parents from the homes of a fifth of the women. Most of the respondents' mothers were full-time homemakers.

The women in our sample had completed an average of 13.0 years of schooling, 43 percent having gone through one year of college. They were much more educated than the older widows. One of the most dramatic conclusions of this study of women aged 25—54 is the decrystallization of the influence of their background and divergence of their life patterns in terms of role involvements. A method most frequently used by them to change the direction of their lives is a return to school. Forty-three percent of the women have obtained additional schooling, with most completing a degree. A high proportion went beyond high school, while many former drop-outs obtained their diploma (Miller, Lopata, and Norr, 1984). The reasons given for each withdrawal from school vary in that family obligations are given as reasons more frequently later in life. The most apt to return at least once is the woman who initially left to get a job but then realized that further or different schooling could enhance her life and ability to enter a better occupation. Furthermore, many women plan on returning to school in the future, and these are definitely aiming at a college degree or a more extensive level of education. However, there are still very few women with Ph.D.s or related degrees. In general, women with discontinuous schooling stayed in the system longer before leaving; more of them completed high school and started college before their first interruption or delay between one level and another.

Two possibilities were predicted concerning continuous versus discontinuous schooling. One is that the more advantaged women, in terms of family background, complete their education without interruption, while their less fortunate counterparts must obtain it in spurts. The other is that less advantaged women simply give up and remain at the level of schooling they initially completed, while those who are better off have more ambitious plans for the future. It is true that women whose fathers or mothers achieved a relatively high educational and occupational level carry this advantage into their own lives, but both categories of women tend to go back to school to finish a program they had begun, be it high school or college. Non-whites are more apt than whites to have stopped going to school in the middle of a program and more of them plan on returning in the future. Younger women are more apt to be considering further education and job training than are older women. Those who have higher levels of education are willing to enter new programs such as graduate school. Returnees are much more apt to be divorced or separated now or in the past and are not likely to have pre-school children in the home. Professional women returned to school after a pause much more often that women in other white-collar, or blue-collar jobs, but few women who never got beyond high school the first time around ever became professional.

Forty-two percent of Chicago-area women are currently full-time homemakers, 15 percent are employed part-time, and the remaining 43 percent hold full-time jobs. Of those employed, 8 percent each hold service or manual jobs, 36 percent are clerical workers, 4 percent are in sales, 7 percent are in managerial positions, and 11 percent are professionals or technicians.

Work Histories

Only a fifth of the women have worked continuously since entering the labor force. The total sample had spent an average of 54 percent of their time since leaving school in paid employment. This pattern does not lead to upwardly mobile career lines or extensive benefits immediately or in later years. There was considerable variation by occupation. For example, the managers of large households had been employed only 27 percent of the time.* Managers and professionals tend to have stayed

---

*Homemakers are defined as managers of households of various complexity based on composition. Small households contain the homemaker, the husband and one or two children. Large households, the parents and three or more children.

in the labor force for longer proportions of their adult lives than women in socioeconomically lower occupations. They are, however, a year or so younger than the average of the sample, which is 37 years. Many of the homemakers plan on returning to work in the future, but most women have interruptions of many years (see Lopata, Barnewolt and Miller, 1985; Miller, Lopata and Norr, 1984 for details about continuous and discontinuous workers). As a general rule, the older a woman is when she enters the labor force, the more likely she is to be a continuous worker. However, as stated above, few women can expect high benefits in retirement based on their employment histories.

On the other hand, the new trends toward delayed childbearing and smaller families can be expected to affect the number of years women are in the labor force and thus their probability of receiving social security at their own retirement. However, the length of employment is not the only variable. Even more important for the size of the social security benefits is the size of the earnings from the job. And, most Chicago-area women in our sample are not earning high salaries and are not contributing heavily to the total family income.

The Economic Situation

The poorest Chicago-area women in our sample are the separated full-time homemakers in the adults-only households and the never-married single parents. They were attempting to live on $2,875 and $3,417 in 1976 (see Table 5.1 for comparisons with women in other marital and occupational situations). By definition, adults-only households do not include anyone under age 18 for whom the respondent is responsible. The never-married managers of single-parent households do not have much more money than the separated managers of adults-only households, but they have children to feed and clothe. Widows in single-parent households are much better off than most of the non-married, full-time homemakers, thanks to social security. Married homemakers fare much better than their counterparts who never married, are no longer married, or who are living with a husband, but the sample falls below that of the employed married women. The never-married, employed women are living on higher incomes than are their separated, divorced, or windowed counterparts. In a separate analysis, we established that most of the unmarried women were living mainly on their own earnings, with the exception of widows, some of whom were employed only part time and received social security benefits. The married employees contributed between 31 percent (saleswomen) and 44 percent (managers) of the total family income. Although the professional/technical workers earned the most, they were married to high wage earners and so their contribution amounted to only 37 percent of the total.

Table 5.1 Total Family Income of Full-Time Homemakers, by Marital Status and Household Composition, and of Employed Women

Occupation	Married		Separated		Divorced		Widowed		Never married	
	n	$	n	$	n	$	n	$	n	$
Homemaker	586	22,741	43	4,605	38	5,250	22	8,432	22	4,750
Adults only	76	20,237	8	2,875	9	6,278	5	6,900	10	6,350
Single parent	—	—	35	5,000	29	4,931	17	8,882	12	3,417
Small household	254	23,117	—	—	—	—	—	—	—	—
Large household	256	23,051	—	—	—	—	—	—	—	—
Employed women	1,207	24,517	84	9,262	147	11,558	52	13,442	172	14,000

Source: Chicago area commitments study, compiled by the authors.

In order to better understand the economic situation of the Chicago-area women, we devised two measures defined as dependency and ade-quacy (see Tables 5.2 and 5.3).* The economic dependency of the women is divided into three categories according to the proportion of their fam-ily income contributed by their own earnings. Women who contribute 30 percent or less are considered economic dependents, those who con-tribute between 30 and 59 percent are defined as shared-income workers, and those who contribute 60 percent or more are seen as economically independent. Obviously, the cut-off is arbitrary and significant for this sample only. The same is true of the concept of income adequacy, created by adjusting the total family income for family size (by subtracting $1,000 for each family member over one) and dividing adjusted income into three equal categories of high, medium, or low. There is no judgment of absolute adequacy, only one within the sample or relative to other women being studied.

The more education the woman has, the more apt she is to be in the high-adequacy column, whether she is dependent on sources of income other than her earnings or shares income maintenance (see Table 5.2). Independent women, who for the most part are living off their own earn-ings, are rarely found in the high-income category; they tend to be low in adequacy if mainly uneducated, medium if they have at least gone to college. An uneducated woman tends to marry an uneducated man, so that the couple's income tends to be low if derived only from his earn-ings, and barely medium if hers are added.

Women who have never been employed outside the home are very likely to be dependent on the husband, unless they are no longer or never married and deriving some sort of socially provided income. Not surprisingly, many are found in the low-adequacy column. So are the service and unskilled or semiskilled manual workers, that is, women whose last job was in these fields if they are currently dependent on the husband's income. A few women who had been limited to such work in the past now have high family incomes although they are not currently employed, and those who are working bring the family total to the higher levels. Professional women tend to marry professional men, so their family income is among the top in our sample, whether they are currently economically dependent or sharing breadwinning.

Age is not as much a determinant of income adequacy as is marital status and the presence of a male head of household (see Table 5.3). Most of the separated, divorced, or widowed women in the "independent" category never get beyond the median-income level, many of those with

---

*Much of this material comes from the Preliminary Report to SSA and was developed by Kathleen Norr.

Table 5.2 Economic Situation (Dependency and Adequacy) by Education and Occupation of Chicago-Area Women

Characteristic	Percentage base	Economic situation								
		Dependent			Shared			Independent		
		Low	Med	High	Low	Med	High	Low	Med	High
Education										
Less than 8 years	56	49	11	9	6	11	0	11	2	0
8 years	32	31	37	0	9	9	0	9	3	0
9 to 11 years	218	35	16	12	3	7	11	11	5	0
12 years	650	12	25	29	1	7	12	6	6	1
13 to 15 years	361	8	12	24	0	7	21	8	18	1
16 years	184	8	10	34	0	4	26	5	10	3
More than 16 years	153	4	14	22	1	1	18	7	27	6
Total	(1,654)	246	299	404	21	102	256	124	176	26
Occupation										
Never worked	89	38	19	27	2	0	1	4	8	0
Professional	289	9	14	29	0	4	22	4	16	2
Managerial	133	6	6	21	0	10	23	7	16	10
Clerical	110	4	26	34	2	0	14	6	11	4
Sales	605	10	20	30	0	7	17	6	9	0
Crafts	19	10	10	32	0	0	21	10	16	0
Operatives	193	26	20	8	1	10	11	16	7	0
Farm	9	89	0	0	0	0	0	0	11	0
Service	209	26	22	13	5	8	9	10	8	0
Total	(1,656)	246	299	404	21	104	256	124	176	26

Dependency is measured by the proportion of income earned by the respondent: 60% or more, independent; between 30% and 59%, shared; less than 30%, dependent. Adequacy is measured by dividing into thirds the total family income adjusted for family size by subtracting $1000 for each family member over one. Figures are percentage distributions.

Source: Chicago area commitments study, compiled by K. Norr.

Table 5.3 Economic Situation (Dependency and Adequacy) by Marital Status, Household Head, and Age of Chicago-Area Women

| | | Economic situation | | | | | | | | |
| | | Dependent | | | Shared | | | Independent | | |
Characteristics	Percentage base	Low	Med	High	Low	Med	High	Low	Med	High
Marital status										
Married	1,201	11	24	32	1	8	20	2	1	0
Separated	83	47	6	7	0	1	4	24	11	0
Divorced	148	26	2	1	1	2	3	26	32	6
Widowed	52	35	8	14	4	0	2	15	19	4
Never married	172	13	2	1	1	1	4	17	55	5
Total n	(1,656)	246	299	404	21	104	256	124	176	26
Household head status										
Respondent	460	26	4	5	1	1	4	21	35	4
Husband	1,196	11	24	32	1	8	20	2	1	0
Total n	(1,656)									
Age										
25–34	764	13	19	20	1	8	16	7	14	1
35–44	503	16	17	27	1	4	14	8	9	3
45–54	389	17	17	29	2	6	16	7	6	1
Total n	(1,656)	246	299	404	21	104	256	124	176	26

*Dependency and adequacy defined as in Table 5.2. Figures are percentage distributions.
Source: Chicago area commitments study, compiled by K. Norr.

159

broken marriages falling in the low category. Married women who share the task of bringing in family income are high in adequacy. They are also the most apt to score high even if they are not employed, thanks to the earnings of the husband. Few have income sources other than his wages or salary. Widowed women are more apt to be dependent and as poor as separated women. Having a male head of household certainly helps bring the family income above the low level. The husbands of very young women tend not to be able to earn enough to place them in the upper third of income adequacy, but many have sharing wives who help pull family income up. There is a strong association between income and whether the woman is head of the household; it is negative if she is, positive if a husband is (gamma = 0.73).

The economic situation of the family often pushes the woman into an employment schedule not of her preference. Only 62 percent of the full-time workers really wish so many hours, 26 percent would prefer part-time work, and 12 percent want to stay home full time. The part-time workers are the most frequently satisfied, three-fourths preferring such a schedule. On the other hand, only 55 percent of the full-time homemakers want to be out of the labor force; almost a third prefer to be employed on a part-time basis. Thus, the women preferring part-time work tend to be divided almost evenly among those able to get such scheduling and those who must be employed full time or must be homemaking full time. This is the reality of their situation. However, part-time work does not bring long-range benefits at retirement and often is devoid of fringe benefits such as health insurance. It does provide contact with the world of work, although not necessarily in the occupation for which the woman is prepared or skilled, as in the case of former professionals or technical workers who are now sales clerks or waitresses.

A total of 57 percent of the women for whom we have complete income data can be considered dependent, mainly on their husbands, because they earn no income or less than 30 percent of the family total. Only 20 percent can be considered financially independent in that their family income comes mainly from their own earnings. This is not a complete picture because there are strong cohort differences in the patterns of role involvement on the part of the Chicago-area respondents. We shall now turn to these differences.

AGE-COHORT CHANGES IN ROLE INVOLVEMENTS*

Dividing the Chicago-area women into three age cohorts, we find definite differences in education; the youngest cohort (25–34) is the most

---

*Most of the material in this section covers Chapter 2 of the Final Report and was developed by Kathleen Norr.

apt to have a college education, especially a degree (see Tables 5.4, 5.5). The youngest women are least likely to be in a blue-collar job and almost a third are in professional/technical or managerial occupations. Their earnings as yet do not reflect this education, and it is the woman in the middle-aged cohort who is most often in the highest earnings range. The same pattern of relatively low rewards on the part of the youngest cohort is visible in the total family income. The youngest cohort is the most apt not to have married and especially not to have entered motherhood. The eldest women, although still in the middle years of 45 to 54, tend to be married or divorced, separated, or widowed more often than the youngest; the middle group has slightly more divorces. It is the oldest group, also, that tends to have the most children. Of course, we cannot know for sure if the youngest cohort will catch up to the oldest.

We do have, however, some evidence that role involvement varies with the age at which women were in school, employment, marriage, and motherhood, and we can use this to compare the younger to the older women. Thus, we can find out what women currently aged 35 to 44 and 45 to 54 were doing when they were as old as, or younger than, the youngest cohort.

We spoke earlier of the tendency of the Chicago-area women to utilize the increasing openness of the educational system by returning to school, even after having initially decided they had had enough of it (see Lopata and Norr, 1979; Miller, Lopata and Norr, 1984). In Table 5.5, we note that the youngest age cohort obtained more schooling than the older two cohorts before first leaving the system. This is true for the women with both continuous and discontinuous schooling. In this table the term *interruption* is used if the person did not finish a level of school, be it primary, secondary, or college, while *delay* refers to time out of school after finishing a level. Although an almost equal percentage of women in the three age cohorts returned to school, the younger women accomplished more the first time around. In addition, since these women are less than 35 years of age, and since the older women had more time to return for more schooling, we can assume that the older women will improve their achievement even more in the future. This is an impressive and important difference, because a higher educational level is positively related to a probability of better jobs, a longer involvement in the labor force, as well as to a higher educational and occupation level of the man the woman marries. Women aged 25 to 29 stayed in school to an older age than any other group. In addition, women in their thirties were more apt to be in school than women in their forties were at the same age. Interestingly, many women aged 50–54 were in school in their later middle years.

The younger women have also been involved in the labor force during the years traditionally devoted to child bearing and rearing in greater proportions than was true of the older women (see Table 5.6). Since this

Table 5.4 Socioeconomic and Familial Characteristics of
Chicago-Area Women, by Age

Characteristic	All women	Current age 25–34	Current age 35–44	Current age 45–54
Education				
Less than 12 years	19	11	24	28
12 years	39	39	40	38
13 to 15 years	21	23	20	20
16 or more years	21	27	17	14
(Percentage base)	(1,872)	(844)	(571)	(457)
Occupation				
Professional or managerial	26	32	23	18
Clerical and sales	48	46	50	48
Blue collar	26	22	27	34
(Percentage base)	(1,267)	(565)	(410)	(292)
Own Earnings (dollars)				
Less than 6,000	24	18	26	35
6,000 to 9,999	33	36	30	32
10,000 to 14,999	28	35	21	23
15,000 and over	15	12	24	10
(Percentage base)	(1,034)	(472)	(308)	(254)
Total Family Income (dollars)				
Less than 10,000	17	16	18	18
10,000 to 14,999	15	18	13	12
15,000 to 19,999	20	25	16	16
20,000 to 24,999	28	24	32	30
25,000 and over	20	18	21	23
(Percentage base)	(1,664)	(770)	(503)	(391)
Marital Status				
Never married	10	16	6	4
Married	74	71	74	78
Divorced, separated, or widowed	16	13	20	18
(Percentage base)	(1,874)	(844)	(571)	(459)
Number of Children				
No children	18	30	9	6
1 child	12	18	7	8
2 children	30	34	31	20
3 or more children	41	18	53	66
(Percentage base)	(1,874)	(844)	(571)	(459)

Figures are percentage distributions.
Source: Chicago area commitments study, compiled by K. Norr.

Table 5.5 Education Interruptions/Delays at First Stop of Full-Time Schooling for Women with Continuous and Discontinuous Schooling, by Age

Age	All women	Women with continuous schooling	Women with discontinuous schooling
All ages			
Elementary/high school interruption	22	25	18
Delay after high school graduation	43	48	36
Interruption of college/graduate*	34	27	45
(n)	(1,877)	(1,062)	(805)
Age 25–34			
Elementary/high school interruption	14	15	14
Delay after high school graduation	41	48	32
Interruption of college/graduate	45	37	54
(n)	(843)	(468)	(375)
Age 35–44			
Elementary/high school interruption	26	31	21

163

Table 5.5 *(continued)*

Delay after high school graduation	46	49	42
Interruption of college/graduate	27	20	37
(n)	(569)	(321)	(248)
Age 45–54			
Elementary/high school interruption	32	36	25
Delay after high school graduation	42	46	38
Interruption of college/graduate	26	18	37
(n)	(456)	(275)	(181)

For women with continuous schooling, these percentages represent their total level of educational attainment; for women with discontinuous schooling these percentages represent their level of educational attainment at their first interruption or delay.

*This category includes an interruption during college, a delay between the completion of college and the start of a graduate-level degree, or an interruption in graduate work.

Source: Chicago area commitments study compiled by K. Norr.

Table 5.6 Percentage Working at Different Ages by Current Age of Chicago-Area Women

Current age (year born)	Percentage working at age*								(n)
	15–19	20–24	25–29	30–34	35–39	40–44	45–49	50–54	
25–29 (1948–1952)	18	61	60	—	—	—	—	—	(489)
30–34 (1943–1947)	10	53	55	54	—	—	—	—	(332)
35–39 (1938–1942)	22	50	44	47	57	—	—	—	(295)
40–44 (1933–1937)	31	54	46	45	51	60	—	—	(224)
45–49 (1928–1932)	19	46	31	27	41	50	60	—	(232)
50–54 (1923–1927)	31	53	43	35	31	47	55	60	(210)

*Proportion working calculated for the single year when members of an age cohort were precisely the indicated ages. Calculations using three-year running averages produced nearly identical results.

Source: Chicago area commitments study, compiled by K. Norr.

is a historical trend, we have included the dates of birth of each cohort. The lowest proportion of workers is among women born between 1928 and 1932, when they were in their child-rearing years. More of them are working now than ever in their adult lives—twice as frequently as when they were in their late twenties and thirties. The eldest women in our sample are likely to have been working during the war years and then withdrew until they hit age 40–44, when there is a dramatic upsurge of return to paid employment. The youngest women, on the other hand, are still employed at ages 25 to 29 at a frequency greater than any other cohort was at that age. Those in their early thirties stayed in school longer and have been consistent in remaining in the labor force, although many are not working now.

Changes in the proportion of women who are currently married reflect the combined influences of changes in the proportion marrying, age at first marriage, and rates of marital dissolution (see Lopata and Norr, 1980:61). The younger women are also delaying marriage. Few married in their teens, and at age 25–29 over a quarter remain without a husband (see Table 5.7). Almost two-thirds of the women who are now 40 to 44 were married during their early twenties, compared to only half of the women under age 35. This change reflects both a tendency of younger women to marry at a later age and a higher percentage of women who have never married. Unlike marriage, the trend in divorce has been one of steady increase. There has been both an increased percentage of women ever divorced and a shift to divorce at earlier ages among the younger cohorts. Nearly twice as many women under age 35 had divorced by their late twenties than had the older cohorts.

The same pattern appears for the age when the women had their first child. Most of the older women (the 45–54 age group) had at least one preschooler during their late twenties or thirties. Among women under age 35, the proportion with preschool children declines and the age of highest concentration increases. For women now in their late twenties, the expected peak has not yet appeared; only half currently have preschool children. It is highly probable that at least some of this difference represents delayed childbearing rather than childlessness (Lopata and Norr, 1980:62).

In order to best understand changes in the ways women have combined their family roles with involvement in the labor force, we have divided the sample into two major categories, not married and married (see Table 5.8). We further divide the respondents according to whether or not they were involved outside the home as student, worker, or both. Mothering status is simplified by dividing women according to whether or not they have at least one child under age 18 living at home. These three sets of role involvements form eight different role clusters. We have used the three ten-year age cohorts for this analysis.

Table 5.7 Proportion Currently Married at Different Ages for Birth Cohorts of Chicago-Area Women

Current age	Proportion currently married at age							(n)
	16–19	20–24	25–29	30–34	35–39	40–44	45–49	50–54	
25–29	7	53	73	—	—	—	—	—	(498)
30–34	13	50	80	82	—	—	—	—	(346)
35–39	16	57	81	79	79	—	—	—	(320)
40–44	18	67	85	88	86	80	—	—	(250)
45–49	13	59	85	90	89	86	84	—	(235)
50–54	16	46	80	89	90	89	86	81	(222)

Source: Chicago area commitments study, compiled by K. Norr.

167

Table 5.8 Employment and Family Involvements at Different Ages for Three Birth Cohorts of Chicago-Area Women

| | Not Married | | | | Married | | | | |
| | Not working or in school | | Working or in school | | Not working or in school | | Working or in school | | |
	Child	No Child	Child	No Child	Child	No Child	Child	No Child	(n)
Current age: 25–34									
Role at age									
19	1	2	2	73	6	0	5	11	(704)
21	2	1	3	52	13	5	8	16	(754)
23	2	1	3	38	17	1	15	22	(818)
25	2	0	5	30	22	2	11	22	(841)
27	2	1	5	24	24	2	19	24	(626)
29	4	1	4	22	30	2	29	9	(487)
34	0	0	1	1	49	2	35	12	(209)
Current	3	0	6	15	34	1	26	14	(821)
Current age: 35–44									
Role at age									
19	1	2	2	64	10	5	6	10	(505)
21	1	1	2	45	19	5	10	16	(527)

23	2	1	3	31	28	5	15	15	(549)
25	2	0	2	11	36	4	21	14	(567)
27	2	0	1	15	44	3	27	8	(566)
29	1	0	3	13	50	1	25	6	(559)
34	2	1	6	11	45	1	32	3	(540)
39	2	0	11	5	39	2	38	4	(319)
44	1	1	5	3	42	3	38	7	(120)
Current	2	1	9	8	30	3	39	8	(518)

Current age: 45–54

Role at age

19	1	4	1	67	9	4	3	11	(437)
21	2	3	2	47	18	10	7	12	(439)
23	1	2	2	27	30	8	11	18	(449)
25	2	1	3	21	42	6	15	10	(457)
27	2	1	2	16	54	1	16	9	(456)
29	2	1	3	12	60	1	16	6	(456)
34	1	0	3	6	61	1	26	6	(453)
39	2	0	4	6	48	1	37	2	(452)
44	1	2	6	5	35	4	40	7	(448)
54	4	1	1	6	33	11	11	32	(72)
Current	3	2	4	8	21	10	26	25	(440)

Source: Chicago area commitments study, compiled by K. Norr.

For the oldest women in our study (45 to 54), it is possible to identify a model, or typical, life pattern. The majority were unmarried students or workers without children at ages 19 to 21. From ages 23 to 39, there were more married housewives with children than any other role combination; the majority of these women were in this traditional role cluster of adult American women from ages 27 to 34. In the younger cohort, distinct changes occur. At ages 19 to 21, role clusters are quite similar to those of the oldest cohort. A high proportion of these young women were unmarried workers or students without children. But beyond these ages, there is a strong movement toward greater diversity in employment and family role involvements than among the older women. Among women now between ages 35 and 44, although the plurality had children and stayed home, almost as many were employed, in spite of their children.

In the ages between 25 and 34, a much larger proportion had been in paid employment than was true of the oldest age cohort. Among the youngest women, married housewives with children are not a clear plurality at any age except 34. Other employment and family combinations that have become more common for younger women include the unmarried student or employee without children and married employee both with and without children. These role combinations represent the increasingly common departures from traditional life patterns of women. The expanding number of employed unmarried mothers among both the young and the middle-aged cohort, especially at ages 30 and on, should also be noted. Many women in this role cluster are especially likely to experience economic problems, even to the point of poverty (see McEaddy, 1976). Younger women find themselves in this situation less often because of the decreasing age of divorce, when marriages are apt to be childless.

Generally speaking, and reflective of national trends, the proportion of mothers of both preschool and older children in the labor force has increased greatly. In spite of this, younger women with young children continue to be withdrawn from paid employment much more often than are women of the same age without childbearing responsibilities. The absence of an age-related drop in employment rates among women under age 35 is due primarily to the great diversity in the age of younger women at the birth of their first child. This diversity of life patterns deserves special emphasis. At least some women are in each employment–family role cluster among all three age cohorts and in each age within each cohort. Even among the oldest women in our sample, at least 40 percent are different from the traditional employment-plus-family role pattern at each age. Thus, at least in recent times, there has been considerably greater diversity in women's role clusters than is usually recognized.

Patterns, however, do exist. A substantial majority of the oldest women in our study, (aged 45 to 54 at the time of the interview) followed a conventional life pattern: employment or school before marriage, housekeeping and mothering after marriage, and either continuing as a housewife or returning to employment at a later age. Among the younger cohorts, there is much more variation, so that no single life pattern includes most women. In addition, the relationship between age and life course patterns seems to be more or less disappearing. As more women decline to enter family roles, delay marriage and/or childbearing, and exit from family roles through divorce, a simple relationship between a woman's age and her family role involvement can no longer be assumed. Not only are women changing their willingness to combine employment and family roles at a particular point in time, they are also expanding the ways in which they integrate involvement in family roles and employment over the course of their lives.

We indicated before how many of the women studied plan to return to school. We can now combine these plans with those related to employment, marriage and motherhood, by their current role involvements (Table 5.9). Women's current family role involvements have strong effects on their expectations for the future. Among women aged 25 to 34, married childless women are most likely to plan to return to school. So are young unmarried respondents with children in the home. They are most often recently divorced. Older women (45 to 54) have fewer such expectations, as we saw before, regardless of family role involvement. Among non-workers, all 24 marrieds without children plan to go to work soon; their lack of involvement in the labor force tends to be due to school roles. Young mothers, whether married or not, tend to express strong plans to return to employment. The least desirous of a job are the older married women with or without preschoolers in the house. Their marital status ensures the absence of felt need but economic dependency on the husband, which they accept. Young married women without children are the most likely to plan to leave their jobs or decrease working hours, doubtless in anticipation of having a baby in the future, as 80 percent of them do. They and the unmarried mothers of young children are least apt to plan on retaining their current level of involvement in employment.

Middle-cohort women without families of procreation are not planning major changes. The patterns are interesting. While a higher percentage of women of all ages expect to be employed in the future than are employed now, this increase is especially high for the youngest women. It seems reasonable to attribute a substantial proportion of this discrepancy to less accurate prediction on the part of the younger cohort. Young women who are not currently mothers have to guess whether they will have children and, if they do, how this will affect their employ-

Table 5.9 Future Plans for Birth Cohorts of Chicago-Area Women, Controlling for Current Family Role Involvements

Future plans	Not Married						Married								
	No child			Child*			No child			Preschooler			School-age		
	25–34	35–44	45–54	25–34	35–44	45–54	25–34	35–44	45–54	25–34	35–44	45–54	25–34	35–44	45–54
Return to school	49	35	25	65	48	30	74	30	19	55	30	20	50	38	25
(n)	(67)	(26)	(32)	(48)	(40)	(30)	(83)	(37)	(129)	(281)	(59)	(10)	(91)	(199)	(145)
Non-employees who plan to be employed	—	—	—	85	67	58	100	46	35	86	79	33	57	69	54
(n)	—	—	—	(27)	(12)	(12)	(24)	(11)	(37)	(236)	(57)	(6)	(28)	(96)	(77)
Employees who plan to															
Increase hours	9	5	6	27	9	26	10	13	8	18	18	0	11	15	11
Decrease hours	10	2	16	11	2	5	14	6	12	11	9	0	5	6	10
Quit work	4	0	0	0	2	0	13	13	6	6	0	0	5	5	4
No change	77	93	77	62	86	68	63	68	74	66	73	100	79	75	76
(n)	(123)	(43)	(31)	(37)	(44)	(19)	(100)	(31)	(102)	(120)	(22)	(2)	(81)	(146)	(104)
Have a baby	56	4	4	25	0	0	81	22	0	45	7	0	12	0	0
(n)	(127)	(47)	(45)	(68)	(57)	(33)	(126)	(54)	(156)	(369)	(81)	(10)	(119)	(274)	(196)
Unmarried who plan to marry	67	34	12	71	13	22	—	—	—	—	—	—	—	—	—
(n)	(108)	(29)	(34)	(52)	(38)	(18)	—	—	—	—	—	—	—	—	—

*Child under age 18 in home.

Dashes represent those instances in which there were too few cases to present.

Source: Chicago area commitments study, compiled by K. Norr.

ment plans. We cannot, however, discredit future projections, in view of the documented incidence of women's continued involvement in all forms of school, including regular universities, community colleges, extension work, and continuing education, such as business and industry training programs (U.S. Department of Labor, 1975).

Another very important trend evident in our data concerns the decrystallization of background influences on current social status. We measured the socioeconomic status (SES) of the family of origin by the education and occupation of the father and, in his absence, of the mother, simply because ignoring the father obfuscated the important differences in background. The SES of the family was defined as *high* if the respondent's father completed college or held a managerial or professional job when the daughter was growing up, *medium* if he was a high school graduate or held a white-collar job that does not fit into the high-status category, and *low* if none of the above conditions is met. We analyzed the influence of the background on current roles.

In general, the younger the age cohort in our sample, the less strongly it is influenced by the socioeconomic status of the parents. There is a much closer association between background SES and the occupational category of the woman for the eldest cohort, aged 45–54 (gamma = 0.61) than for the youngest, aged 25–34 (gamma = 0.30). This trend applies also to the relation between race and occupation (gamma = 0.82 for the oldest cohort, gamma = 0.30 for the youngest). In other words, the younger women, both white and non-white, are less disadvantaged than are older women, since fewer came from low-status families, and those who do are less likely to remain in the lowest segment of the society in adulthood. A reverse pattern is visible in the association between the occupation of the wife and that of her husband, in that there is a greater similarity in occupation among the younger than among the older women (gamma = 0.63 for youngest, gamma = 0.57 for oldest). The differences are not as dramatic here. What the differences and similarities mean is that older women are more locked into the class system than are the younger ones, an important finding.

The changing employment and family role involvements of women from families of different socioeconomic statuses are shown in Table 5.10. Many more of the low-status women now aged 45–54 were married, full-time homemakers with children before age 25 than their high-status counterparts. The women who came from higher-status families were much more likely to be unmarried, without a child, and employed until age 29 than were the less fortunate respondents. In later years the three groups of women aged 45 to 54 are quite similar in their role involvement, except that the higher-status women are much more likely to be currently employed.

Looking now at the women age 35–44 we find fewer lower-class women to be married, full-time homemakers, and mothers up to age 34

Table 5.10 Employment and Family Roles at Different Ages, Controlling for Socioeconomic Status of Family of Origin for Birth Cohorts of Chicago-Area Women

	Currently 25–34								
	Not Married				Married				
	Not working or in school		Working or in school		Not working or in school		Working or in school		
	Child	No Child	Child	No Child	Child	No Child	Child	No Child	(n)
High family status **Role at age**									
19	0	2	0	85	2	0	2	10	(203)
21	0	1	2	68	6	0	3	19	(213)
23	0	0	3	49	6	2	9	31	(245)
25	0	1	4	36	10	2	13	33	(255)
27	1	0	2	35	18	0	16	27	(191)
29	1	2	2	30	28	4	23	10	(157)
34	0	0	0	0	62	0	25	12	(64)
39	—	—	—	—	—	—	—	—	—
44	—	—	—	—	—	—	—	—	—
49	—	—	—	—	—	—	—	—	—
54	—	—	—	—	—	—	—	—	—
Current	1	0	4	20	32	0	23	20	(249)
Medium family status **Role at age**									
19	0	2	1	77	3	0	2	14	(214)
21	1	1	3	55	10	3	8	19	(234)
23	1	0	5	38	18	0	10	28	(252)
25	0	0	7	30	26	1	9	27	(261)
27	0	2	8	19	20	2	15	33	(182)
29	2	1	4	21	38	2	28	4	(130)
34	0	0	1	3	42	0	51	3	(71)
39	—	—	—	—	—	—	—	—	—
44	—	—	—	—	—	—	—	—	—
49	—	—	—	—	—	—	—	—	—
54	—	—	—	—	—	—	—	—	—
Current	0	0	6	17	33	1	26	17	(255)
Low family status **Role at age**									
19	2	2	3	61	13	1	10	9	(273)
21	3	1	4	38	21	10	13	11	(291)

Table 5.10 *(continued)*

23	4	3	4	27	24	1	26	12	(305)
25	3	0	5	22	29	4	28	9	(309)
27	3	1	7	17	30	1	25	16	(239)
29	6	0	6	16	24	0	35	12	(192)
34	0	0	1	1	45	3	27	22	(71)
39	—	—	—	—	—	—	—	—	—
44	—	—	—	—	—	—	—	—	—
49	—	—	—	—	—	—	—	—	—
54	—	—	—	—	—	—	—	—	—
Current	5	0	7	9	38	3	30	8	(301)

	Currently 35–44								
	Not Married				Married				
	Not working or in school		Working or in school		Not working or in school		Working or in school		
	Child	No Child	Child	No Child	Child	No Child	Child	No Child	(n)
High family status Role at age									
19	2	0	0	73	9	2	2	12	(124)
21	0	0	0	51	17	3	5	24	(130)
23	0	1	0	35	21	4	15	23	(136)
25	0	0	2	24	31	1	15	27	(140)
27	0	0	1	19	37	0	22	20	(140)
29	0	0	3	15	50	3	14	14	(138)
34	2	0	2	18	45	0	30	4	(136)
39	0	0	8	7	42	0	38	5	(74)
44	0	0	3	0	26	0	58	13	(31)
49	—	—	—	—	—	—	—	—	—
54	—	—	—	—	—	—	—	—	—
Current	0	0	4	14	26	0	47	8	(133)
Medium family status Role at age									
19	0	0	0	78	6	0	4	12	(96)
21	0	0	2	55	17	5	7	14	(104)
23	0	2	1	34	36	6	6	14	(110)
25	2	0	0	22	37	4	16	19	(109)
27	0	0	1	16	47	7	25	4	(108)
29	1	0	1	13	53	0	29	3	(107)
34	1	0	6	11	46	0	35	2	(107)
39	2	0	10	2	42	0	42	2	(48)
44	0	0	0	0	46	9	46	0	(22)

Table 5.10 *(continued)*

								(n)
49	—	—	—	—	—	—	—	—	—
54	—	—	—	—	—	—	—	—	—
Current	1	0	8	3	34	2	42	11	(101)

Low family status
Role at age

								(n)
19	2	3	3	58	9	8	8	9	(257)
21	2	3	3	41	18	6	13	14	(265)
23	3	2	5	30	28	6	17	11	(275)
25	2	0	3	21	38	5	24	7	(289)
27	3	0	1	15	46	2	27	6	(288)
29	2	1	4	13	49	0	28	3	(284)
34	3	2	7	8	46	1	30	3	(269)
39	2	0	12	6	37	0	39	4	(178)
44	0	2	7	7	47	3	30	5	(60)
49	—	—	—	—	—	—	—	—	—
54	—	—	—	—	—	—	—	—	—
Current	4	1	11	8	32	4	34	6	(256)

	Currently 45–54							
	Not Married				Married			
	Not working or in school		Working or in school		Not working or in school		Working or in school		
	Child	No Child	Child	No Child	Child	No Child	Child	No Child	(n)

High family status
Role at age

	Child	No Child	Child	No Child	Child	No Child	Child	No Child	(n)
19	0	2	0	83	6	0	2	7	(102)
21	2	5	0	68	8	7	3	8	(102)
23	0	3	0	41	23	5	5	23	(104)
25	0	2	2	28	32	10	10	15	(106)
27	0	0	2	21	55	3	5	15	(106)
29	0	1	2	14	60	1	10	11	(106)
34	1	1	1	8	62	0	24	4	(106)
39	0	1	4	6	45	0	42	2	(106)
44	0	1	7	6	38	2	40	6	(104)
49	0	0	10	4	28	8	28	24	(51)
54	0	0	0	0	50	12	12	25	(16)
Current	0	1	6	5	23	8	35	23	(104)

Medium family status
Role at age

	Child	No Child	Child	No Child	Child	No Child	Child	No Child	(n)
19	3	6	0	72	3	0	0	16	(68)
21	0	0	3	59	13	6	6	13	(68)

Table 5.10 (continued)

23	0	0	3	34	17	11	13	21	(70)
25	0	0	3	26	31	10	19	11	(70)
27	4	0	0	20	53	0	17	6	(70)
29	3	0	4	14	56	0	20	3	(70)
34	0	0	4	9	59	3	23	3	(70)
39	3	0	4	9	54	0	26	4	(70)
44	3	1	4	7	26	3	51	4	(70)
49	5	0	0	5	24	10	37	20	(41)
54	15	0	8	0	15	15	15	31	(13)
Current	6	2	6	11	21	6	33	15	(66)
Low family status									
Role at age									
19	0	4	2	61	12	8	4	10	(254)
21	2	3	2	36	23	12	8	14	(256)
23	2	3	2	21	38	8	12	14	(262)
25	2	2	3	18	49	3	15	8	(268)
27	2	2	2	14	55	1	18	6	(267)
29	2	1	3	11	60	1	17	4	(267)
34	2	0	3	4	62	1	26	1	(264)
39	2	0	3	5	48	2	37	2	(263)
44	1	2	6	4	37	5	36	9	(261)
49	6	4	3	6	26	12	20	25	(153)
54	2	2	0	10	34	10	10	32	(41)
Current	4	3	4	8	22	12	20	27	(257)

The socioeconomic status of a family of origin is considered *high* if the respondent's father has completed college or has a professional or managerial job, *medium* if he is a high school graduate or has a white-collar job but does not fit into the high-status category, and *low* if none of the above conditions is met. For respondents who did not live with their fathers before 18, the mother's education and occupation are used.

Source: Chicago area commitments study, compiled by K. Norr.

than was true of the older women of the same class background. Many more of them were combining the roles of wife and mother and employment. The younger, upper-class women were more likely to be married at age 19 and 21 than were older women of the same class. In the middle years these upper-class women appear to be more diversified than the older, upper-class women or same-age, lower-class women. We find an even greater diversification among the youngest women in our study. The main difference is the dramatic number of high-status women who are unmarried and without children while in the labor force as late as age 29. This is not true of those who are now aged 35–44: most of them were married and with at least one child at those ages (up to 29). The women who are currently 35–44 are similar to the oldest women in this respect.

All in all, the younger women at the time of the interview have moved from the traditional way of combining home and employment roles and from entering and exiting different roles at the same ages as older women. Thus, they change roles rather freely (except for motherhood), and they have a longer and stronger attachment to the labor force if they come from higher status homes—except that they tend to stay home when the children, which they have later in life than any other group, are very young.

The decrystallization of life patterns means that no single set of policies can benefit all women. It also means that the male model of continuous attachment to the labor force still does not cover most women. Many become dependent on an earning husband for their family income at one point in life, although not as continuously among the younger as the older women. As we saw earlier, those who are employed often do not earn enough to support themselves and their children. Of course, those with husbands do not have a financial need to commit themselves fully to work, since they are able to take part-time employment or refuse demands that would interfere with their childcare responsibilities. And need for money does not necessarily translate itself into adequate earnings, when the need to care for a family competes with such commitment. Until society does something to help families meet multiple role obligations, the only way women can do so is to sacrifice their earning power. In the long run, it also means a sacrifice of pension or social security benefits, and either poverty in old age or dependence on a living or deceased husband's benefits. This does not cover, of course, women no longer married, or separated from a husband who does not continue to provide support.

RETIREMENT EXPECTATIONS

The rapid changes in rates and patterns of labor-force participation among American women led us to expect awareness on their part of the social security system and of the best ways of taking advantage of benefits in the future.* The question is: How do women prepare for retirement years? The answer that came quickly is that they do not. In addition, few know the conditions under which they or their husband (if any) would receive benefits, or the probable sources of income that

---

*Most of the material in this section comes from Chapter 1 of the Final Report and was developed by Kathleen Norr.

will be available to them in retirement. Younger women were especially ignorant and lacking in planning for the future as far as social security is concerned. Older women have retirement expectations that are much closer to what their actual retirement experiences will be. More of the events that determine retirement resources and demands have already occurred in their lives, and they are more likely to have begun thinking seriously about retirement plans. On the other hand, we must remember that our cut-off age for the sample is 54 and that there are relatively few women in their fifties whose attitudes and expectations we can examine here.

The women in the Chicago metropolitan area were asked when they expect to retire, whether they expect to work for pay after retirement, and what they expect to be their main sources of income at age 65. Contrary to our predictions, only a quarter of the women think they will retire at the ages of 62 or 65, which were the key social security years as of 1978 (when they were interviewed). Only 8 percent plan to retire at age 62, and 17 percent at age 65 (Table 5.11). The largest group, (37 percent) do not know when they will retire, and an enormous 28 percent expect to withdraw from the labor force before age 62. We assumed that early retirement would be tied to being married to an older man. However, as Table 5.12 indicates, this is not so. Fifty-three percent of the married women think they will retire when the husband is less than 62 years of age; 86 percent of the women whose husband will be that young when the wife retires plan to retire before age 62 themselves. All the other distributions are less concentrated. This does not sound as if the women were gearing their plans to an age at which social security benefits are possible, except in reduced amounts. On the other hand, only 19 percent of the 1,877 women do not expect to receive social security at age 65 in their own right, mainly because they have not been employed in occupations covered by the system.* Most of these women are currently full-time homemakers.** The surprising finding is that 81 percent of the women expect to receive social security benefits in their own right when they reach age 65. In addition, 77 percent expect to receive benefits from their husband's record. The distributions are interesting in terms of several characteristics of the respondents (Table 5.13).

Thus, expectations vary by occupation; for example, many manual workers do not anticipate benefits from the husband's social security because of the type of work the men do. Homemakers count on the husband more than anyone but the sales workers, many of whom are also

---

*Seventeen women never have been employed, 166 did not work long enough, and 106 contributed nothing to social security.

**Forty-two are professionals, mainly in occupations which are not automatically covered by social security. For example, we have several artists in the sample.

Table 5.11 Retirement Expectations, by Age and Race for Chicago-Area Women

Expectations	All women	Age			Race	
		25–34	35–44	45–54	White	Non-white
Expected retirement age						
Less than 62	28	29	30	24	29	26
62	8	5	11	11	6	13
63 or 64	1	1	2	1	1	0
65	17	18	14	19	18	15
Over 65	8	10	7	7	8	9
Don't know	37	37	36	39	38	37
(n)	(1,585)	(767)	(475)	(343)	(1,234)	(345)
Work expectations after retirement						
Work	23	21	20	29	21	28
Not work	45	39	52	48	46	39

It depends, don't know	33	40	28	23	33	33
(n)	(1,507)	(718)	(453)	(336)	(1,178)	(332)
Expected main source of income at age 65						
Own pension	9	10	8	7	8	9
Husband's pension	37	42	34	31	44	14
Own social security	16	14	19	16	9	40
Husband's social security	15	11	16	22	13	22
Savings or investments	12	11	13	12	14	4
Own earnings	3	4	1	2	2	4
Husband's earnings	6	6	6	8	7	4
Other's contributions	2	2	3	2	2	3
(n)	(1,755)	(784)	(538)	(433)	(1,368)	(390)
Mean number of expected sources of income at age 65	3.9	4.2	3.7	3.5	4.0	3.2

Source: Chicago area commitments study, compiled by K. Norr.

181

Table 5.12 Husband's Expected Age at Wife's Retirement for Currently Married Chicago-Area Women

Husband's age at wife's retirement	All women	Wife's expected age at retirement					
		Under 62	62	63–64	65	Over 65	(n)
Under 62	53	86	3	1	10	1	(344)
62	6	65	20	5	10	1	(40)
63–64	7	30	43	0	28	0	(47)
65	5	20	27	7	40	7	(30)
Over 65	29	4	17	3	63	13	(188)
Total							(649)

Source: Chicago area commitments study, compiled by K. Norr.

married. Among the service workers, the least likely to see themselves receiving benefits from either their own or the husband's work record are those in personal and protective occupations, mainly because so many work minimal hours or get income from unrecorded tips and have husbands who are not employed steadily. Aside from the homemakers, the least likely to expect benefits from their own record are professional and technical workers, and from the husband's record, manual workers and managers. Among the homemakers, it is not surprising that only 37 percent of those managing single-parent households expect social security benefits from a husband's account; those are mainly widows. We had hypothesized that homemakers with large households (three children or more) would be less likely than those with fewer children to count on benefits from their work, but the opposite is true (68 percent for large and 56 percent for small households).

Table 5.13 Percentage of Women Expecting to Receive Social Security from Their Own and from Their Husband's Work Record at Age 65, by Occupation

Occupation	Own social security	Husband's social security
Service	87	74
Manual	95	65
Clerical	92	76
Sales	95	82
Homemaker	68	81
Manager	90	71
Professional/technical	81	73
Total	81	77

Source: Chicago area commitments study, compiled by the authors.

One's earnings, the husband's earnings, or other sources are rarely mentioned as the main source of income at age 65, and only 12 percent of the women expect their savings or investments to be the main source; only 9 percent think their own pensions will make the main contribution (Table 5.14). These expectations in some sense reflect America of the 1970s rather than of the 1930s, but they appear quite unrealistic. So is the number of expected sources of retirement income (4.2 for young women, 4.0 for whites). On the national level, O'Rand and Henretta (1982:27–28) document that, although the number of women in paid employment has increased steadily, their interrupted work histories and "their tendency to be concentrated in only a few occupations" with "lower levels of earnings and fringe benefits (including pension coverage)," and limited upward mobility, as well as their location in industries with low levels of unionization, "small firm size and low wages and fringe benefits, produce a large number of retirement-aged women with very low retirement incomes." They used the Longitudinal Retirement History Study to discover the determinants on retirement incomes and concluded that

> The results of the analysis are very similar for unmarried women and wives. Discontinous work throughout life, a late age at first job, and industrial location have important and large effects on expected retirement income. In the case of unmarried women, disadvantage on one of these factors may be very serious, since their average expected income is very low. The problem is not so severe for married women, yet their work histories can have a surprisingly large effect on the couple's retirement income (O'Rand and Henretta, 1982:42).

The concept "expected" used in the quotation refers to the income projected by the analysts, not by the woman herself.

Not only do the women expect multiple important sources of income in retirement, but also many count on the pension or benefits of the husband. Schulz (1980:127), however, estimates that only 42 percent of the wage and salary labor force was covered by private pension plans in 1975 and that only 46 percent by private pension and/or profit sharing. Fifty-two percent of the men and only 36 percent of the women employed full time were covered at that time, so the woman's assumption that she will not receive benefits from private plans is realistic. Also, as Schulz (1980:190) notes, "Vesting requirements of 10–15 years penalize women who move in and out of the labor force." Finally, he states that

> ...social security income drops sharply when a spouse dies. Typically, private pension income also drops when the worker-recipient dies and sometimes ceases entirely. Often pensions that were barely adequate be-

Table 5.14 Retirement Expectations by Work and Family Roles in 1977 for Chicago-Area Women

	All women	Not married				Married			
		Not working		Working		Not working		Working	
Expectations		Child	No child	Child	No child	Child	No child	Child	No child
Expected retirement age									
Under 62	28	19	14	18	24	26	14	31	34
62	8	6	0	11	10	0	14	8	1
63 or 64	1	0	0	0	2	0	0	2	1
65	17	25	14	16	24	14	10	13	24
Over 65	8	3	57	11	10	7	3	6	11
Don't know	38	47	14	44	30	47	59	40	22
(n)	(1,500)	(32)	(7)	(110)	(204)	(334)	(29)	(520)	(264)
Work expectations after retirement									
Work	28	46	67	32	44	14	37	31	20
Not work	55	29	17	39	41	80	47	55	53
It depends, don't know	16	25	17	29	15	7	16	14	27
(n)	(1,143)	(28)	(6)	(84)	(171)	(228)	(19)	(398)	(209)
Expected main source of income at age 65									
Own pension	9	9	0	27	29	2	3	7	6
Husband's pension	37	4	6	5	4	52	40	43	41
Own social security	16	60	35	44	34	7	13	10	11
Husband's social security	15	13	24	7	5	19	23	16	15
Savings or investments	12	4	6	8	19	9	9	14	15
Own earnings	2	6	12	5	9	8	11	7	3
Husband's earnings	6	2	6	0	0	0	0	0	8
Other contributions	2	2	6	5	1	2	0	2	2
(n)	(1,661)	(47)	(17)	(101)	(197)	(494)	(70)	(484)	(251)

Figures are percentage distributions.
Source: Chicago area commitments study, compiled by K. Norr.

came inadequate when one spouse dies. A large proportion of poverty among women can be traced to the inadequacy of mechanisms to provide sufficient financial support to survivors.

Two important findings emerge when we look at the expectations for retirement income sources for Chicago-area women: one is the lack of knowledge and realism, and the second is continued dependence on the husband. Regardless of whether a women is employed and contributes to the family income when she is earning, in the long run she will not earn enough to become independent in retirement. The major source of income will usually come from the husband's work record and, if there is no husband, the woman is likely to be poor. Economic independence is still not available to many unmarried women, at least in middle age and retirement.

Retirement expectations, however, vary considerably among the different types of women included in our sample. Background characteristics of age and race, education and employment, economic situation, and family roles are related to these future expectations. We first discuss the retirement expectations of women in different categories of each of these variables and then explore the joint effect of all these factors.

Background Factors

Age is a critical variable influencing life circumstances and construction of reality of women. If younger women differ greatly from older women in their retirement expectations, we would have to determine whether this is an age or cohort effect. In spite of variation in career commitment and labor force participation, younger women in our sample do not differ from older women in the age at which they think they will be retiring, or even in the certainty of the time (see Table 5.11).* Younger

---

*The career commitment index was developed from answers to the following:
a. "Please tell me which of these roles is most important to you *now.*" (Respondent is handed a card with 12 major roles of American women). *Career woman* selected from a list of 12 roles common to women as first in importance = 4, second = 3, third = 2, fourth = 1; fifth or lower = 0
b. "Thinking about when you were age 24, which of these roles was the most important to you then?" (score same as above)
c. "Looking ahead, which of these roles do you think will be the most important one when you are 55?" (score same as above)
d. "At present, do you think of yourself as having a career?" (Yes = 4; No = 0)
e. Did you plan to follow a career in the jobs you held in the past?" (Yes = 4; No = 0)
f. "Do you plan to follow a career in the jobs you hold in the future?" (Yes = 4; No = 0)

women are somewhat less likely to say that they will definitely work or not work after retirement, tending to state that their employment status will depend on circumstances. Younger women less often expect social security on the husband's account, and more often think his pension will be the main source of income after they reach age 65. This may reflect greater optimism on the part of the youngest age cohort in our sample and a greater realism of the oldest, or it may be an accurate reflection of expanded pension plans and the generally more favorable economic circumstances for younger men. One's own pension and social security do not feature as main sources of income for most young women, in spite of their probable longer attachment to the labor force. Dependency has not decreased for them more than for the oldest cohort. However, the young women expect multiple income sources much more often than the respondents aged 45 to 54. It is quite apparent that most of these women, regardless of age, do not organize their lives toward the eventuality (which is very probable statistically) of widowhood.

Other characteristics of the woman and of her current life influence retirement expectations. There is little difference between whites and the non-whites in expected age of retirement or in whether they anticipate working for pay after that time, but considerable variation as to sources of income anticipated after age 65. Whites expect the husband's pension to be the main source in 44 percent of the cases, while only 14 percent of non-whites count on it. The latter count on their own social security (40 percent) much more often than do whites (9 percent).

The higher the eduction, the later the woman expects to retire, but the differences are not signficant (data not shown). High school graduates assume that their husbands will receive a pension much more often than other women, and there is a 20-point difference (45 to 25 percent) between this and less educated groups. Very few of the college graduates count on their own social security or that of the husband at age 65, with most assuming the main source will be pensions and investments. They expect 4.5 sources of income in retirement, compared to 3.0 on the part of grade school or high school drop-outs.

Role Involvements

We assume that current marital status would strongly affect expectations regarding age and main sources of income at retirement. Almost a third of married women who are not household heads expect to retire before age 62, while 37 percent have no idea when they will retire. Household heads who have never married are more likely to expect employment after age 65, but this is only 12 percent of the respondents. Widows are most likely to state that whether they continue working after retirement depends on their circumstances. There are some interesting differences in the expected sources of income at age 65 by marital status. A married woman whose husband is head of the household generally expects his pension to be the mainstay, while the separated, divorced and, to a lesser degree, the widowed look to their own social security. Women who have never married count on their pension, social security, and investments, ignoring the possibility that they may become dependent on funds brought in by a husband. Even part-time work does not decrease the dependency expectations of married women, and in that respect they differ considerably from full-time employees. For example, 63 percent of full-time homemakers, 56 percent of part-time employees, but only 40 percent of full-time workers expect to be dependent mainly on the husband's pension or social security. On the other hand, only 15 percent of employees expect their own pension, and 22 percent their own social security to be the main source of their income in retirement, or at least at age 65.

When we combine marital, motherhood, and employment roles, we find those most likely to cite 65 as their expected retirement age are unmarried full-time homemakers with no young children (25 percent). Those who cannot even guess their age of retirement are married full-time homemakers with no young child (59 percent). Those who are very definite about not working after retirement are non-employed married mothers of children under age 18 (80 percent, compared to 55 percent for the group as a whole). They are counting on the husband's pension amazingly often (52 percent) when compared to the group as a whole (37 percent), and especially compared to non-married women, very few of whom count on a husband's pension, although more expect to receive the husband's social security. Generally speaking, the most likely to list their own social security are the unmarried mothers who are not now employed. One wonders how adequate the benefits will be when they reach age 65, in view of their employment history.

The most likely to anticipate early retirement are clerical workers, whereas over half of the limited number of craftswomen do not estimate their age at retirement. Sales workers expect to leave the labor force later than others, and few of them think they will be employed after that. They tend to be married to white-collar men and count on the husband's pension as a main source of income. It surprised us to find that many professional and technical workers assume dependency on the same source, rather than on their own pension. Few expect to depend mainly on social security, theirs or their husband's. The women in lower-status positions appear quite realistic in not anticipating savings or investment to make a major contribution to their family income at age 65. Professionals and managers expect 4.2 sources of such income, manual workers an average of only 3.3.

Economic Situation

The total 1976 family income also influences the age of expected retirement and the anticipation of a need to work for pay afterwards. Few women with an income at that time of $25,000 or more intended to work for pay after age 65. Those living on less than $15,000 expected to have to work longer; few even dream of retiring before they are 62, and relatively many of the very poor expect to be relying mainly on their social security at age 65. We must remember that the poorest women in our sample are unmarried and heads of households. The absence of a husband is reflected in their total family income, and both facts are reflected in their failure to list a husband's pension or earnings. More affluent women expect the pension to be the most important source of income in retirement. The woman's own earnings affect her anticipation of continued dependence or independence, in that the less a woman earns herself, the more she expects to depend on the husband's pension and even social security. Women who earned less than $6,000 in 1976 also expect the husband to still be earning after the wife has reached age 65 much more often than other women. The higher the earnings of the woman, the more she expects to have a pension or savings, investments, and several other resources to fall back on. Interestingly enough, the proportion of time a woman has been employed since leaving school does not significantly affect her expectation of a pension. Of course, those who have worked 80 percent or more of the time tend to be young and expect an interruption in involvement in the labor force when they have children.

We can now look at the statistics summarizing the relation between economic dependency and adequacy, as measured by the indices previously discussed (see also Table 5.2). The pattern is somewhat unclear as to expectations for retirement (see Table 5.15). Those likely to be uncertain regarding retirement age are economically dependent respondents, particularly the poorer ones, while shared-income women are likely to think they will have to postpone retirement until age 65 or later. The dependent woman living on a high income is very likely to state that she would never work for money after retirement, which is not surprising in view of the fact that she is not currently employed. The independent respondent with a medium income expects to live off her own pension or social security. Expectations of social security in her own right are high among independent, low-income women. Very few of the respondents think that they will have an employed husband when they themselves have reached age 65.

The occupation of the husband will naturally affect the sources and amount of retirement income of married women. Wives of professional and other white-collar men are representative of the sample as a whole in the expected age of retirement of the woman. Wives of skilled and crafts workers are more likely to be uncertain as to their own age of retirement, while the wives of blue-collar workers are slightly more likely to select age 62 or 65, the traditional ages for such action, and less frequently consider retiring before age 62. The sources of income expected by wives vary considerably by the occupational category of the husband. The women married to professionals and skilled craftsmen most often think they will rely on the husband's pension. Blue-collar men in less complex jobs are married to women who most often consider their own social security to be a main source, while wives of both professionals and other white-collar workers count on savings and investments. The "other white collar" husbands are expected to have many, and the "other blue-collar" men few, income sources in retirement.

ATTITUDES TOWARD SOCIAL SECURITY

As we stated previously, the social security program has been the target of a great deal of attention, usually critical, throughout its history. Feminists especially find it unfair to women in general, or to special categories of women (Treas, 1983). Waite (1981) states one set of arguments; others can be found in Chapter 3 of this book.

> The automatic availability of dependent benefits to wives of fully insured male workers creates two types of inequities. First, working women married to working men pay more in social security taxes for the benefits they receive than do any other workers, because married women are guaranteed 50 percent of their husband's retirement benefits regardless of their own contributions. As in the case of the progressive income tax, the dependency assumption built into the social security system reduces the real wages of married women relative to single women and men and discourages their labor force participation. A second inequity results from the assignment of social security credit only to the workers and not to the dependent spouse; housewives became eligible for benefits only as dependents, not in their own right. So a woman who marries an insured worker before he retires receives the same benefits as a wife of many years and a homemaker divorced after less than ten years of marriage receives no benefits (Waite, 1981:34–35).

As we saw just above, however, it is unlikely that women are discouraged from labor force participation by the awareness of future benefits from the husband's work record unless they are reaching late middle age and do not expect to be able to earn high wages or salaries. They have certainly given up hope of offsetting the non-employed years by that time.

Table 5.15 Retirement Expectations by Economic Situation (Dependency*) and Adequacy**) of Chicago-Area Women

	All women	Economic situation								
		Dependent			Shared			Independent		
Expectations		Low	Med	High	Low	Med	High	Low	Med	High
Expected retirement age										
Less than 62	29	14	28	36	10	46	32	22	24	46
62	8	7	7	6	5	9	7	19	6	31
63 or 64	1	2	1	1	0	0	1	0	1	0
65	18	25	14	12	29	14	26	17	25	4
Over 65	9	8	9	8	24	14	5	9	10	8
Don't know	34	44	41	37	33	17	29	33	34	12
(Percentage base)	(1,411)	(167)	(207)	(330)	(21)	(104)	(256)	(124)	(176)	(26)
Work expectations after retirement										
Work	29	28	25	22	35	28	27	30	50	24
Not work	55	53	66	73	47	48	51	42	32	68

It depends, don't know	16	19	9	5	18	25	22	28	17	8
(Percentage base)	(1,096)	(126)	(144)	(241)	(17)	(80)	(212)	(106)	(145)	(25)

Expected main source of income at age 65										
Own pension	9	4	1	4	0	6	10	17	32	23
Husband's pension	38	29	53	54	11	48	42	4	6	12
Own social security	16	31	6	3	50	11	4	53	30	4
Husband's social security	15	24	21	9	28	20	18	8	8	0
Savings or investments	12	3	8	16	11	3	15	8	14	58
Own earnings	3	4	1	0	0	0	3	7	7	0
Husband's earnings	6	2	6	10	0	12	5	2	0	0
Other's contributions	3	3	3	4	0	0	2	1	2	4
(Percentage base)	(1,559)	(236)	(291)	(371)	(18)	(100)	(232)	(115)	(170)	(26)

*Dependency measured by the proportion of income earned by the respondent: 60% or more = Independent, between 30% and 59% = Shared, less than 30% = Dependent.

**Adequacy measured by dividing into thirds total family income adjusted for family size by subtracting $1000 for each family member over one.

Figures are percentage distributions.

Source: Chicago area commitments study compiled by K. Norr.

We asked our respondents if they considered social security policies to be fair to women and, if not, to which types of women and in what ways is it unfair. The mass media and other sources of information available to Chicago-area women appear to have convinced almost half of them that policies are unfair (see Table 5.16). However, 38 percent are sufficiently unaware of the policies and the arguments to state that they do not know whether they are unfair. The knowledge on the part of the 832 women who feel there is discrimination is also a bit shaky. Half state that the program is unfair to all women, 44 percent that only some kinds of women are treated unfairly, and 6 percent could not answer this general question. As we continue to the reasons given for the unfairness, we find the greatest amount of agreement over the statement that "taxes are unfair." The feeling that benefits are too limited refers to the family size limitation and lack of additional benefits when the wife is also working. Perceived distributive injustice comes from the judgment that since the system is based on men, women do not get back what they put in, married women workers do not benefit and, in general, that they get less benefits than men. Multiple reasons are frequently given, and the summary statement of unequal treatment of women draws agreement from over seven of ten respondents.

In order to better understand the influences on women's attitudes toward social security, we examine several sets of factors: age and social background (such as race and education), marital status and whether the woman is head of the household, role involvements, work factors (such as the proportion of time employed since first leaving school and occupation), economic factors of total family income, own earnings, and economic situation.

Background Factors

Younger women are more likely than older women to be unaware of policies and answer "I don't know" when asked if the program is unfair to women (see Table 5.16). Even if they state that it is unfair, they frequently cannot specify which category of women is most discriminated against. There is little difference among the age groups in the details given as to how some women are treated unfairly, except that older respondents are more likely to say that women get less in benefits and do not gain from working if they are married, while younger respondents simply state that women do not get back what they put in. In other words, distributive injustice and limitations of benefits bother different age cohorts. There are some differences by race in attitudes toward social security. Non-whites, almost entirely black in our sample, are more likely to say that the system is unfair (50 versus 43 percent) and less frequently claim ignorance. They feel the policies are unfair to all women much more often than do whites. Those who select a specific kind of womàn as discriminated against point to separated and divorced members of their gender, possibly because so many are in that situation. Nonwhites also state that unfairness results from limitations on family benefits and that no additional benefits came from the employment of wives. These racial differences thus appear to reflect divergent experiences in role involvements. More heavily discriminated against in the larger society, non-whites also perceive more unfairness in social security policies for women. The heavier concentration of non-whites at the lowest end of the economic scale means that they are more dependent on social security, and their concerns about the policies focus more on the adequacy of benefits than on the distributive justice in the system.

We expected greater variation among the respondents in relation to education than actually occurred. One of the differences is that women who never finished high school are considerably more likely than others to feel that social security policies are fair. Contrary to usual findings on American attitudes, the proportion of answers of "don't know" actually increases slightly with an increase in education. More educated women often say that policies are unfair for particular types of women, rather than for the group as a whole, and they mention working and divorced females as those who are disadvantaged. Women with less than a high school education feel that the system discriminates against all women, or mention widows as the most disadvantaged (45 versus 20 percent for all respondents). It is true that there are more widows per age among the poor, but widows are actually better off than are divorced or separated women, especially if they have young children.

Less educated women differ from others in assigning reasons for policy unfairness. They mention lower benefits far more often, and mention more often that the system is based on men's work patterns. The more educated respondents stress the failure of women to get back what they put in as the source of unfairness. Thus, higher education leads to the realization that the situation is complex and to an emphasis on distributive injustice rather than on the situation of one's own category of potential beneficiary. It also makes people more aware of media-publicized controversies.

Women's household arrangements and marital status also relate to their views of social security policies. Household heads and those in homes headed by others do not differ much in perception of policies, but the former mention working women less often and far more often mention single, separated, divorced, or widowed women (the marital statuses of nearly all female heads of households) as the most discriminated against. Altogether, nearly half of the household heads, compared to only a quarter of the non-heads, say social security policies are most un-

Table 5.16 Attitudes about Social Security Policies for Women by Age and Race, for Chicago-Area Women

Attitude	All women	Age			Race	
		25–34	35–44	45–54	White	Non-white
Social security policies toward women are						
Fair	17	17	17	19	17	19
Unfair	44	41	47	47	43	50
Don't know	38	42	36	34	40	31
(n)	(1,874)	(844)	(571)	(459)	(833)	(326)
Social security policies are unfair to						
All women	50	48	55	49	47	61
Particular women	44	47	40	44	47	34
Don't know	6	5	5	6	6	5
(n)	(832)	(348)	(268)	(216)	(625)	(208)

Social security
policies are most unfair for

Working women	17	13	17	23	16	18
Married women	13	10	15	15	17	12
Single women	4	3	5	3	4	3
Separated or divorced women	8	9	8	8	7	13
Widowed women	20	19	20	20	20	18
Others, don't know	39	47	36	31	41	31
(n)	(365)	(163)	(106)	(96)	(105)	(71)

Social security
policies are unfair because

Benefits are too limited	47	43	50	50	43	60
Unequal treatment of women	72	74	74	68	72	74
Taxes	90	89	90	91	90	89
(n)	(832)	(348)	(268)	(216)	(625)	(208)

Figures are percentage distributions.
Source: Chicago area commitments study, compiled by K. Norr.

fair to women who are not currently married. They mention nearly every reason for thinking this way and have stronger, better articulated feelings of unfairness, especially toward women in their own situation, than the women with a male head of household.

An examination of the respondents' marital statuses clarifies the relationship between being a household head and attitudes toward social security. The scarcity of cases of separated and widowed interviewees means that their distributions must be interpreted cautiously. Widows are much more likely, and women who have never been married are least likely, to feel that social security policies are unfair, with little difference among those in other marital situations. Thus, the category of female household head includes those most and those least opposed to social security policies. Divorced women are likely to feel policies are unfair to all women. Respondents who feel the policies are unfair to particular groups of women again select the category of their own marital status. Never-married women are more than two and a half times as likely to mention single women than are the other groups; twice as many divorced and separated women say divorced and separated women are most discriminated against, and 60 percent of the widows (versus 20 percent for all women) feel policies are most unfair for them. Only married women do not seem to feel their marital status is treated most unfairly; they more frequently mention women in other marital situations. The policies are seen as unfair because of limitations in benefits and distributive injustices (by never-married women), because of limitations on family benefits and taxes (by widows), and because women get less benefits (by divorced and separated respondents). The last named are also prone to state that the system is based on men, that women do not get back what they put in, and that there are no additional benefits for wives who work.

Role Involvements

Combining now the attitudes toward social security and the three major roles in role clusters (employment and marital and parental), we find that those most likely to consider policies fair are married women without young children in the house, whether employed or not. This is surprising, since employed women are not likely to receive returns from their record and probably will be treated the same as the full-time homemakers. The least likely to know whether the system is fair or not is the married homemaker without young children. We are not talking here of very old women but of those who at the most are in their early fifties. Those feeling that working women are most discriminated against are employed wives, regardless of active parental roles. This is logical, yet we are talking now of only about 7 percent of those without a child under age 18 in the house and 6 percent of those with a child. The variation in the reasons given by the 789 women who consider social security policies unfair to women are very interesting and reflective of their own situation. The non-employed, unmarried mothers focus on limitations on family benefits, which affect them. They also stress the male base of the system but are not unusually concerned with taxes, since they pay none. On the other hand, unmarried employed mothers state that no additional benefits accrue to the wife if she works, and the married, non-employed women without small children state that women get less in benefits in general. These points are harder to understand since they cover people in situations different from the respondents. The non-married, employed women select the male base of the program.

Work-related factors, besides current involvement in the labor force, include the proportion of time the women have spent in the labor force since first leaving school and occupation in current or last job. Women who have been employed a longer proportion of time are more likely to feel that social security policies are unfair to all women; if they select a particular group it tends to be the workers. The differences in reasons given for this judgment are especially interesting. The longer they have been working, the more often they mention distributive injustice (women do not get back what they put in and the system is male based) and the less likely they are to mention taxes.

Economic Situation

Total family income has very little impact on whether women consider social security policies to be unfair, or whether they see them as unfair to all women or to particular groups of women. Income does relate to reasons given for a negative judgment. Respondents with lower incomes more often than others mention taxes and benefit limitations. Women with both high and low incomes, rather than those in middle levels, feel that policies are unfair due to distributive injustice. The earnings of workers relate to their occupations, experience, and competence, and to their attitudes. Women earning in middle ranges in 1976 (between $6,000 and $9,999) are rather distinctive for unknown reasons. They are more likely than the others to think social security policies are fair, or, if not, that widows are discriminated against most and that limitations on family benefits are the main problem. Those who earn the least say all women are treated unfairly. Respondents with higher earnings mention taxes less often and more often mention issues of distributive injustice, again reflecting their education and other economic characteristics.

Among women who feel policies are unfair for particular categories of women, the economically independent at all income levels are more likely than the others to state that married women are most discriminated against, rather than they themselves. Working women in general are mentioned as disadvantaged under the system by both independent, low-income and by shared-income women with high incomes. Respondents with high shared incomes, or independently obtained ones at all income levels, are more concerned about distributive justice issues, while dependent women are least concerned about social security policies in general.

MULTIPLE REGRESSION ANALYSES OF EXPECTED MAIN RETIREMENT INCOME SOURCE AND ATTITUDES TOWARD SOCIAL SECURITY

The tabular analysis of retirement expectations and attitudes toward social security shows the importance of several classes of variables: background factors, labor force participation, family characteristics, employment-related factors, and economic characteristics. To go beyond the impact of single variables, we used regression analysis.

Main Expected Income Sources in Retirement

We examined three aspects of the main income source women expect at age 65; whether they anticipate it to be their own or their husband's social security, pension, or earnings, and whether they count on savings and investments. The 18 variables included in the regression explain 22 percent of the total variation in dependence on social security and 22 percent of the total variance in depending on an income source of one's own (Table 5.17).

Race, age, education, total family income, and being married all have significant independent effects on dependence on social security.* Women who expect social security to be their main income source at age 65 are more likely to be non-white, older, less well educated, not currently married, and of low family income (adjusted for family size). What all these factors have in common is their indication of the limitations of

---

*Cross tabulations with variables that have small impacts have been omitted.

economic resources available to women. The fewer a woman's economic resources, the more likely she is to expect to depend on social security for her main income source at age 65, either on her own or her husband's account.

Whether women expect to depend on their own pensions, social security, or earnings as a main income source is most strongly influenced by marital status ($r = -0.45$). Married women at all economic levels are much more likely to expect to be dependent on their husband than to provide their own main income source at retirement. Being married and older, non-white, and less-educated and having a lower adjusted family income lead to greater expectations of dependence on the husband's social security. Unmarried women at all economic levels realize that, in all probability they will have to depend on themselves for retirement income. Being older, non-white, and having relatively high job earnings also influence the expectation of dependence on oneself.

Only 8 percent of the total variance in whether women expect savings or investments to be the main source of their retirement income can be explained by all 18 variables. Not surprisingly, women who are white, of a religion other than Catholic, who have worked a high proportion of time since leaving school, are career committed, are earning relatively good salaries or wages, and are living on a relatively high family income are much more likely to expect savings and investments to be the main source of income at age 65 than are the others. Affluence, commitment to careers, and steady involvement in the labor force are anticipated to produce definite independent benefits in retirement.

Attitudes toward Social Security

All factors taken together can explain only about 2 percent of the variation in whether women feel social security policies are unfair. Part of the reason for the very low explained variance is technical: there is restricted variation because the question is a dichotomy, and because only a minority of women thought policies were fair (about 20 percent).

This extremely low relationship between evaluation of social security policies and a whole set of factors that measure aspects of a woman's "objective" situation vis-à-vis social security, taken together with the distributions showing the relationships between individual factors and social security attitudes, suggest two conclusions. First, despite widespread media controversy about social security policies for women, most women are quite uninformed about social security, and their attitudes are not well articulated or very strongly held. Second, women's feelings about

Table 5.17 Factors Influencing Expected Main Income Sources at Age 65 and Attitudes of Chicago-Area Women toward Social Security Policies for Women

Influencing factors	Own or husband's social security main expected income		Savings or investments main expected income		Own pension, social security, or earnings main expected income		Feel social security policies toward women are unfair	
	r	b*	r	b*	r	b*	r	b*
Background factors								
Father's education	−0.14	0.08	0.07	−0.02	0.04	0.09	−0.01	0.01
Mother's education	−0.19	−0.04	0.08	−0.06	0.00	0.02	−0.02	−0.06
Mother worked	0.00	−0.04	0.01	0.03	−0.02	0.04	0.05	0.04
Age	0.10	0.12[a]	0.01	−0.01	0.01	0.11[a]	0.03	−0.02
White	−0.34	−0.22[a]	0.12	0.09[a]	−0.24	−0.15[a]	−0.06	−0.10[a]
Catholic	−0.02	0.03	−0.07	−0.09[a]	−0.08	−0.02	0.00	0.02
Education	−0.27	−0.11[a]	0.19	0.11	−0.03	−0.08	0.03	0.00
Family characteristics								
Married	−0.27	−0.17[a]	−0.01	−0.05	−0.45	−0.43[a]	0.04	0.06
Husband's education	−0.30	−0.08	0.18	0.04	−0.09	−0.02	0.04	0.04
Number of children	0.12	0.00	−0.08	−0.01	−0.06	−0.01	0.06	0.08
Child under 6	−0.02	0.05	−0.08	−0.04	−0.06	0.06	−0.04	−0.06
Work factors								
Proportion of time worked	0.00	0.02	0.02	0.11[a]	0.16	0.08	−0.03	−0.03
Currently working	0.01	0.01	0.08	0.07	0.10	0.03	−0.01	0.00
Professional job	−0.15	−0.04	0.07	−0.04	0.00	0.04	0.00	0.04
White-collar job	−0.11	−0.04	0.08	0.02	−0.10	0.01	0.10	0.14[a]
Career commitment	−0.10	0.00	0.17	0.09[a]	0.10	0.03	0.08	0.11[a]
Economic factors								
Adjusted family income	−0.33	−0.13[a]	0.21	0.13[a]	−0.18	0.04	0.02	−0.01
Current earnings	−0.06	−0.03	0.17	0.10[a]	0.07	0.09[a]	0.02	0.00
R^2		0.22		0.08		0.22		0.02

[a] F level statistically significant, $p > 0.05$.

Source: Chicago area commitments study, compiled by K. Norr.

200

social security do not appear to relate in a simple way to their life situation. That is, all housewives do not see things one way and working women another, nor do women who are affluent see things differently from those who are poor. Our analyses of the cross tabulations suggest that there are two very different groups of women who feel policies are unfair for two very different reasons. Poorer women feel they are unfair because benefits are limited; women more involved in work feel they are unfair because of inequities. These findings certainly emphasize the need for caution in responding to media and special interest-group pressures for policy change.

Race, commitment to career, and having a white-collar job are the factors with the greatest independent effect on social security evaluation, highlighting again the importance of studying women's definitions of their situation as well as their current behavior.

SUMMARY AND CONCLUSIONS

In this chapter we have been examining the economic situation of a sample of women residents of metropolitan Chicago aged 25 to 54 when interviewed in 1978. A major conclusion, which reflects the national scene, is that, although many women are currently delaying marriage and motherhood, and decrystallizing the effects of parental socioeconomic background by returning to school and by life pattern variations, most still reach a period of the life course when they drop out of the labor force to meet family obligations. Thus, most become highly dependent on a husband and his earnings, during a decreasing number of years than was true of the past, but still, when the children are small. Their employment histories tend to be discontinuous because the heavy burden of family care falls entirely on them, with no help from society. Since the wife and children are dependent on the husband's income, he cannot take time off to solve crises or domestic problems, and the world of work is quite inflexible in the demands it makes on full-time employees. Non-married women usually still retain the main responsibility for child care, which competes with occupational demands at the cost of the latter. Such women tend to be much poorer, especially when the children are small; it is hard for them to hold a job and the benefits they can get from Aid to Families with Dependent Children tend to be minimal.

Changes are occurring in life patterns, education, and both employment and occupational histories; younger women are getting more schooling, delaying marriage and motherhood, and becoming more committed to jobs and occupations than is true of the oldest cohort in our sample (aged 45–54). The youngest women do not follow a modal pattern of involvement in social roles, so that is difficult to predict their role cluster at any age, much more so than has been true of women in the past 100 years.

In spite of the changes and increased orientation to the world outside of the home, these women are still not earning enough, for the most part, to live comfortably without the husband's earnings, and they themselves contribute only about a third to the total family income. They also are not making long-range plans for retirement, to ensure that they will have high pension and social security benefits, again relying on a husband's work record instead. For these Chicago-area women aged 25 to 54, both retirement plans and attitudes toward social security policies are low in salience, a fact reflected in the high proportion responding "don't know." An unexpectedly high number of them expect to retire from paid employment before age 62, before eligibility for full benefits from social security and even some pensions. In addition, few are in jobs that ensure pensions. Most women expect to receive social security benefits, but lower than those received by the husband, which is no different from what they would have obtained if they had never been employed. The more economically well off, in white-collar jobs and married to men in similar occupations, expect the husband's pension to be the major source of retirement income. What many do not consider is that they may lose that income if the husband dies. In addition, few men have adequate pensions when living (Schulz, 1980).

Differences in women's retirement expectations and attitudes toward social security policies for their gender are best explained in terms of three underlying causal factors: economic need, dependency status, and level of involvement in work. Nearly all the relationships between social background and family factors, work-related factors, and economic factors can be interpreted in terms of these three underlying dimensions.

Women expect to retire later and to work after retirement if they have higher economic needs and if they must be economically independent, which explains the positive relationships with race, household head status, and lower family incomes. A different group of women plans to retire later and work after retirement because working is an important part of their lives—therefore career commitment, higher-status occupations, current work status, and the proportion of time since leaving school all relate positively to retirement age and plans to work after retirement, even though the women with these characteristics tend to have lower economic needs. The presence of these two very different groups of women planning to retire later and to work after retirement also explain why variables such as age, job earnings, and education bear little or no relationship to plans to retire and to work after retirement. Younger, more educated women earning higher wages tend to have higher incomes and a greater desire to work, and the opposite effects of these two different factors result in little overall relationship.

Women's expected main income sources at retirement are very strongly influenced by economic dependency and by economic need. Women with higher economic need are much more likely to expect their own or their husbands' social security to be their main income source at age 65 and less likely to expect pensions or savings to be their main income source. Non-whites, blue-collar workers, and women with lower earnings, family income, and education are all much more likely to depend on social security sources. Women who are now household heads are also more likely to expect social security to be their main income source at age 65, presumably because they have fewer economic resources and do not anticipate having a husband in the future. An examination of marital status shows that divorced, separated, or widowed women are affected; single women are no more likely than married women to expect to depend on social security as their main retirement income resource.

Women's economic dependency status also influences their retirement expectation whatever their income level; married women expect that their main income at age 65 will come from their husbands' pension or social security. This relationship holds whether one examines economic dependency, whether the woman is household head, or whatever her marital status or earnings. A substantial minority of divorced, widowed, or separated women expect their main income at age 65 to come from some source connected with a husband. The continued differentials between men and women in earnings, occupational level, and time spent in the labor force make it unlikely that a wife will have a higher pension or social security benefits than her husband, even if she has worked a relatively long time in a medium-level job. Married women's continued dependence on their husbands for retirement income means that their needs and expectations regarding social security are quite different from the needs of unmarried women. This continued economic dependence on a husband further accentuates the plight of divorced, widowed, or separated women who do not have access to any benefits from a prior marriage.

In this regard, it is appropriate to look at a recent report issued by the Social Security Administration reviewing the period from 1960 to 1982 (Lingg, 1983). The report states:

> The number of women receiving benefits based on their own earnings record increased 247 percent during this period, while the number of women receiving benefits solely as dependents and survivors increased only 94 percent (Lingg, 1983:11).

The key word here is "solely," since women receiving benefits based on being "dually entitled" are counted among those receiving benefits based on their own earnings record. The high percentage increase is due to the previously low number of employed women. Dual entitlement occurs when a woman has earned a benefit of her own, but this is an amount less than the wife's or widow's benefit to which she is entitled. The report goes on to say:

> Although the number of women who have worked long enough in covered employment to qualify for benefits based on their own earnings record has grown, these benefits are often lower than the benefits they would receive as dependents and survivors (Lingg, 1983:11).

This point deserves major emphasis. If we look at the issue from another perspective, not focusing on whether she earned some portion of the benefit she received, but whether the amount of benefit was based on her own or her husband's past work, we see that the amount most women receive comes from benefits as dependents. There is an accounting record of the benefit they earned themselves, but the actual amount of benefit is not affected by their prior work even in cases of dual entitlement.

The percentage of women whose benefit amounts were based on their husband's work record was 61.3 in 1960. This percentage decreased to a low point of 57.4 in 1972 and had risen to 59.0 by 1980. Table 5.18 comes from the report, with an added column showing the percentage of women who were dependent or dually entitled. Two points are apparent. The percentage of women whose benefit amounts are unaffected by whether they worked has shown only minor changes from 1960 to 1980, the last year for which data on dual entitlement is available. There has been a slow but steady increase since 1974 in the percentage of women receiving benefit amounts based on the husband's earning record.

The data indicate that while more women are working, the beneficiary group as of 1980 was still dominated by those receiving benefits as dependents. The majority of women did not have earnings records that entitled them to benefits that surpassed what they could get as their husband's dependents. Rather than decreasing consistently over time, the percentage of such women has been increasing in the past decade in response to program changes and economic events.

The views of Chicago-area women concerning social security policies show how different is a representative sample of women from the allegedly "average" woman discussed in the mass media. The Chicago-area respondents for the most part do not have definite opinions about the fairness of social security policies for women. Their views do not appear to be influenced by changes in women's work patterns or by news media coverage of social security policy issues.

Dissatisfaction with social security policies for women is high, certainly much higher than is desirable for a major government program, but women who feel these policies are unfair have widely differing views about how they are unfair and the people who are disadvantaged by them. Again, there appear to be two quite different clusters of reasons for feeling social security policies are unfair. Women who are less well off economically (the same group that is most likely to expect their main income at age 65 to come from social security) are likely to feel that the unfairness comes from family limitations. Non-whites, less educated women, household heads, non-workers, and those with lower family income (all factors that relate to lower economic position) are more likely than the more affluent women to mention limitations in benefits. Involvement in paid employment also relates to feelings of unfairness. It is the woman most involved in the labor force who is most likely to focus on problems of unfairness in the treatment of women versus men, or of working women versus non-workers. Current employment status, education, proportion of time worked since leaving school, career commitment, and being head of the household all relate positively to thinking that social security policies are unfair because of problems in distributive justice. Unmarried status as well as being head of the household relate to mentioning both limitations to benefits and distributive injustice, because more unmarried women are poor and working. Divorced, separated, or widowed women are particualrly likely to feel social security policies are most unfair to women in their own marital statuses.

These findings highlight the importance of examining both commitment to work and involvement in family roles in order to understand the needs and expectations regarding social security for different kinds of women in U.S. society today. And, the fact remains that women in a variety of life situations are still likely to be dependent on a husband's income through his earnings or benefits, during the marriage and in widowhood. With the exception of the highly educated unmarried women of the younger or even middle-aged cohorts, those without a husband's earnings or benefits tend to be economically disadvantaged.

Table 5.18 Number and Percentage of Female Beneficiaries Aged 62 or Older, with Benefits in Current-Payment Status, by Type of Entitlement, 1960–1982

At end of year	Percentage dependent or dually entitled[a]	Total number[b]	Entitlement based on— Own earnings record Number	Percentage of total	Entitled as— Retired worker Number	Number dually entitled	Percent dually entitled	Disabled worker	Husband's or child's earnings record Number	Percent of total	Entitled as— Wife	Widow	Parent
1960	61.3	6,619	2,866	43.3	2,845	303	10.6	21	3,753	56.7	2,174	1,546	33
1961	60.2	7,162	3,185	44.5	3,160	331	10.5	25	3,977	55.5	2,247	1,697	33
1962	60.2	7,806	3,526	45.2	3,494	422	12.1	32	4,280	54.8	2,388	1,858	34
1963	60.1	8,283	3,804	45.9	3,766	497	13.2	38	4,479	54.1	2,436	2,009	34
1964	60.0	8,710	4,056	46.6	4,011	571	14.2	45	4,654	53.4	2,463	2,157	34
1965	59.4	9,143	4,327	47.3	4,276	612	14.3	51	4,816	52.7	2,475	2,308	33
1966	59.0	9,711	4,685	48.2	4,624	699	14.3	61	5,026	51.8	2,504	2,490	32
1967	58.7	10,084	4,929	48.9	4,859	761	15.1	70	5,155	51.1	2,479	2,645	31
1968	58.6	10,524	5,189	49.3	5,111	832	15.7	78	5,335	50.7	2,521	2,784	30
1969	58.4	10,924	5,449	49.9	5,363	910	16.3	86	5,475	50.1	2,524	2,922	29

1970	57.9	11,374	5,753	50.6	5,661	967	17.0	92	5,621	49.4	2,546	3,048	27
1971	57.7	11,853	6,077	51.3	5,975	1,060	17.1	102	5,776	48.7	2,576	3,174	26
1972	57.4	12,379	6,440	52.0	6,325	1,170	17.7	115	5,939	48.0	2,613	3,301	25
1973	57.6	13,015	6,880	52.9	6,754	1,361	18.5	126	6,135	47.1	2,678	3,433	24
1974	57.5	13,539	7,270	53.7	7,126	1,516	20.2	144	6,269	46.3	2,701	3,546	22
1975	57.7	14,010	7,586	54.1	7,424	1,660	21.3	162	6,424	45.9	2,745	3,659	20
1976	57.8	14,489	7,926	54.7	7,744	1,812	22.4	182	6,563	45.3	2,781	3,763	19
1977	58.0	15,012	8,302	55.3	8,106	1,992	23.4	196	6,710	44.7	2,824	3,868	18
1978	58.1	15,452	8,632	55.9	8,430	2,163	25.7	202	6,820	44.1	2,844	3,960	16
1979	58.5	15,913	8,978	56.4	8,777	2,380	27.1	201	6,935	43.6	2,856	4,064	15
1980	59.0	16,350	9,304	56.9	9,101	2,594	28.5	203	7,046	43.1	2,884	4,148	14
1981	—c	16,781	9,629	57.4	9,428	—c	—c	201	7,152	42.6	2,905	4,234	13
1982	—c	17,198	9,933	57.8	9,734	—c	—c	199	7,265	42.2	2,931	4,322	12
Percentage change, 1960–1982	160	247	—	242	—	—	848	94	—	35	180	-64

Numbers in thousands.

aData computation based on original table.

bExcludes special age-72 beneficiaries and adults receiving benefits because of childhood disabilities.

cData not available.

Source: Social Security Bulletin, 1983, 46, no. 9 (September).

REFERENCES

Anderson, Karen. 1947/1981. *Wartime Women: Sex Roles, Family Relations and the Status of Women During World War II.* Contributions to Women's Studies, no. 20. Westport, CT: Greenwood Press.

Bird, Caroline. 1979. *The Two-Paycheck Marriage.* New York: Rawson-Wade.

Davis, Kingsley. 1972. The American family in relation to demographic change. In *Demographic and Social Aspects of Population Growth,* edited by Charles F. Westoff and Robert Parke, Jr., pp. 235–265. Volume 1 of the U.S. Commission on Population Growth and the American Future Research Reports. Washington, D.C.: Government Printing Office.

Friedan, Betty. 1963. *The Feminine Mystique.* New York: Norton.

Gans, Herbert. 1962. *The Urban Villagers: Group and Class in the Life of Italian-Americans.* New York: Free Press.

Keller, Suzanne. 1972. The future status of women in America. In *Demographic and Social Aspects of Population Growth,* edited by Charles F. Westoff and Robert Parke, Jr., pp. 269–304. Volume 1 of the U.S. Commission on Population Growth and the American Future Research Reports. Washington, D.C.: Government Printing Office.

Lingg, Barbara A. 1983. Female Social Security beneficiaries aged 62 or older, 1960–1982. Notes and brief reports. *Social Security Bulletin* 46, no. 9 (September): 10–12.

Lopata, Helena Znaniecka. 1984. Social construction of social problems over time. *Social Problems* 31, no. 3. (February): 249–272.

———. 1976a. *Polish Americans: Status Competition in an Ethnic Community.* Englewood Cliffs, NJ: Prentice-Hall.

———. 1976b. Polish immigration to the United States of America: Problems of estimation and parameters. *The Polish Review* 21, no. 4:85–108.

———. 1971a. *Occupation: Housewife.* New York: Oxford University Press.

———. 1971b. Living arrangements of urban widows and their married children. *Sociological Focus* 5, no. 1: 41–61.

Lopata, Helena Znaniecka, Debra Barnewolt, and Cheryl Miller. 1985. *City Women: Work, Jobs, Occupations, Careers. Volume 2: Chicago.* New York: Praeger.

Lopata, Helena Znaniecka, with Cheryl Miller and Debra Barnewolt. 1984. *City Women: Work, Jobs, Occupations, Careers. Volume 1: America.* New York: Praeger.

Lopata, Helena Znaniecka and Kathleen Norr. 1980. Changing commitments of American women to work and family roles. *Social Security Bulletin* 43, no. 6 (June): 3–14.

———. 1979. Changing commitments of Chicago-area women to work and family roles and their consequences to Social Security. Report to the Social Security Administration. Contract no. SSA600-75-0190.

———. 1978. Changing commitments of American women to work and family roles and their future consequences for Social Security. Preliminary report to the Social Security Administration. OMB no. 72-S-77003.

McEaddy, Beverly J. 1976. Women who head families: A socioeconomic analysis. *Monthly Labor Reivew* 99: 3–9.

Miller, Cheryl Allyn, Helena Znaniecka Lopata, and Kathleen Norr. 1984. A cohort-historical analysis of the educational histories of American urban women. Paper presented at the Annual Meeting of the American Sociological Association, San Antonio (August).

Norr, Kathleen Fordham, Helena Znaniecka Lopata, and Cheryl Allyn Miller. 1979. Changing involvements in employment and family roles among Chicago area women: New ways of growing old. Paper presented at the Annual Meeting of the Midwest Sociological Society, Milwaukee (April).

O'Rand, Angela, and John C. Henretta. 1982. Midlife work history and retirement income. In *Women's Retirement: Policy Implications of Recent Research*, edited by Maximiliane Szinovach, pp. 25–44. Beverly Hills, CA: Sage.

Pearce, Diana, and Harriette McAdoo. 1984. Women and children: Alone and in poverty. In *Families and Change: Social Needs and Public Policies*, edited by Rosalie G. Genovese, pp. 161–176. New York: Praeger.

Riesman, David, Nathan Glazer and Ruel Denney. 1950. *The Lonely Crowd*. New Haven, CT: Yale University Press.

Schulz, James H. 1980. *The Economics of Aging*, 2nd ed. Belmont, CA: Wadsworth.

Skolnick, Arlene. 1983. *Intimate Environment: Exploring Marriage and Family*, 3d ed. Boston, MA: Little, Brown.

Smuts, Robert W. 1959/1971. *Women and Work in America*. New York: Schocken.

Treas, Judith. 1983. Trickle down or transfers: Postwar determinant of family income inequality. *American Sociological Review* 78 (August): 546–559.

U.S. Bureau of the Census. 1975. *Historical Statistics of the United States, Colonial Times to 1970*. Washington, D.C.: Bureau of the Census.

U.S. Department of Commerce, Bureau of the Census. 1978. Child support and alimony. Special Study. Series P-23, no. 106. Washington, D.C.

U.S. Department of Labor. 1977. *Dictionary of Occupational Titles*. Washington, D.C.: U.S. Government Printing Office.

———. 1975. *Handbook on Women Workers, 1975*. Washington, D.C.: U.S. Government Printing Office.

Waite, Linda J. 1981. *U.S. Women at Work*. Population Bulletin 36, no. 2. Washington, D.C.: Population Reference Bureau.

———. 1983. Working wives and the family life cycle. *American Journal of Sociology* 86, no. 2 (September): 272–294.

Wyse, Lois. 1983. *The Six-Figure Woman and How to Be One*. New York: Linden Press/Simon & Schuster.

6

Summary and Implications

The purpose of this book is to analyze the processes by which American wives and children became economic dependents of the husband/father, and the consequences of society's definition of them as a social problem to be solved by federal policies when they lose this economic support. As in the case of worker disability and medical care needs of the elderly, the Federal government decided that the economic situation of elderly widows and father-orphaned children created a problem and tried to solve it through the Social Security program.

SUMMARY

Most human history has involved complex work groups organized around families or at least households. Although a division of labor by gender and age appears to be universal, the content of tasks and the way these have been woven into social roles vary considerably (see Beneria, 1982, for discussions of rural women). In addition, the clear-cut segregation of life along gender and age categories that has evolved in recent history was not as apparent because of the interdependence and cross-over of activities. Hareven (1977) makes this point very clearly:

> The historical experience actually shows that the increase in role segregation among family members (a direct product of nuclear-family isolation) has tended to diminish the opportunity for equality within the family. It also shows that sex and age segregations in family roles have been inventions of the past century rather than permanent features of family behavior. Mother as a full-time vocation has emerged only since the middle of the nineteenth century (Hareven, 1977:68–69).

As communities and then societies grew larger, division of labor proliferated and various forms of money exchange supplemented barter of goods and services. Even in pre-industrial societies of Europe and Asia, work became increasingly organized into social roles or jobs—entrepreneurial, as in the streets of London and the marketplace—or organized in groups such as banks and trading companies. Braudel (1981, 1982, 1984) traces in three volumes the shift of production from the home and farm to outside organizations, and the growing dependence on modern capitalism with the expansion of surplus goods and markets. Finally, states coordinated the economic activity of their members, to the extent that they had the power to do so. The work that remained in the home became relatively invisible and devalued because it did not bring direct economic rewards. Even now it is not counted in the gross national product of "modernized" societies. Industrialization, urbanization, and ideological changes finally concentrated much of production, distribution, and services in the public sphere of life, away from the home and its private territory.

American society inherited much of English-based culture and thrust of change, adding its own peculiar bent. Starting without the burden of an established social structure heavily dominated by the upper classes, the United States moved quickly into industrialization and urbanization and away from dependence on family work on farms. The Protestant Reformation provided an ideological base to its emphasis on the economic institution as the focal institution not to be interfered with by the others, such as the family or religion itself.

The transformation of work (or at least much of it) into paid jobs for employer organizations for money with which to maintain the worker and others, and the removal of other forms of economic support from the members of society, produced a large number of dependents. Those people who could not hold a job had to be supported by others. Few people had sufficient inheritance or property to maintain themselves without jobs. This is certainly true of the modern era. The disabled were always in such a situation. Gradually, however, more and more people were added to the category of dependents.

Early industrialization began through the "putting out" or "cottage industry" system, where early capitalists sent raw material to people's homes for families to turn it into finished or partially finished products. Women and children worked along with the men. When factories were finally introduced, women and children followed the work into them. English and American social scientists have documented the work of very young children (Oakley, 1975; Hareven and Langenbach, 1978). Reform movements accompanied an ideological redefinition of children, from small adults to needing a completely different life from that of adults, freed from work in the home or from paying jobs, schooled and protected from physical harm. The removal of children from all day work was followed, as Hareven (1977) and others have pointed out, by a redefinition of motherhood as a full-time occupation requiring women's withdrawal from work outside of the home. Rather than being part of a work team, women became defined as potential or actual mothers, wives, homemakers, servicing a small private unit to be supported by the husband/father. In fact, women were gradually removed from cooperative entrepreneurial work with their husbands and from many other goods or money-earning activities in the public sphere of life (Oakley, 1975). Wives and children had already been legal dependents of the husband/father, according to English common law, which was brought over to America. This did not necessarily translate itself into economic dependency until the last one or two centuries. The prior assumption of early industrialization was that people could support themselves independently of other adults and that mothers could somehow provide for children too young to assist in their support.

The "discovery" of childhood and motherhood was accompanied by an even more dramatic ideological shift. The world became divided into the public sphere, expanding rapidly with industrialization, urbanization, and the creation of large policial and national culture societies, and the private, domestic sphere (Cott, 1977; Welter, 1966; Znaniecki, 1952). For a variety of historical reasons, the public life became defined as male, ignoring all the previous public activity of women. The domestic and "voluntary" (meaning non-paid) sphere was assigned to women, ignoring the private activity of men. The reorganization of much work into paid jobs and people into spheres was accompanied by a revolutionary change in self- and other-concepts along age and gender lines. Different personalities became necessary for different functions: work in the home and its surroundings required different types of people from those in competitive activity in the economic and political spheres of life. Male children needed to be trained into transition from one to the other; female children did not need to make such a shift, so each gender had to be socialized and educated differently. In the meantime, as societies grew more complex, education was extended to cover an increasing number of years, and girls were finally admitted to its various levels—not in all specialties, and not in preparation for a public career, but to function better as wives and mothers.

The result of this creation of a two-sphere world, each with its own activities, has made most Americans (until recently, when dramatic changes have occurred) incompetent in the sphere to which they were not assigned at birth. This further removed women and young children from activities that could ensure their economic support, increasing their dependence on people who can earn income through jobs, mainly fathers and husbands, while the wage earners are able to work for pay.

The number of dependents in American society was expanded by quite a large proportion of the total population through the introduction of retirement policies. People above a certain age "should" not work for pay because of their increasing incompetence and in order to open up jobs for younger men (since older women were not likely to be working, the emphasis was on men). This policy was accentuated by the Great Depression (Elder, 1974).

In spite of its insistence that some categories of people should not be employed, American society has not been able to work out a consistent method for supporting them. A major problem has been the assignment of responsibility for their support. Value systems that prohibit some solutions were carried over from the Elizabethan Poor Laws and the Puritanical suspicion of all people who were not self-supporting, even if they could not be. Such dependency accompanied the dramatic social-economic upheaval that followed the English enclosure acts and occurred during the American depression of the 1930s. Responsibility for the poor was assigned at times to parishes, communities, families, states, and the Federal government, depending on the category of person and the mood of the times. Americans tried to convince adult men to support not only their wives and children, but also elderly or disabled kin. This solution to the problem of economic dependence was incompatible with the increasingly nuclear family structure, with its decreasing sense of obligation of the breadwinner to the elderly and to former wives and children of divorce.

One solution to the problem of dependent children would be to return to having them support themselves. This is not realistic—small children are definitely not allowed to work for pay by law, and there is no chance that this law would be rescinded. Older, especially little educated, youth is not desired by employers forced to pay the minimum wage. The present Federal administration is recommending lowering the minimum wage for unemployed youth out of school. Such a move will also not solve the dependence problem, since a lowered wage cannot lead to economic self-sufficiency. Children are no longer taken away from families lacking a breadwinner and put in workhouses, as they were as late as at the turn of the century. Americans decided that neither the children nor the community benefited from such action. Leaving them with the mother proved to be the preferred policy since the 1909 White House Conference on Dependent Children, but the solution of that time, mothers' pensions, proved totally inadequate because of state variation and depression politics that channeled money to the unemployed. Even the latter policy had been fought since "charitable" organizations wished to retain control over the allocation of funds to the poor to ensure that "undesirables" did not receive them. Undesirability was often claimed on the basis of a foreign life style, the failure of the husband to find work, or his absence because of other than "appropriate" reasons. The economic support of dependent children lacking a wage-earning father or mother gradually came to be taken over by two government approaches: welfare, in the form of Aid to Families with Dependent Children, based on a means test with strong negative overtones, and, as of 1939, the Social Security program based on the record of a deceased or retired insured worker. We shall examine the consequences of this solution later in this chapter.

What about women who have the potential of becoming an economic problem of themselves, rather than being the only available solution to the problem of the economic dependence of their children? Women lacking a father or husband serving as a breadwinner of their children? Women lacking a father or husband serving as a breadwinner can be expected to earn their own support. At the same time, they must be socialized in such a way so as not to become so committed to an occupation and a career as to refuse to have children or to rear them with full-time activity. Since, however, they can be expected to leave an occupation upon marriage or motherhood, they are not especially desirable as employees, except in low-paying, female-intensive jobs with easy entrance and exit lines, training, and replaceability. They are desirable only under those conditions. What about women who are taking care of children or disabled family members, so that they cannot work for pay? If divorced, they were initially expected to receive alimony and child support with which to support the family. The realization that women could have paid jobs, even after divorce or if they were mothers, has decreased the demand by courts to assign or to enforce such means of economic maintenance. What about older women? Their problems came to the attention of American society only after the problem of dependent older men was "solved" through the Social Security Act of 1935.

The situation of men out of work due to unemployment, disability, or retirement has also bothered Americans. The companion volumes to this study deal with the various economic consequences of physical and psychological disability as it relates to the situation in each state and the cost of medical care for the elderly. The situation of the increasing number of elderly has been defined as a social problem requiring federal action since the 1930s. The depression and the Townsend Movement, including the pressure from a variety of groups on the government during the administration of a socially conscious president, resulted in the formation of a policy to guarantee economic security to all retired workers in covered occupations. It was not until the passage of the 1939 amendment to the Social Security Act of 1935 that the presence of dependents for whom that worker is responsible was recognized, so that funds were allocated for them. Older women workers were to receive benefits on their own account, but complicated formulas were devised to determine how much a wife and dependent children could receive on the husband/father's record. In addition, provisions were made for economic benefits of widows and father-orphaned children before they reached adulthood, defined then as 18 years, or 22 if they went to college. The latter age was designated from a combination of wishes to educate youth and to keep it out of the labor force as long as possible.

The Social Security Act and its various amendments were built on the ideological base of American society, leading to some interesting assumptions. For example, it was assumed that people would be influenced in their life-course behavior by knowledge of the program and its provisions. Studies of Chicago-area women indicate that this assumption is incorrect. For example, the study of widows in five beneficiary situations (older beneficiaries, mothers of dependent children, women who received lump-sum payments to help defray funeral costs, former beneficiaries whose children have grown, and former beneficiaries who have remarried) finds them quite ignorant of the policies and programs. Three-fifths of the widows did not even know about the earnings test let alone about the amount of money they could earn without cutting into their benefits. It is doubtful if families regulate the number of children they have in order not to exceed the family maximum in benefits when the husband dies. All evidence indicates that few families ever plan for that event. In actual experience, we found the best situated economically to be the mothers of dependent children, whose benefits helped considerably to maintain the family. Next best off were the remarried widows who have a husband's earnings plus the children's benefits from the late husband's record. However, two-thirds of the women lost income in widowhood and one-third had incomes that fell below the poverty line. Widows whose children were growing up worried about sources of income in the future. The poorest widows were the recipients of old-age benefits, and they were followed by lump-sum beneficiaries who were unable to get a good job. The two main sources of income for women in American society, employment or remarriage, were not available to the majority of the Chicago-area widows.

The economic situation of the women in middle years presented in Chapter 5 again documents their ignorance of social security policies and programs and their dependence on a husband's income if married. In fact, if there is only one earner in the family, it had better be a male rather than a female, since his contribution is generally twice as large as hers. Although the more education a woman has, and the higher her occupational status, the more she earns, this does not necessarily translate itself into a higher proportion of her contribution to the family income. Interestingly enough, never-married women out-earn their married or formerly married counterparts. It is possible that the lack of competing roles of wife and mother enables them to concentrate on their careers.

Of course, many are younger than the sample at large, which averaged 37 years of age and was limited to women aged 25 to 54.

Although younger women in Chicago have begun to decrystallize the effects of family background, mainly through returns to education, and display no modal life patterns as far as entrances into, and exits from, major roles are concerned, most are and will be dependent on a male's earnings and expect to carry this dependence into retirement. The more affluent anticipate several sources of income at that indefinitely perceived time; the poorer have no such expectations, pointing only to the husband's or their own social security. In spite of this, they are not really familiar with relevant policies and have not planned their employment histories with them in mind. Since the husband earns more than the wife, and in keeping with the history of American society, the burden of meeting family crises and the care of the home and small children still falls on the wife. More than eight in ten of the Chicago women feel that a mother should stay home after the birth of a child to care for her/him, although they disagree as to how old the child should be when it is all right for them to return to paid employment. It is the family obligation, leading to an interrupted work history and accompanied by the pay inferiority of most women's jobs, that continues to make American women dependent on another breadwinner, who is usually the husband. At the same time, their contribution enables the family to enjoy a better life style than it would otherwise be able to experience. Society at large has done little to enable women to maintain themselves above the poverty level if they have children and no support from the father, which is the usual situation in cases of separation or divorce. Welfare is not the preferred solution to the economic problems of such women, who often, however, do not know how to get training and decent jobs without leaving the children. Even self-maintenance can be difficult for women reared in traditional norms, which discourage aggressive stances vis-`a-vis the world of work outside of the home. Minority women lacking advanced education are suffering the most.

We shall now review and discuss the implications of the societal attempts to deal with the social problem of women and children deprived of a bread-winning husband/father in "respectable" circumstances of his death, rather than through his desertion or imprisonment.

IMPLICATIONS FOR SOCIAL SECURITY AND OTHER AMERICAN POLICIES

When we started this project, we had planned on focusing only on the Social Security program and assumed that the focus of its planners was the social problem of the economic situation of women upon the death of the husband. Our expected starting point for analysis was the question of whether the policy and program dealing with this situation matched the dimensions of the problem as defined. In conceptualizing this issue we discovered the need to broaden our analysis to the processes by which women became economically dependent on their husband and the consequences of this dependency for all women. This broadening of interest is in keeping with the wider frame of reference used in the public examination of the treatment of women under Social Security. For our purposes, dependent women include all those who now or previously had relied primarily on their husband for economic support.

The expansion of our concern to all categories of women so defined made us realize that the social problem to be solved by the planners of Social Security was never the situation of dependent women. Rather, the problem was defined from the perspective of a male breadwinner as the need for economic protection of his dependent family members if he could no longer provide support. The problem was defined to include only selected categories of dependents, and the program was designed with two major thrusts: financial support of people for whom a disabled or dead worker had primary responsibility and financial support for the aged. The family for whom the worker was responsible was defined as minor children. Support for a widow was available only if she were caring for an eligible minor child, or if defined as aged. A dependent wife's benefits were available if the husband were living but retired only if the woman herself had reached the age when old-age benefits were payable, or, as of 1950, if she were caring for her husband's children eligible for benefits. Women not old enough to qualify for old-age benefits and without eligible children in their care were not entitled to either a widow's benefit or to benefits based on being their retired husband's dependents. Divorced women were not defined as a problem for policy or program concern unless they had been married a certain number of years, the man had died or retired, and the ex-wife had met the requirements of care of his eligible children or of her own old age.

Nowhere in the policy or program statements of Social Security is there any effort to see dependent women and their needs for economic security as a social problem in its own right deserving or warranting a comprehensive solution. To do so would require treating widows, divorced women, and the wives of retired husbands as women whose economic security was affected by the loss of income from the earnings of a male breadwinner. This threat to economic security after the death of the spouse is less likely now, when many couples plan on a small number of children and two incomes as a permanent way of life, except when the children are very small. The death of the husband disrupts the plan, and an earnings replacement program that does not recognize this fact is denying reality.

Excluding from benefits wives and widows not caring for eligible children or who are not old enough for benefits based on age, distorts the social concept of dependency within the family. If a man retires at age 62 or, for that matter, at age 65 or later, his wife's age does not make her any more or less dependent on him economically if she has not been in the paid labor force for many years. However, the payment of dependent benefits for the wife is based on both the husband's age and retirement status and the wife's age and retirement status. Currently, women can receive actuarially reduced benefits as either dependent wives or as workers starting at age 62.

If benefits for dependent wives were payable at an earlier age than for workers it would be more in accord with a rational definition of dependency. However, it would raise some serious issues. It could, if not carefully controlled, provide a stimulus for men with younger wives to leave the labor force earlier than might otherwise be the case. Second, such benefits might entice working wives out of the labor force at earlier ages. These are undesirable prospects to the current administration, particularly in view of its attempts to find ways to cut program expenditures and/or increase program revenues for the long as well as the short term. However, that situation by itself does not justify conceptual inequities in the program. Do we want to force a retirement-age man to stay in the labor force longer because of his wife's age? At a minimum, cognizance should be taken of such considerations in planning program changes around the issue of equity in the treatment of women.

If dependent benefits for wives at earlier ages than for workers were considered, definitions of dependency could be applied, as well as additional actuarial reductions, so that the potential of benefits would not entice married women out of the labor force, or younger women to marry older men. For example, a test of recency of attachment to the paid labor force and duration of marriage could be used where the woman is under age 62.

An interesting question is raised by the use of actuarial reduction for dependent wives. What is the basis for the age-related actuarial reduction in this situation? For a worker, the reduction is based on the program definition of 65 (as of now) as the "proper" retirement age, so that if retirement is permitted before that age, a reduction in benefits compensates for the longer period of time the individual will receive benefits. For dependents' benefits, the actuarial reduction does save the program money and compensates for the longer time period benefits will be received as compared to age 65. But what does age 65, or age 62, represent for a dependent wife who did not work enough to collect a benefit in her own right as a worker? It has no significance, since no event accompanies it. There is no change in the basic dependency relationship between husband and wife that has existed for most, if not all, of the marriage. Neither is it the age at which the dependent wife leaves the labor force or no longer should be regarded as capable of labor force participation. It appears to be a straight application of the age used for workers.

Paying dependent benefits for wives at an earlier age than retirement benefits for workers would not resolve the issue of equity in the treatment of workers as opposed to dependent women. If anything, it would add a dimension to the issue. We do not propose such benefits for consideration or expect that they would be seriously entertained, particularly under the current conditions of severe fiscal restraint in the area of domestic policy. We point out this aspect of dependents' benefits only to indicate the inconsistency in the concept of dependency growing out of the lack of focus on the needs of women.

Another difficulty emerges when we examine the match between the problem, the policy, and the program. The benefit structure for widows was established on the basis of the wife being an economic dependent of the husband. However, if a woman were not to be part of the labor force but to be dependent on the husband/breadwinner, how could she be expected to sustain herself if he died after the last child reached maturity but before she could receive a widow's benefit based on old age? Was she expected to go to work at this point because she had no minor children to care for? If so, was this realistic in view of her lack of experience? Was private insurance expected to provide? Was it simply too expensive to consider? Was it too low in social value in a priority listing of social problems? This restricted definition of the problem did not consider reality from the perspective of the woman. If she had not worked for much or any of her married life, she was ill-equipped to enter or return to paid employment—a condition that would be problematic if she were widowed in this "in between" period.

It may be argued that adult children would have been expected to take the responsibility to support a widowed mother in the event she was widowed before being old enough to receive benefits based on her age. However, was it any more realistic to expect adult children to contribute to the support of widows under age 65 than those over 65? If not, why was it a necessity to pay older widows but not younger ones benefits based on their deceased husbands' work histories? For adult children still living in the household with a widow, the obligation to contribute to her support may have been felt and honored. Similarly, widows in the "blackout" or "in between" years could move in with their adult children and be supported by them. However, to force this dependence by economic strain would be contrary to the original intent of the social insurance program of support for dependents and survivors. At best, the expectation of support from children would be a weak basis for assuming these younger widows do not need the same public base of support as did older widows.

However, the program of old-age benefits for widows may have been established on a different conception of the order of events in a woman's life. How could retirement benefits to a dependent wife be abruptly terminated on the death of the husband/breadwinner? This was probably the focus rather than the expectation of a woman becoming a widow at an earlier age and having to find some other means of support until she reached the age for old-age widows' benefits. That focus may have made it illogical not to provide old-age widows' benefits. However, was it logical and consistent not to have provided a benefit for a woman with grown children whose husband died when she was in her fifties or to terminate the benefits of a widow after her last child reached maturity?

The data from Chicago does not indicate substantial planning or preparation for the financial realities of old-age widowhood let alone widowhood during a period of life when there would be no payment of social security survivors' or old-age benefits. If a woman with dependent children had worked along with her husband, she was not prepared to sustain the loss of his earnings without receipt of any compensating benefits, an event that would undoubtedly occur because of the earnings test if she continued working, unless there were enough dependent children, so that the family maximum provisions would not come into play. But the Chicago and other data indicate that women with more dependent children tend not to work as much as women with fewer children.

The Social Security policy assumed financial preparation in the form of savings and investments, so that benefits only needed to partially fulfill income requirements on the retirement or death of the breadwinner. The data from Chicago, suggesting the most effective route out of poverty for a widow is through work or remarriage rather than income from the past, does not point to this as a realistic assumption. The program implemented this policy, and extended various provisions, such as the retirement test, to the widow without modification, thereby restricting a widow's own earning rights before replacing her dead husband's earnings. The result of this action may well have been muted by the low-level of awareness of this provision, even among those most affected. However, overall the level of poverty among widows is quite high.

The social problem of "widowhood" has undergone change, along with the changing role of women in society. While the percentage of women in the labor force is unquestionably higher than in earlier years, the proportions of women working are not the same as those of men. However, within at least a segment of the population there are women who are economic equals to men as opposed to dependents. The Social Security system permits women to be treated as dependents according to the original model, or as independent workers. It has no provision for movement between or a combination of the two, which would recognize that many women have not attained fully independent status. The need for social security to adjust to the concept of equal treatment of the genders and to the actual and expected changes in the work and dependency status of at least a major proportion of American women has been recognized in recent years.

It is uniquely widows without dependent children who are not old enough for old-age benefits and who have not been firmly attached to the labor force who are caught between the two models of women currently existing in society: the traditional and "modern" woman. Treating them as either workers or dependents will not solve their problem. Treatment in the traditional mode will not provide them with a benefit under social security, and raises the questions posed earlier; treatment as a worker provides no help at the point needed. They are not currently attached to the labor force and need assistance in establishing or reestablishing independence. A program of transitional assistance would be needed to deal with this period and problem. Such a program would require a new policy to deal with a newly defined social problem. The prior definiton made it justifiable not to pay direct benefits to these widows. However, many have left the job market, and while they may be capable of reentry, not all are currently equipped to do so. The problem arises in part because of the changing (as contrasted to changed) role of women and the gap between the original program and the definition of the problem. The problem and policy were not viewed as a need to help a widow reorganize her life. A concern for dealing with the circumstances of these widows would be a departure from the formulated policy underlying social security.

The present generations of older widows, as reflected in the Chicago-area women we studied, has characteristics and problems unlike those of generations to follow. This must be taken into consideration in planning any modifications of the present program to deal with the difficulties facing them. The oldest two generations contain a higher proportion of widows who were either born outside the United States or married to foreign-born men than should be the case in the future. They and their husbands often received only minimal education. Many of the women did not work under social security themselves and had husbands who earned relatively low levels of benefits. Program provisions to care for their needs would not necessarily be appropriate for future generations of widows, more of whom will have been born in this country, obtained more education, been married to more educated men, and been in the labor force and earned benefits in their own right. Their husbands will have had better jobs and have earned higher benefits for themselves and for their widows than was the case with past generations.

All but the very young widows had been socialized in families that idealized patriarchal authority and family-focused life. They were taught to be women in the traditional meaning of the term, to become homemakers in their own homes. The man was expected to be the bread-winner, the woman the homemaker and the bearer and nurturer of children.

Medical advances have added years of life to the wife/mother. To-day, she can expect to live in her home with only her husband 15–16 years and alone for another 15–16 years. Most women of the older gener-ations are not prepared to reenter the labor market, even in the face of the probability that they will become divorced, widowed, or both, and will have inadequate economic support unless they rely, in part, on their own efforts. In the future, however, women will not face many of the problems that older widows typically encounter now. Any action soci-ety undertakes to help solve some of the problems experienced by widows like those studied in the Chicago area will not necessarily be a burden to it in the future.

On the other hand, the widows in the Chicago area and in the soci-ety at large are a heterogeneous aggregate. Policies designed to allevi-ate some of the problems and restrictions of one segment may be irrele-vant to others. In fact, the heterogeneity may be expected to increase considerably in the future, as women decrystallize their lives and se-quencing of role-involvement patterns. Adjusting policy and program to deal with such a multifaceted problem issue and a heterogeneous popu-lation will require a flexible approach. Widows and their problems re-flect the diversity of women in their relationship to society, to men, and to the changing but not yet changed social values governing these rela-tionships.

RECENT ISSUES AND DEVELOPMENTS IN THE TREATMENT OF WOMEN UNDER SOCIAL SECURITY

In the last several years much attention has focused on the treatment of women under social security and on possible ways to deal with de-fined inequities in the program between men and women. There is a public recognition of the changes in the relationship between the genders from the 1930s to the present. Marriage is not as stable in the 1980s as it was then, and women are less likely to play the role of full-time homemaker with a husband as the sole breadwinner. Women, includ-ing married women with children, are much more likely to be in the paid labor force. Two-earner families are common. However, while most women now spend a considerable portion of their lives in paid employ-ment, this is not a universal experience. There is a diversity of life styles. Additionally, child bearing and rearing and other home and family responsibilities create significant gaps in employment, even for those women with extensive work histories; and the earnings of women are still lower than those of men.

A major concern created by the interaction of the changes in social reality from the 1930s to the 1980s and the structure of the Social Security program based on the 1930s model has been the inequity in benefits for one- versus two-earner families. Almost three of five women beneficiaries aged 62 and over are receiving benefits either as dependents only or as dually entitled receivers. In the latter case the benefit amount is unaffected by their prior earnings. Dependent spouse benefits for women with no earnings record from work in the labor force are similar to benefits of most women with limited and in some cases fairly extensive personal work histories. The basis is a percentage of the husband's earned benefit as an eligible survivor or aged spouse. There is no extra benefit based on the woman's own prior earnings and contributions to the program in those two-earner families where the worker benefit a wife would receive is less than the dependent benefit to which she is entitled on her husband's work record. The result often is lower benefits for two-earner couples than for one-earner couples with the same prior family earnings.

The dependent benefit built into the Social Security program by the family protection concept of the 1939 amendment's focus on the adequacy of benefits for the family unit results in the inequities just discussed. Married women who do not earn a larger worker benefit on their own will receive no benefit above the same dependent spouse or survivor benefit a non-working wife would receive. This creates the inequity between one- and two-earner families. Dependent benefits also produce inequities between single and married workers since both are taxed at the same rate.

Beyond these equity matters a series of adequacy issues is of current concern. As we have noted, the widow in between (when the youngest child is too old for any benefits to be paid and the widow herself is not old enough for benefits to be paid based on her age alone) receives no benefit. Reduced benefits are payable based on age at 60, and at 50 if the widow is disabled. The widow in between may not have been in the labor force for years, but is not entitled to any benefit. A divorced wife gets a 50 percent benefit as a dependent. The 50 percent add-on may be adequate for a wife's benefit in an intact couple, but not for a divorced homemaker living alone. As our analysis shows, many aged widows have insufficient total incomes with little to supplement their social security benefits.

Various approaches, including earnings sharing, have been considered in an effort to find the best solution to the problems with the present system as we have moved away from the social realities of the 1930s. Too many women fall between the cracks in the current program and none of the proposals fills all the cracks. In part, this is because, as we have hopefully documented, the system was not designed to deal with the problems of women. Initially it was to provide retirement income for those too old to work, and later to provide benefits for a worker's dependent family in the event of his death or retirement. Disability protection was added later. The program always has focused on the worker and benefits provided to replace some part of lost wages. The complication with the present program and all the proposed modifications is that they still leave certain categories of women without protection in the event of the loss of that primary base of support. Society accepts the legitimacy of these women not working, but does nothing to ensure their support. This could be considered unavoidable and could be left to individual responsibility. However, we as a society are uncomfortable with such a solution to the economic problems of such women and consider the situation worthy of debate. A major recent focus on this debate is the economic contribution of the homemaker, not just to the family unit as a matter of individual choice, but also to society as a whole. Her unpaid work can be seen as contributing to the gross national product.

Mikulski and Brown (1983) provide a series of case studies of hypothetical individuals as a way of pointing out the difficulties encountered by women in different roles and circumstances of life in their treatment under the Social Security system.* Their article was reprinted in the report of the hearing before the Task Force on Social Security and Women entitled *Inequities Toward Women in the Social Security System.*** By their account, the case studies are not a comprehensive chronicle of the problems that affect women, but point to changes needed in the system that could be accomplished within the context of current fiscal reform. The case studies focus on the following issues: (a) Women with patterns of movement in and out of the labor force often find their benefits as dependents are higher than their own earned benefits. They receive the same benefit amount as if they had never worked, thus their contributions into Social Security are a subsidy to the system. (b) A one-earner couple with exactly the same average monthly wage as the combined wage of a two-earner couple will receive more in monthly benefits because of the dependent benefit. This difference is accentuated when survivor benefits are payable. (c) Married wage earners receive greater protection from the system than single workers because of dependent and survivors' benefits, yet both pay in at the same rate. (d) Disability benefits are not payable if a woman has been a full-time homemaker long

---

*Barbara Mikulski is a member of the United States House of Representatives, and has represented the third district of Maryland since 1976.

**The Task Force was of the Subcommittee on Retirement Income and Employment and the Select Committee on Aging, House of Representatives, 98th Congress, 1st session, September 22, 1983, Comm. Pub. no. 98-413. Washington, D.C.: U.S. Government Printing Office, 1983.

enough so that she does not meet the recency of attachment to the labor force requirements. Similarly, survivors' benefits are not payable on the death of a full-time homemaker. (e) There is a "widow's gap" of benefits between the time the youngest dependent child reaches 16 and the widow herself reaches 60. (f) Aged widows, particularly those who have to claim actuarially reduced benefits at age 60 and continue on the rolls for a long period, receive relatively low benefits and are least likely to have other economic resources. (g) No benefits are payable to the divorced wife on death or retirement if the marriage did not last at least ten years. (h) A divorced wife could not receive even the 50 percent dependent benefit unless the ex-husband was receiving retirement benefits. If the ex-husband was only semi-retired, the divorced wife received 50 percent of the reduced benefit.*

The Social Security amendments of 1977 required the secretary of Health, Education, and Welfare "...to study and prepare a report on proposals to eliminate dependency as a factor in entitlement to social security spouse's benefits and to eliminate sex discrimination under the social security program."** The report explores two options for dealing with the adequacy and equity issues that arise from the present system of providing dependents' benefits. The two options are earnings sharing and a double-decker benefit structure, described as follows:

> Under earnings sharing, a couple's annual earnings would be divided equally between them for the years they were married for purposes of computing retirement benefits. The earnings would be divided when the couple divorced or when one spouse reached age 62. This would entitle each spouse to a primary benefit which would replace aged dependent spouse's and surviving spouse's benefits provided under present law (*Social Security Bulletin* 1979:27).

> Under the double-decker option, each U.S. resident would have retirement, survivors, and disability protection. This universal protection would be the first tier of a two-tier system. Tier I would be a flat-dollar payment of $122 for U.S. residents beginning at age 65 (or upon disability). Reduced benefits would be paid as early as age 62. Tier II would

---

*This situation was altered in the 1983 Social Security amendments. Effective January 1985, a divorced spouse aged 62 or over may receive benefits based on the earnings of a former spouse who is eligible for retirement benefits, independent of the former spouse's retirement status, if the couple has been divorced for at least two years.

**Men and Women: Changing roles and Social Security. *Social Security Bulletin*, 1979, 42, no. 5 (May): 25–32. This article provides extensive excerpts form the summary of the report entitled *Social Security and the Changing Roles of Men and Women*, Department of Health, Education, and Welfare, February 1979.

be a benefit equal to 30 percent of a person's average earnings in covered employment. Tier II benefits would be payable as early as age 62 (reduced if taken before age 65). The benefit for an aged or disabled worker would be equal to the sum of a tier I and a tier II benefit (*Social Security Bulletin*, 1979:29).

The earnings-sharing concept includes the following modifications, so that the benefits paid are somewhat comparable to those under present law:

1. When one spouse dies, the survivor would be credited with 80 percent of the total annual earnings of the couple during the marriage, but not less than 100 percent of the earnings of the higher earner.

2. For purposes of benefits for young survivors—children and young surviving spouses caring for children—earnings would not be transferred between the spouses with regard to a marriage in effect at the time of death. Benefits for young survivors would be based on any earnings credits the deceased person had from paid work (while unmarried or during a current marriage), plus any credits acquired as a result of a prior marriage terminated by death or divorce.

3. For purposes of disability benefits, earnings would not be shared with regard to a marriage still in effect at the time of disability. Disability benefits would be based on any earnings credits the disabled person had from paid work (while unmarried or during the current marriage), plus any credits acquired from a prior marriage (*Social Security Bulletin*, 1979:28).

Certain additional features were included in the earnings-sharing option presented to illustrate one way of dealing with concerns raised or to limit costs to those of the present system. Benefits would be payable to surviving mothers only until the youngest child was seven. On the plus side, an adjustment benefit equal to 100 percent of the deceased worker's benefit would be payable to the surviving spouse for one year following the worker's death, regardless of whether there were any children eligible for benefits.

The double-decker option similarly included features that are not a basic part of such a proposal. These include the 50–50 split, inheritance of earnings by a surviving spouse (for Tier II benefit computation), and an adjustment benefit as under earnings sharing.

The two options are compared in the review article as to how they would resolve a series of issues. The comparisons are complicated by the different benefit structure introduced under the double-decker proposal. The decision is that a variety of issues affecting women are either resolved or improved as a result of one or both of these options. These include: the need for additional benefit protection for aged widows; gaps in protection for divorced women; low benefits for women workers because of child-care and homemaking time out of paid employment; disability protection; and, the fact that for married women benefits as paid workers largely duplicate rather than supplement their benefits as dependents. However, two issues we have raised are not affected by these options. There are no benefits provided for widows in the "in between" category, with the exception of the proposed one-year adjustment benefit, if it were indeed included in either an earnings-sharing or a double-decker plan. Second, on the death of the major breadwinner in a two-earner family with or without dependent children, the surviving wife cannot receive any benefit for herself based on her deceased husband's earnings record, despite the clear evidence the family counted on the earnings of both.

Concern for the problems of women under Social Security has focused most recently on the issue of earnings sharing. Public Law 98-21, the Social Security amendments of 1983, provides for study of the implementation of an earnings-sharing plan. Presumably this is based on the assumption that this appraoch offers the best possiblilty for providing equity between men and women and among different categories of beneficiaries. For most observers this seems to be the best way to go because it rights more wrongs than any other proposed solution. But even here, it is by no means a total remedy. As an analysis by O'Grady (1982) shows, the issue is not a simple one. O'Grady compared earnings sharing, child-care dropout years, and special minimum benefit with the provisions of the present law to determine their relative effect on compensating for the years of caring work in computing OASI benefits for women. As she points out,

> ...the present law's benefit structure implies that either a woman's labor force participation must parallel that of a man's—that is, strong labor force attachment—or she must behave like her counterpart in the 1930s and fulfill the role of a lifelong homemaker. If she falls between these roles, it is possible for her to receive a benefit based on her own earnings that is inadequate. If she is dually entitled, then the lower return on her contributions is inequitable since those contributions have not added to her retirement income (O'Grady, 1982:188–189).

The analysis used hypothetical work histories and calculated the OASI benefits for women retiring in 1991 under the present law and the three alternate potential policy approaches. These alternate approaches recognize caring work and assume equality in the work roles of women and men.

The higher replacement rates for retired women worker's benefits was seen with earnings sharing. However, this approach resulted in benefits less than poverty for divorced women of 12- or 16-year marriages with certain types of work histories. For the benefit payable to a couple as contrasted to a retired woman worker, child-care dropout years provided a more adequate benefit than earnings sharing, particularly as computed at age 62. For some couples the situation changed for computation at age 65. For them the three years of assumed higher earnings resulted in earnings sharing having a higher replacement rate.

In considering all the issues of equity and adequacy, O'Grady (1982) concludes that the special minimum benefit is the best policy choice, but with a qualified recommendation. This approach targets filling the gaps due to years out of the paid labor force in caring work. It is also designed especially for low earners. While not everyone gains, as is clearly not possible, no one loses, as does the husband under earnings sharing. Those with the lowest lifetime average earnings gain.

The determination in this analysis that the special minimum benefit is the "best" policy choice is linked to a particular assessment of equity and adequacy concerns and of the most appropriate focus and balance to be taken relative to these issues. It points out the complexity of the issue of resolving a defined inequity in treatment between the sexes based on the view of the world from a 1930s male vantage point and the continuing differences between men and women in their involvement in the world of work outside and inside of the home. It addresses the different potential needs for benefits of a previously dependent wife if she becomes a young or old widow, a divorced wife, an older woman, or half of a retired couple. It addresses the relative importance of equity and adequacy and different categories of women in relation to men.

On a totally distinct level, the question can be asked whether the concerns for equity center on the present Social Security system with its separate revenue mechanism. If the program were funded out of general revenues, would the same concerns arise? Many programs funded from general revenues provide differential benefits for different segments of the population, and we all pay taxes that go to services and programs we do not use. In fact, the Medicare program, which is funded primarily from the separate trust fund, is heavily inequitable in its return relative to contributions. The more sick aged receive far higher returns on their contributions than the less sick aged. The issue is need for care, not the equity of return on contributions. We are being somewhat facetious in presenting this example. However, it points out the fallacy of carrying the equity issue too far. Not all aspects of a benefit program can be equitable, as Social Security traditionally views the issue, if the concern is for human needs. Clearly, this does not imply that benefits should not relate to prior earnings. It does suggest that it may be time to reexamine what are the underlying social problems with which we want to deal, and what are the policy and program approaches that could deal with them most effectively. This is not the time in American history to propose new programs requiring additional tax revenues, whether these are from general revenues or Social Security trust funds. However, this does not mean it is inappropriate to view the various situations in which women in current society find themselves as a legitimate focus of problem-defining attention, rather than seeing the issue solely as an aspect of the problem of wage replacement for retired, deceased, or disabled workers. Fair and equitable treatment of women may call for a reassessment of the ideology and opportunities affecting different groups of women and the potential social and economic risks some may face in American society. Such a reassessment would provide at least some basis for arraying a priority of values for the types of problems society helps create for women. The equity issue here is quite different from the concept of equity of return on contributions. We may wind up recognizing that the effort to remold the Social Security program to deal with these situations as defined into problems is not the most appropriate route. We may wind up recognizing the need to reallocate existing social resources in a different pattern from what has been developed or contemplated.

While reexamining the assumptions, policies, and programs of Social Security we may also find the need to question the system that has created a two-sphere world, making integration of men and women so difficult, and which punishes half of the population. The punishment is in the form of economic dependency and the inability of many women to maintain themselves economically at the level available to many men. The system also places the total burden of organizing home and family care on the woman, making it impossible for her to maintain a career line if she also wishes to marry and have children. This book is not devoted to other results of the way our society has moved in its process of modernization; it focuses mainly on economic consequences for women deprived of a male breadwinner through his death, and only in cases where the society has taken the responsibility of supporting widows caring for eligible children, neglecting the analysis of supports for mothers deprived of a male breadwinner through his voluntary action. Although changes are occurring in society that may lead to an increasing opportunity for people now defined as dependent to reach economic independence, such changes are so slow and inadequate as to leave most women still dependent on a husband or the government—those who support themselves and especially those who manage female-headed households are frequently economically impoverished. Many members of this society are trying to do away with the social problem created by the ideology and set of values which created it in the first place—but they are fighting an overwhelming battle. Their goal in the redefinition of the interdependency of the spheres of life on a non-monetary basis.

REFERENCES

Aries, Philippe. 1965. *Centuries of Childhood*. New York: Vintage Books, Random House.

Beneria, Lourdes, ed. 1982. *Women and Development*. New York: Praeger.

Braudel, Fernard. 1980–1984. *Civilization and Capitalism, 15th–18th Century*, translated by Sian Reynolds. Vol. 1, *The Structures of Everyday Life*, 1981; Vol. 2, *The Wheels of Commerce*, 1982; Vol. 3, *The Perspective of the World*, 1984. New York: Harper & Row.

Cott, Nancy. 1977. *The Bonds of Womanhood: Women's Sphere in New England, 1780–1885*. New Haven, CT: Yale University Press.

Elder, Glen. 1974. *Children of the Great Depression*. Chicago, IL: University of Chicago Press.

Hareven, Tamara K. 1977. Family time and historical time. *Daedalus* 106, no. 2 (Spring): 57–70.

Hareven, Tamara K., and Randolph Langenbach. 1978. *Amoskeag: Life and Work in an American Factory City*. New York: Pantheon Books.

Mikulski, Barbara A., and Ellyn L. Brown. 1983. Case studies in the treatment of women under Social Security law: The need for reform. *Harvard Women's Law Journal* 6, no. 1 (Spring): 29–49.

Oakley, Ann. 1975. *Women's Work*. New York: Vintage Books.

O'Grady, Regina A. 1982. Caring Work and women's OASI benefits: An analysis of proposed changes in the Social Security law. Waltham, MA: unpublished dissertation, Florence Heller Graduate School for Advanced Studies in Social Welfare, Brandeis University.

Social Security Bulletin. 1979. Men and Women: Changing roles and Social Security. *Social Security Bulletin* 42, no. 5 (May): 25–32.

Task Force on Social Security and Women. 1983. Inequities toward women in the Social Security system. Washington, D.C.: U.S. Government Printing Office.

Welter, Barbara. 1966. The cult of true womanhood: 1820–1960. *American Quarterly* 18, no. 2 (Summer): 151–160.

Index

About the Authors

Index

About the Authors

HELENA ZNANIECKA LOPATA is Professor of Sociology and Director of the Center for the Comparative Study of Social Roles, Loyola University of Chicago. Her prior books include *Occupation: Housewife, Widowhood in an American City, Polish Americans: Status Competition in an Ethnic Community, Women as Widows: Support Systems,* and *City Women.* She is presently editing a series on *Research on the Interweave of Social Roles* (JAI Press).

HENRY P. BREHM is Associate Professor of Sociology at the University of Maryland Baltimore County. He was previously Chief, Research Grants and Contracts, in the Office of Research, Statistics, and International Policy of the Social Security Administration.

Dr. Brehm has authored and coauthored a series of journal articles and other presentations in the area of sociology. He also is a coauthor of the following books: *Disease, the Individual, and Society, Preventive Health Care for Adults, Disability, from Social Problem to Federal Program,* and *Medical Care for the Aged, from Social Problem to Federal Program.*

Dr. Brehm holds a B.A. and an M.A. from New York University and a Ph.D. from the University of Maryland College Park.